Study Guide

for use with

ADVANCED ACCOUNTING

Sixth Edition

Charles H. Griffin

Thomas H. Williams

James R. Boatsman

Don W. Vickrey

Prepared by
Ula K. Motekat
Old Dominion University

IRWIN

Homewood, IL 60430
Boston, MA 02116

Printed in the United States of America.

ISBN 0–256–06963–8

1 2 3 4 5 6 7 8 9 0 EB 7 6 5 4 3 2 1 0

Preface

This Study Guide is intended to supplement the Sixth Edition of <u>Advanced Accounting</u> by Griffin, Williams, Boatsman, and Vickrey. It is designed to help you understand and master the advanced accounting concepts and procedures discussed in the textbook.

Each chapter in the Study Guide first outlines the corresponding chapter in the textbook. This chapter outline is followed by fifteen True or False Statements designed to test how well you retain the material of the chapter. These Statements are succeeded by Exercises similar to those in the textbook. They give you the chance to apply the concepts and procedures introduced in the chapter. Answers to the True or False Statements and solutions to the Exercises are given at the end of each chapter.

For maximum benefit you should first read the chapter in the textbook. Then you should use the chapter outline of the Study Guide to review the material you have just read. If you do not understand a concept or its application, again go over the detailed information in the textbook.

After you have studied a chapter in this manner, answer the True or False Statements and work the Exercises. Then compare your answers to the solutions for immediate feedback on how well you understand the material. For any items you missed you should study the correct solution to determine the reason for your mistake. After this sequence of steps you should have a better understanding of the material in each chapter and be better able to work the exercises and problems assigned from the textbook as homework.

I hope this Study Guide will help you to master and enjoy Advanced Accounting. Any suggestions and comments you have will be greatly appreciated.

Ula K. Motekat

Contents

v

Chapter 1
Economic and Accounting Issues in Business Combinations

Chapter Outline

I. Economic Motivations for Business Combinations

   A. The decision to enter into a business combination is a form of capital budgeting decision. Assets are purchased if the cost of acquisition is less than the net present value of the estimated future income stream.

     1. A firm may acquire one asset or several assets in a basket purchase.

     2. A firm may acquire common stock of another company and thereby acquire control over the other firm's net assets.

   B. The reason for acquiring a group of assets is the expectation of profits. In a business combination the purchaser expects incremental, or synergistic, value from the acquisition in four ways:

     1. through the elimination of duplicate fixed costs.

     2. through the coordination of successive phases of a production process, e. g. when the acquired firm is a supplier or a customer of the acquiring company.

     3. through more efficient asset management.

     4. through capturing otherwise unused tax advantages, such as the utilization of a net operating loss carryforward.

II. Mechanisms for Business Combinations

   A. In a business combination the common stock of the acquired company can be obtained either for cash or for common stock of the acquiring company.

     1. If the stock acquisition is for cash, the ownership of the acquired company has changed and a sale and purchase have occurred. Therefore, the net assets acquired should be recorded at their cost to the buyer.

     2. If the stock acquisition is for common stock, the owners of the acquired company, by becoming shareholders in the acquiring company, continue to own an interest in the acquired company. An argument can therefore be made that the transaction should not be accounted for as a sale and purchase of assets but rather as a pooling of the interests of the shareholders of the two companies. In

1

this case the net assets should continue to be carried at their book values.

B.   No matter whether the shareholders of the acquired company received cash or common stock for their stock, the business combination can be structured in three ways:

1.   In an <u>acquisition</u> both companies continue to exist, but the acquired company becomes a subsidiary of the acquiring company, called the parent. Each company prepares its own financial statements which are then combined to show the results of this economic entity in the consolidated financial statements.

2.   In a <u>merger</u> the acquired company is absorbed by the acquiring company so that only one company, namely the acquiring one, survives.

3.   In a <u>consolidation</u> a new corporation is formed which receives the net assets of both the acquiring and the acquired company. In this case, too, only one company exists after the business combination.

III. Accounting Methods for Business Combinations

A.   Under the purchase method the assets and liabilities of the acquired company are revalued at their fair values. The purchase method MUST be used if any one of the 12 conditions for a pooling of interests is not met.

B.   Under the pooling of interests method the assets and liabilities of the acquired company retain their book values. In addition, the acquiring company's share of the retained earnings of the acquired company can be transferred to the books of the acquiring company. The pooling of interests method MUST be used if all of the 12 conditions set out in <u>APB Opinion No. 16</u> are met. These conditions are:

1.   Each of the combining companies must be autonomous and must not have been a subsidiary or division of another corporation during the two-year period prior to the initiation of the combination plan. However, this does not exclude companies that were newly incorporated within the preceding two years, unless they were successors to part or all of a company that was not autonomous.

2.   At the dates the plan of combination is initiated and consummated, none of the combining companies can hold as intercorporate investments more than 10 percent of the outstanding voting common stock of any combining company, unless the shares held were exchanged for shares that are issued to effect the combination plan. In other words, each of the combining companies must be independent of the other combining companies.

2

3. The combination must be effected by a single transaction, or in accordance with a specific plan within one year after the plan is initiated.

4. The surviving (or resultant parent) corporation must issue <u>only</u> common stock with rights identical to those of the majority of its outstanding voting common stock, in exchange for "substantially all" of the voting common stock of the other (combining) companies outstanding at the date the plan of combination is consummated. <u>Opinion No. 16</u> specifies a detailed set of procedures for determining whether the requirement is satisfied that "substantially all" of the voting common stock be exchanged. The essence of the requirement is that 90 percent or more of the outstanding common stock of a combining company must be exchanged (between the dates the plan of combination is initiated and consummated) for the voting common stock issued by the surviving or parent (issuing) corporation.

5. Each of the combining companies must maintain substantially the same voting common stock interest; that is, none of the companies may change those interests by exchanges, retirements, or distributions to stockholders in contemplation of effecting the combination.

6. The combining companies may reacquire shares of voting common stock <u>only</u> for purposes other than business combinations, and no company may reacquire more than a normal number of shares after the date the plan of combination is begun.

7. The ratio of the interest of an individual common stockholder to those of other common stockholders in a combining company must remain the same as a result of the exchange of stock to effect the combination.

8. The voting rights of the common stock interests in the resultant combined corporation must be exercisable by the stockholders; no mechanisms, such as a voting trust, can be used to deprive or restrict the common stockholders from exercising their voting rights.

9. The combination must be resolved at the date the plan is consummated, with no pending provision of the plan relating to the issue of securities or other consideration. Thus, the combined corporation cannot agree to contingent issuances of additional shares or other consideration to the former stockholders of a combining company.

10. The combined corporation must not agree directly or indirectly to retire or reacquire all or part of the common stock issued to effect the combination.

11. The combined corporation must not enter into other financial arrangements for the benefit of the former stockholders of a combining company, such as a guaranty of loans secured by stock issued in the combination.

12. The combined corporation must not intend to dispose of a significant part of the assets of the combining companies within two years after the combination, except to eliminate duplicate facilities or excess capacity and those assets that would have been disposed of in the ordinary course of business of the separate company.

C. Since fair values tend to exceed historical cost valuations, the net income of the combined companies tends to be higher under the pooling of interests method than under the purchase method. Therefore, managers whose income is dependent on their firm's net income, favor poolings.

IV. Unopposed and Opposed Business Combinations

A. In an unopposed business combination the management of one company negotiates with the management of another company for the acquisition of the latter company's stock. When a mutually satisfactory agreement is reached, it is submitted to the target company's stockholders for approval. A favorable vote binds all stockholders to the transaction so that the 90 percent requirement for a pooling of interests is met.

B. In an opposed business combination the management of the target company is against the acquisition and refuses to submit the offer to the stockholders for a vote. Therefore the prospective parent company has to deal directly with the target company's stockholders through a public offer. In this case the 90 percent requirement for a pooling will probably not be met and the combination must be accounted for as a purchase.

C. Target companies have developed various strategies to defend themselves against unwanted takeover attempts. Among them are:

1. Greenmail is the premium paid for treasury stock purchased from a would-be acquiring company who was unable to obtain enough stock.

2. A white knight is another would-be parent who is more to the liking of the target company's management.

3. A poison pill is taken by a target company when it sells prime assets to make itself less attractive as a takeover object.

4. In a <u>leveraged buyout</u> the management and/or employees of the target company borrow money to acquire a majority of the target company's stock.

5. <u>Golden parachutes</u> are executive compensation contracts made between a target company and its top management providing for generous payments to individuals displaced in a takeover.

V. Tax Factors Affecting Business Combinations

A. Acquisitions are generally taxable to the shareholders of the acquired company who surrendered their shares unless:

1. The transaction is a merger under state law and a significant part of the total consideration received is common stock of the acquiring company, or

2. The transaction involves the acquisition of at least 80 percent of the acquired company's common shares solely in exchange for common shares of the acquiring company.

B. The change in stock ownership generally has no effect on the tax basis of a company's net assets.

1. If the transaction is nontaxable to the target company's shareholders, the tax basis of the company's assets and liabilities remains the same.

2. If the transaction is taxable to the target company's shareholders, the target company can elect to be taxed as if it had sold its net assets and repurchased them at fair value.

   a. If the company makes this election, it will recognize gains and losses on the differences between fair value and former tax bases. If the combination is accounted for as a purchase, the assets and liabilities of the acquired company will have the same values for book and tax purposes.

   b. If the company does not make this election, it will retain the old tax bases and not recognize any gains or losses. If the combination is accounted for as a purchase, differences will exist between the fair values and tax bases of the assets and liabilities of the acquired company.

C. The members of an affiliated group can elect to file consolidated or separate income tax returns. To qualify as an affiliated group, the parent must own at least 80 percent of the common shares of its subsidiary.

5

VI. Appendix A: Working with the Authoritative Literature of the SEC, FASB, and AICPA

t min wt to invests   *regulate tradizin*

A. The structure of accounting authority rests on the Securities Act of 1933 and the Securities Exchange Act of 1934, both of which are administered by the Securities and Exchange Commission (SEC). Registration statements required by the SEC are:

1. Form 10 is the initial form filed by firms when they become subject to the authority of the SEC. It contains audited financial statements.

2. Form 10-K is filed annually and contains audited annual financial statements.

3. Form 10-Q is filed quarterly. It contains abbreviated financial statements which may be unaudited.

B. The SEC has implicitly delegated some of its authority to:

1. The Accounting Principles Board (APB).

2. The Financial Accounting Standards Board (FASB).

3. The American Institute of Certified Public Accountants (AICPA).

C. The most important source materials for accounting research are:

1. Pronouncements by the SEC:

   a. Accounting Series Releases.
   b. Staff Accounting Bulletins.
   c. Financial Reporting Releases are the replacement of Accounting Series Releases. Financial Reporting Release No. 1 codifies previous Accounting Series Releases.
   d. Regulation S-X and Regulation S-K.

2. Pronouncements by the APB:

   a. Opinions.
   b. Interpretations of APB Opinions.

3. Pronouncements by the FASB:

   a. Discussion Memoranda.
   b. Exposure Drafts.
   c. Statements of Financial Accounting Standards.
   d. Interpretations
   e. Technical Bulletins.
   f. Consensus Positions by the Emerging Issues Task Force.

6

4. Pronouncements by the AICPA:

    a. <u>Accounting Research Bulletins</u>, superseded by <u>APB Opinions</u>.
    b. <u>Statements of Position</u> by the Accounting Standards Executive Committee.
    c. <u>Issues Papers</u> by the Accounting Standards Executive Committee.
    d. <u>Industry Accounting Guides</u>.
    e. <u>Industry Audit Guides</u>.

VII. Appendix B: Negotiations of Business Combinations

A. In a cash for common stock exchange the price to be paid for the target company's shares is negotiated.

B. In a common stock for common stock exchange the ratio of shares to be exchanged is negotiated. If the combination is expected to produce synergistic values, the limits of the stock exchange ratio are:

    1. The maximum exchange ratio for the acquiring company allocates the total synergistic value to the shareholders of the acquired company.

    2. The minimum exchange ratio for the acquired company allocates the total synergistic value to the acquiring company.

C. The computations for the maximum and minimum exchange ratios are:

    1. Maximum number of shares to be issued: $\dfrac{P}{P + Y} \times FV = MV\text{-}P$

    2. Minimum number of shares to be issued: $\dfrac{Y}{P + Y} \times FV = MV\text{-}S$

    3. Exchange ratio: Y : S

    4. The symbols mean:
        P   =   number of outstanding shares of parent (acquiring) company before acquisition
        Y   =   number of additional shares of parent company to be issued for the acquired company's shares
        FV =   the future value of the combined companies
        MV-P =   the total market value of the outstanding parent shares before acquisition
        MV-S =   the total market value of the outstanding subsidiary shares before acquisition
        S   =   number of outstanding shares of subsidiary (acquired) company before acquisition

Test Your Understanding of Chapter 1

True or False

Instructions: Indicate your choice by circling either T, if you think the statement is true, or F, if you think the statement is false.

T F 1. The primary motivation for business combinations is synergy.

T F 2. A consolidation is a business combination in which both the parent and the subsidiary survive.

T F 3. A merger is a business combination in which the acquiring and the acquired company are merged into a newly-formed company.

T F 4. When a business combination does not meet all of the conditions of APB Opinion No. 16 it must be accounted for as a purchase.

T F 5. The fundamental difference between the purchase and pooling of interests method is that under the purchase method the acquiring company's assets are recorded at fair value, whereas under the pooling method they remain at book value. acquired

T F 6. To qualify for pooling of interests treatment, the business combination must meet all 12 conditions specified by APB Opinion No. 18.

T F 7. Purchasing treasury stock to honor executive stock opinion plans does not violate the prohibition against treasury stock transactions and means that the combination can still qualify for pooling of interests treatment.

T F 8. If a business combination qualifies as a nontaxable transaction, it should be accounted for as a pooling of interests.

T F 9. To qualify as a nontaxable transaction to the shareholders of the acquired company, the acquiring company must obtain at least 90 percent of the acquired company's outstanding stock.

T F 10. If a business combination is taxable, the tax bases of the acquired company's assets and liabilities changes.

T F 11. A parent and its subsidiary may file consolidated income tax returns if the parent owns at least 80 percent of the subsidiary's outstanding common stock.

T F 12. Financial Reporting Releases are issued by the FASB.

T F 13.   In a <u>Discussion Memorandum</u> the FASB does not take a
                position.

T F 14.   The maximum number of shares the stockholders of the
                parent company are willing to exchange for subsidiary
                company shares allocates the total synergistic value to
                the subsidiary's shareholders.

T F 15.   The minimum number of parent company shares the
                stockholders of the subsidiary company are willing to
                accept allocates the total synergistic value to the
                parent's shareholders.

Exercises

P Company is negotiating with the shareholders of S Company for the
acquisition of their shares. Relevant data for the two companies and
the combined companies are as follows:

	P Company	S Company	Combined
Net income	$500,000	$100,000	$700,000
Common shares outstanding	200,000	50,000	
Earnings per share	$2.50	$2.00	
Common share market price	$30.00	$12.00	

Both firms expect the combined companies to have a total market value
of approximately $7,000,000 after the combination.

1. Required: Determine the maximum acceptable stock exchange ratio.

2. Required: Determine the minimum acceptable stock exchange ratio.

3. Required: Determine earnings per share assuming
                a. the maximum stock exchange ratio

                b. the minimum stock exchange ratio.

Solutions to Chapter 1 Exercises

True or False

1. T	4. T	7. T	10. F	13. T
2. F	5. F	8. F	11. T	14. T
3. F	6. F	9. F	12. F	15. T

Exercises

1. $[200,000 : (200,000 + Y)] \times 7,000,000 = 6,000,000$
   $200,000 \times 7,000,000 = 6,000,000 \times (200,000 + Y)$
   $1,400,000 = 1,200,000 + 6Y$
   $6Y = 200,000$
   $Y = 200,000 : 6$
   $Y = 33,333$
   Maximum acceptable exchange ratio: $Y : S = 33,333 : 50,000 = .667$

2. $[Y : (200,000 + Y)] \times 7,000,000 = 600,000$
   $Y \times 7,000,000 = 600,000 \times (200,000 + Y)$
   $7,000,000Y = 120,000,000,000 + 600,000Y$
   $6,400,000Y = 120,000,000,000$
   $64Y = 1,200,000$
   $Y = 1,200,000 : 64$
   $Y = 18,750$

   Minimum acceptable exchange ratio: $Y : S = 18,750 : 50,000 = .375$

3. a. EPS under maximum exchange ratio = $700,000 : (200,000 + 33,333) = \$3.00$

   b. EPS under minimum exchange ratio = $700,000 : (200,000 + 18,750) = \$3.20$

Chapter 2
Balance Sheet Issues in Purchase Transactions

Chapter Outline

I. Reasons for the Acquisition Form of Business Combination

    A.   It is cheaper to acquire a subsidiary's stock than to acquire its net assets, since control of the net assets is achieved with the ownership of less than 100 percent of the outstanding voting stock.

    B.   In case the acquisition is less profitable than expected, it may be easier to dispose of the shares of a subsidiary than individual assets.

    C.   The parent, like any corporate stockholder, has limited liability.

    D.   A disadvantage of the acquisition form is that both parent and subsidiary may be subject to a state franchise tax levied on the corporate assets. In the parent's case, these assets include the investment in the subsidiary's stock.

II. Determining the Cost of an Acquired Company

    A.   Only the direct, incremental costs of an acquisition are included in the cost of the investment.

    B.   When securities are issued to acquire the stock of a subsidiary, the costs of issuing and registering these securities affects the proceeds from the securities, not the cost of the investment.

    C.   An acquisition agreement may specify the issuance of additional stock contingent on a future event. The issuance of such additional shares should be added to the cost of the investment only if it is based on earnings, not if it is based on security prices.

    D.   The date of acquisition is normally the date assets are received and other assets are given or securities are issued.

III. Consolidated Balance Sheet

    A.   The consolidated balance sheet differs from the parent company's balance sheet only in detail. Instead of the parent's Investment in S Company account the consolidated balance sheet contains the assets and liabilities of S and the minority interest in S, if applicable.

11

1. P acquires 100 percent of S at book value and book value equals fair value. The disaggregation of P's investment account substitutes the assets and liabilities of S with no differential remaining.

2. P acquires 100 percent of S at a price other than book value and book value does not equal fair value. The disaggregation of P's investment account leaves a differential between P's cost and the book value of S. This differential is allocated to differences between fair and book value with any positive remainder termed goodwill.

3. P acquires less than 100 percent at book value and book value equals fair value.

   a. In a proportionate consolidation the disaggregation of P's investment account substitutes P's share of each individual asset and liability of S with no recognition of the minority interest.

   b. In a full consolidation the disaggregation of P's investment account substitutes S's assets and liabilities and recognizes the minority interest in the net assets of S.

4. P acquires less than 100 percent at a price other than book value and book value does not equal fair value. The disaggregation of P's investment account leaves a differential between P's cost and P's share of the book value of S. This differential is allocated to differences between fair and book value with any positive remainder allocated to goodwill. In a full consolidation the minority interest can be handled in two different ways:

   a. Under the entity theory 100 percent of the fair value of S is determined by dividing P's cost by its percentage of ownership in S. The assets and liabilities of S are recorded at 100 percent of fair value and the minority interest, too, is shown at fair value, including its share of goodwill, if any.

   b. Under the parent company theory only P's share of the difference between fair value and book value is recognized (including any goodwill paid for by P), while the minority interest is shown at its percentage of S's book value.

B. A consolidated balance sheet working paper is used to facilitate the preparation of a consolidated balance sheet.

12

1.   The working paper has the following five columns: one each for P's and S's balance sheet, two for the debit and credit side of the elimination entries, and one for the consolidated amounts.

2.   The elimination entries are numbered: the first one eliminates the equity accounts of S and the investment account of P and sets up the differential and the minority interest; the second one allocates the differential.

3.   The elimination entries result in:

   a.   the elimination of the stockholders' equity of S,

   b.   the elimination of the parent company's investment account,

   c.   the establishment of the minority interest,

   d.   the allocation of the differential to the differences between fair value and book value of S's net assets and the recognition of goodwill.

4.   Elimination entries are not recorded on the books of either the parent or the subsidiary.

C.   Other intercompany transactions, such as receivables and payables, and subsidiary treasury stock are also eliminated.

D.   Consolidated and separate parent company balance sheets do not give the same picture of financial position.

   1.   The shareholders equity section is the same in both statements.

   2.   Total assets and total liabilities, as well as ratios based on balance sheet items, are usually different.

IV.   Requirements for Consolidated and Separate Company Statements

A.   Both the SEC and the FASB consider consolidated statements to be more meaningful than separate parent company statements. Therefore, separate parent company statements are viewed as supplements to the consolidated statements. Consolidated statements are required:

   1.   Under the SEC's Regulation S-X when one company controls another one.

   2.   Under the FASB's SFAS No. 94 when one company owns a majority of the outstanding voting stock of another one.

3. Generally, majority ownership means control. However, control may be temporary, e. g. if the subsidiary has outstanding convertible debt, or may be exercised by somebody else, e. g. when the subsidiary is in bankruptcy.

B. Separate company statements of the subsidiary may be prepared using push down accounting. In this case an entry is made on the subsidiary's books to adjust the book values by the parent's share of the difference between fair value and book value, record the parent's share of goodwill, and eliminate the subsidiary's retained earnings as of the acquisition date.

1. Under the SEC's Staff Accounting Bulletin No. 54 and Staff Accounting Bulletin No. 73 the subsidiary's assets and liabilities should be shown at the same values as they have in the consolidated statements. This means book value plus the parent's share of the difference between fair and book value, including the parent's cost allocated to goodwill.

2. Staff Accounting Bulletin No. 54 requires push down accounting if the parent acquires at least 90 percent of the subsidiary's outstanding voting stock in a single transaction, unless the subsidiary has either public debt or preferred stock outstanding.

3. Consensus Position No. 86-16 specifies valuation of the subsidiary's assets and liabilities at book value plus the parent's share of the difference between fair and book value.

V. Accounting for Leveraged Buyouts

A. In a typical leveraged buyout (LBO) a newly created holding company acquires all the outstanding common shares of an existing company. It exchanges the old company shares held by the organizers of the LBO for shares of the new holding company. The remaining outstanding shares of the old company are acquired with cash borrowed and received for the issuance of new company stock. The old company is then merged into the new company.

B. Under Consensus Position No. 88-16 the assets and liabilities of the old company on the books of the new company should be valued at fair value, except for the percentage of net assets represented by the old company shares exchanged for new company shares. In other words, the net asset valuation results in the same valuations as the parent company theory applied to purchase acquisitions.

14

VI. Differential Allocation

A. Fair value is determined according to <u>APB Opinion No. 16</u>:

1. Marketable securities at current net realizable values.

2. Receivables at present values of amounts to be received determined at appropriate current interest rates, less allowances for uncollectibility and collection costs.

3. Inventories:

   a. Finished goods at estimated selling prices less the sum of disposal costs and a reasonable profit allowance for the selling effort.

   b. Work in process at estimated selling prices of finished goods less the sum of costs to complete, costs of disposal, and a reasonable profit allowance for the completion and selling efforts.

   c. Raw materials at current replacement costs.

4. Plant and equipment:

   a. To be used: at current replacement costs for similar capacity unless the expected future use of the assets indicates a lower value to the acquirer.

   b. To be sold or held for later sale rather than used: at current net realizable value.

   c. To be used temporarily: at current net realizable value recognizing future depreciation for the expected period of use.

5. Intangible assets than can be identified and named, including contracts, patents, franchises, customer and supplier lists, and favorable leases, at appraised values.

6. Other assets, including land, natural resources, and nonmarketable securities at appraised values.

7. Accounts and notes payable, long-term debt, and other claims payable at present values of amounts to be paid determined at appropriate current interest rates.

8. Other liabilities and commitments, including unfavorable leases, contracts, and commitments and plant closing expense incident to the acquisition, at present values of amounts to be paid determined at appropriate current interest rates.

9. Pension plans, as amended by SFAS No. 87:

   a. Liabilities at the excess of projected benefit obligations over plant assets.

   b. Assets at the excess of plant assets over projected benefit obligations.

B. Deferred taxes are required under SFAS No. 96. They should be set up for the differences between fair values and tax bases. If present book values differ from tax bases, the present balance of deferred taxes should be adjusted for the differences between fair and book values.

C. Net operating loss carryforwards can be assigned a value if, under the laws of the applicable taxing jurisdiction, they can reduce the parent's tax liability.

   1. If a value is assigned to a net operating loss carryforward, the amount allocated to goodwill is reduced.

   2. If no value is assigned to a net operating loss carryforward at acquisition, its subsequent realization will reduce goodwill. After goodwill is reduced to zero, income tax expense is decreased.

D. A residual credit differential results when P's purchase price is below its share of the fair value of S. Under APB Opinion No. 16 it is used to reduce the assigned values of noncurrent assets, except long-term investments in marketable securities, proportionately. If a credit differential remains after P's share of the noncurrent assets has been reduced to zero, it is classified as a deferred credit and amortized like goodwill.

E. Preacquisition contingencies, such as pending litigation, should be reflected in the determination of fair values, if they are resolved during the allocation period (generally understood to mean one year after acquisition). If they are resolved later, they should affect earnings. Litigation arising from the acquisition itself are contingencies of the purchaser.

Test Your Understanding of Chapter 2

True or False

Instructions: Indicate your choice by circling either T, if you think the statement is true, or F, if you think the statement is false.

T F 1. An acquisition is the only type of business combination that creates a parent-subsidiary relationship.

T F 2. An advantage of the parent-subsidiary relationship is that the subsidiary has limited liability.

T F 3. A disadvantage of the parent-subsidiary relationship is that it is more difficult to sell the shares of a subsidiary than individual assets.

T F 4. In a purchase acquisition the value of the stock acquired is measured by the fair value of the shares received or the consideration (cash or securities) given, whichever is more clearly evident.

T F 5. Costs of maintaining an acquisition department should be allocated directly to the investment cost of any acquisitions made during the period.

T F 6. The cost of an acquisition should be increased by the amount of any contingent consideration given after the date of acquisition, if the additional consideration is based on stock price performance.

T F 7. Consolidated balance sheets essentially contain a summation of the affiliates' assets and liabilities that have resulted from transactions with nonaffiliates.

T F 8. If P acquires 100 percent of S's stock at a cost that is equal to book value, there is no differential to be allocated to goodwill, no matter what the fair value is.

T F 9. If the parent company owns 80 percent of the subsidiary's voting stock, only 80 percent of the subsidiary's assets and liabilities are combined with those of the parent company under a proportionate consolidation.

T F 10. A debit differential is the excess of the parent's cost over the parent's share of the fair value of the subsidiary's net assets.

T F 11. If the book value of a subsidiary's net assets is $100,000 and the parent pays $90,000 for an 80 percent interest, a debit differential of $10,000 results.

T F 12. If S Company has treasury stock in its capital structure when P Company obtains a majority of S's voting stock, P Company's percentage of control is based on the total number of S shares outstanding rather than shares issued.

T F 13. The investment elimination entry avoids double counting of subsidiary net assets when the subsidiary's individual assets and liabilities are combined with those of the parent.

T F 14. Except possibly for disclosure of minority interests, the consolidated owners' equity section reports just the parent's owners' equity accounts.

T F 15. To be effective, all elimination entries are booked by the parent.

Exercises

1. P Company acquired all of S Company's 1,000,000 outstanding shares of common stock in exchange for 250,000 shares of P Company common stock. P's stock has a par value of $1 and a market value of $25. P Company paid $100,000 for a preacquisition audit and $75,000 to register the shares it exchanged for S's stock. The cost of operating P Company's acquisitions department was $4,000,000, which worked exclusively on the S Company acquisition for at least 3 months during the past year.

Required:
a. Compute the cost of the investment to P Company.

b. Record the acquisition on P's books

18

2. On January 1, 19x1, S Company prepared the following balance sheet:

	Book Value	Fair Value
Cash	$ 20,000	$ 20,000
Receivables	50,000	45,000
Inventories	60,000	75,000
Land	25,000	55,000
Plant and Equipment	200,000	180,000
Patents	5,000	15,000
Total assets	$360,000	$390,000
Liabilities.............	$100,000	$100,000
Common stock	120,000	
Paid-in capital	80,000	
Retained earnings	60,000	
Total equities	$360,000	

Assume that P paid $400,000 in cash for 100 percent of S's stock.

Required:

a. Compute the differential and indicate whether it is a debit or a credit.

b. Prepare the investment elimination entry for the consolidated working paper at acquisition.

c.   Prepare the elimination entry to allocate the differential.

3.   Use the balance sheet from Exercise 2 but assume that P paid $300,000 for 80 percent of S of S's stock.

Required:
a.   Compute the differential and indicate whether it is a debit or a credit.

b.   Prepare the investment elimination entry for the consolidated working paper at acquisition.

c.   Prepare the elimination entry to allocate the differential.

4.   Use the balance sheet from Exercise 2 but assume that P paid $200,000 for 90 percent of S's stock.

Required:
a.   Compute the differential and indicate whether it is a debit or a credit.

b.   Prepare the investment elimination entry for the consolidated working paper at acquisition.

c. **Prepare the elimination entry to allocate the differential.**

Solutions to Chapter 2 Exercises

True or False

1.	T	4.	T	7.	T	10.	F	13.	T
2.	F	5.	F	8.	F	11.	T	14.	T
3.	F	6.	F	9.	T	12.	T	15.	F

Exercises

1. a. Market value of P stock issued:
          250,000 shares x $25 = $6,250,000
          Preacquisition audit   100,000
          Investment in S Company $6,350,000

    b. Investment in S Company   6,350,000
              Cash or liability to auditors   100,000
              Cash or liability for registration   75,000
              Common stock, 250,000 shares @ $1   250,000
              Paid-in capital [250,000 x
                (25 - 1)] - 75,000   5,925,000

2. a. P's cost................................. $400,000
        Less P's share of S's book value -260,000
          x 100%   260,000
        Debit Differential $140,000

    b. Common stock   120,000
        Paid-in capital   80,000
        Retained earnings   60,000
        Differential   140,000
            Investment in S Company   400,000

    c. Inventories (75,000 - 60,000)   15,000
        Land (55,000 - 25,000)   30,000
        Patents (15,000 - 5,000)   10,000
        Goodwill*   110,000
            Receivables (45,000 - 50,000).   5,000
            Plant and equipment (180,000 -
              200,000)   20,000
            Differential   140,000

        *P's cost $400,000
        Less P's share of S's fair value -
          (390,000 - 100,000) x 100%   290,000
        Goodwill $110,000

3. a. P's cost $300,000
        Less P's share of S's book value - 260,000 x 80%   208,000
        Debit Differential .... $ 92,000

23

b. Common stock 120,000
   Paid-in capital 80,000
   Retained earnings 60,000
   Differential 92,000
         Minority interest (260,000 x 20%)   52,000
         Investment in S Company   300,000

c. Inventories (15,000 x 80%) 12,000
   Land (30,000 x 80%) 24,000
   Patents (10,000 x 80%) 8,000
   Goodwill* 68,000
         Receivables (5,000 x 80%)   4,000
         Plant and equipment (20,000 x 80%)   16,000
         Differential   92,000

   *P's cost $300,000
   Less P's share of S's fair value - 290,000 x 80% 232,000
   Goodwill .... $ 68,000

4. a. P's cost $200,000
      Less P's share of S's book value - 260,000 x 90% 234,000
      Credit Differential .... $(34,000)

   b. Common stock 120,000
      Paid-in capital 80,000
      Retained earnings 60,000
            Differential   34,000
            Minority interest (260,000 x 10%)   26,000
            Investment in S Company   200,000

   c. Inventories (15,000 x 90%) 13,500
      Land (30,000 x 90%) - 13,420* 13,580
      Patents (10,000 x 90%) - 3,660* ... 5,340
      Differential 34,000
            Receivables ((5,000 x 90%) ...   4,500
            Plant and equipment
            (20,000 x 90%) + 43,920* ...   61,920

   Allocation of residual credit differential:
                         Fair value   Percent   Allocation
   Land   55,000   22   13,420
   Plant and equipment   180,000   72   43,920
   Patents   15,000   6   3,660
   Totals   250,000   100   61,000

   Computation of residual credit differential:
   P's cost $200,000
   Less P's share of S's fair value - 290,000 x 90% 261,000
   Residual credit differential .... $(61,000)

24

Chapter 3
Income and Retained Earnings Statement
Issues in Purchase Combinations

Chapter Outline

I. The Cost Method

A. This method basically reflects the assumption that the initial cost of an investment in a subsidiary should remain unadjusted over time.

B. Subsidiary profits and losses are not reflected on the parent's books.

C. The parent recognizes its share of the subsidiary's income only when the subsidiary declares a cash dividend.

D. The exception is a subsidiary's dividend in excess of the accumulated, undistributed earnings since acquisition by the parent. Such excess is classified as a liquidating dividend and credited to the investment account.

II. The Equity Method *reduction of inv*

A. This method is based on the premise that the parent's investment account should present the parent's interest in the subsidiary's net assets. As the book values of the net assets change, the parent's investment account is adjusted periodically for the parent's interest in the changes.

B. The parent's share of a subsidiary's net income is debited to the investment account and credited to a suitably named account, such as Equity in Subsidiary's Earnings.

C. The parent's share of a subsidiary's net loss is debited to Equity in Subsidiary's Earnings and credited to the investment account. No more entries are made if the investment account is reduced to zero, unless the parent guaranteed the subsidiary's debts.

D. Dividends declared by the subsidiary are credited to the investment account because the declaration of cash dividends by the subsidiary decreases its net assets.

E. The equity method is a relaxation of the traditional realization criterion. It incorporates the belief that the economic impact of a corporation's profits and losses immediately accrues to its stockholders, regardless of when dividends are declared and paid.

III. Entry Comparison

    A.   <u>APB Opinion No. 18</u> requires the equity method for financial reporting of unconsolidated subsidiaries.

    B.   The method chosen by the parent to account for its investment in a subsidiary (cost or equity) does not affect the consolidated statements, but it does affect the consolidated working paper entries.

IV. Statements of Consolidated Income and Retained Earnings

    A.   The consolidated income statement summarizes the revenues, expenses, gains and losses of the affiliated companies and eliminates balances resulting from intercompany transactions. From this total income the minority interest in the net incomes of subsidiaries is subtracted to arrive at consolidated net income. This definition reflects the parent company theory and is based on the assumption that the consolidated statements are prepared for the parent company's stockholders and creditors.

    B.   An alternative definition of consolidated net income treats the minority interest's share of subsidiary net income as a distribution of, rather than as a deduction necessary to determine, consolidated net income. This definition reflects the entity theory.

    C.   The consolidated statement of retained earnings starts with beginning consolidated retained earnings, adds consolidated net income and deducts the parent's dividends to arrive at ending consolidated retained earnings.

V. The Three-Division Working Paper--First Year Subsequent to Acquisition

    A.   The three-division working paper format can be used whether the financial information of the affiliated companies is arranged in financial statements or in trial balances. Under this format the nominal accounts have not yet been closed. The retained earnings section of each company therefore starts with the beginning retained earnings balance, adds the net income from the income statement and deducts the dividends declared to arrive at the ending balance.

    B.   In Case 1 the data for the first year assume an acquisition at book value.

    C.   The elimination entries for Case 1 substitute the subsidiary's account balances for the parent's Equity in Subsidiary Earnings and Investment accounts and set up the minority interest. This is done in three entries:

1. The first entry reverses the entry made on the parent's books to recognize its share of the subsidiary's income or loss. If the parent owns less than 100 percent of the subsidiary, this entry also sets up the minority interest in the income statement and the balance sheet.

2. The second entry eliminates the dividends declared from the subsidiary's retained earnings. The corresponding debits reverse the credit recorded in the parent's investment account for its share of these dividends and, if appropriate, reduces the minority interest for the dividends it received.

3. The third entry deals only with balances as of the beginning of the period. Since this case is for the first year after acquisition, the beginning balances are those at acquisition. The entry eliminates the stockholders' equity of the subsidiary and the investment account and sets up the minority interest.

D. After the elimination entries are made, the elimination columns are successively added with the sub-totals entered on the appropriate line of the next statement.

E. The working paper reveals certain important relationships:

1. Consolidated net income is identical to the parent's net income. The consolidated income statement merely substitutes the subsidiary's income and expense balances for the parent's Equity in Subsidiary Earnings. For this reason the equity method is called a "one-line consolidation."

2. The same amounts appear in the parent's and the consolidated columns of the retained earnings section.

3. The entries to the minority interest in the income statement, retained earnings section, and balance sheet equal the ending minority interest in the balance sheet when added together.

4. Total consolidated assets probably do not equal the total assets of the parent, since the subsidiary's net assets (i. e. assets less liabilities) are substituted for the parent's investment account.

VI. Consolidated Statement Working Paper--Second Year Subsequent to Acquisition

A. For the second year after acquisition and any period thereafter the consolidated working papers are set up and completed in essentially the same way as the working papers for the year of acquisition.

B. The same three elimination entries are made as in the first year after acquisition. The third entry again deals with balances as of the beginning of the year, in this case the beginning of year 2.

VII. Other Intercompany Transactions

A. In addition to the parent's investment in the subsidiary the two companies may engage in other intercompany transactions. The effects of these transactions must also be eliminated.

B. Intercompany sales and cost of goods sold should be eliminated in total. These transactions present special problems when some of the merchandise purchased from an affiliate remains in the ending inventory of the buyer.

C. Other types of intercompany transactions that must be eliminated result from the rendering of services, such as intercompany loans, including interest income and expense, management fee income and expense, etc.

VIII. Multicompany Affiliations

A. If a parent company has more than one subsidiary (i. e. a multicompany affiliation), the principles of consolidation are the same as for a parent and one subsidiary.

1. In the working paper a separate column is used for each subsidiary.

2. The elimination entries are similar to the ones for a parent with one subsidiary.

3. In the working paper the minority interests in the two subsidiaries are kept separate.

B. A reconsideration of basic definitions points out different ways of calculating consolidated net income and consolidated retained earnings without the preparation of working papers.

1. Consolidated net income can be computed in the following two ways:

a. A residual determination of consolidated net income adds the net incomes of the parent and each subsidiary, subtracts the parent's share of the net income of each subsidiary and the minority interest in each subsidiary.

b. An incremental determination of consolidated net income takes the parent's net income from its own operations and adds to it the parent's share of the net income of each subsidiary.

28

2. Consolidated retained earnings at acquisition are the parent's retained earnings. For any period ending retained earnings is obtained by taking beginning retained earnings, adding consolidated net income and deducting the parent's declared dividends. If the parent uses the equity method, the parent's retained earnings are identical to consolidated retained earnings.

IX. Accounting for Investments in Joint Ventures

A. A joint venture is an entity owned and operated by a small group of investors termed venturers. Usually no single investor is in control.

B. Joint ventures are frequently used for particularly risky undertakings requiring large capital investments.

C. A joint venture can be organized as a corporation, a general partnership, a limited partnership, or an undivided interest.

D. Corporate joint ventures must use the equity method of accounting for the venture according to APB Opinion No. 18 on the assumption that the venturers are exercising joint control over the venture. If, however, one corporation controls the venture, then the venture is deemed a subsidiary and the other venturers should use the cost method to account for their investment in the venture.

E. Partnerships and undivided interests should also use the equity method according to Accounting Interpretation No. 2 of APB Opinion No. 18. Since partnerships and undivided interests are not taxed directly, income taxes attributable to venture profits and losses should be accrued.

F. Proportionate consolidation is used for investments in undivided interests, especially in the oil and gas industry. In this case each investor includes its proportionate interest in assets, liabilities, revenues, and expenses, and no minority interest is reported.

G. Real estate joint ventures should, according to the AICPA's Statement of Position 78-9, use control, not the exercise of influence, as the determinant for selecting the method of accounting. In other words, if one venturer has control, this venturer should consolidate the investment. The other venturers should use the cost or equity method, depending on their ability to exercise significant influence over the operating and financial policies of the venture. If the venture is subject to joint control, all venturers should use the equity method.

X. Appendix: Consolidated Working Paper Techniques Using the Cost Method

A. In the first year after acquisition the consolidation of the parent's and subsidiary's account balances is accomplished with the following elimination entries:

1. The first entry eliminates the subsidiary's dividends declared by debiting the parent's dividend income and the minority interest's share of the subsidiary's dividends.

2. The second entry debits (credits) the minority interest in the income statement and credits (debits) the minority interest in the balance sheet for the minority interest in the subsidiary's net income (net loss).

3. The third entry deals with balances as of the beginning of the year, i. e. at acquisition. It eliminates the stockholders' equity of the subsidiary and the parent's investment account and sets up the minority interest in the subsidiary's net assets.

4. When the parent uses the cost method, consolidated net income and consolidated retained earnings will not equal the corresponding amounts on the parent's books, as they do under the equity method.

    a. Consolidated net income equals the parent's net income plus the subsidiary's net income, less the parent's dividend income and the minority interest in net income. It can also be obtained by summing across the net income line on the working papers.

    b. At acquisition the parent's retained earnings is the consolidated retained earnings. It is increased by consolidated net income and decreased by the parent's dividends to arrive at the ending consolidated retained earnings. The ending consolidated retained earnings can also be computed by adding the parent's share of the change in the subsidiary's retained earnings after acquisition to the parent's retained earnings.

5. The consolidated column under the cost method is identical to the same column under the equity method.

B. In the second year after acquisition the consolidation of the parent's and subsidiary's account balances is accomplished with the following elimination entries:

1. The first entry again eliminates the subsidiary's dividends declared with debits to the parent's dividend income and the minority interest's share of the subsidiary's dividends.

2. The second entry again debits the minority interest in the income statement and credits the minority interest in the balance sheet for its share of the subsidiary's net income. If the subsidiary reports a net loss, the entry is reversed.

3. Whereas the first two entries are the same for the first and second year after acquisition, the third entry differs significantly, as follows:

   a. 100 percent of the subsidiary's contributed capital (common stock and paid-in capital) is eliminated.

   b. The debit to the subsidiary's retained earnings is for the parent's share <u>at acquisition</u> plus the minority interest's share as of the beginning of the year, i. e. Year 2 in this case.

   c. The credit to the investment account is for the cost at acquisition, since no entries have been made to this account under the cost method.

   d. The credit to the minority interest is for its share of the stockholders' equity as of the beginning of the year.

4. When the parent uses the cost method its net income and retained earnings will differ from their consolidated counterparts.

   a. Consolidated net income can be computed in any year as described for the first year after acquisition or by summing across the net income line of the working papers.

   b. Consolidated retained earnings at the beginning of any year is equal to the parent's beginning retained earnings plus the parent's share of the change in the subsidiary's retained earnings since acquisition. It is increased by consolidated net income and decreased by the parent's dividends to arrive at ending consolidated retained earnings. The difference between the parent's ending retained earnings and consolidated retained earnings is again the parent's share of the change in the subsidiary's retained earnings since acquisition.

5. The consolidated columns under the cost method are again identical to those under the equity method.

31

Test Your Understanding of Chapter 3

True or False

Instructions: Indicate your choice by circling either T, if you think the statement is true, or F, if you think the statement is false.

T F 1. The cost method of accounting for an investment in a subsidiary records the declaration of a cash dividend by the subsidiary as a reduction in the book value of the investment.

T F 2. Under the equity method of accounting for an investment in a subsidiary the investment account is adjusted periodically for the parent's proportionate share of the subsidiary's income, losses, and dividends declared after the date of acquisition.

T F 3. The account Equity in Subsidiary Earnings is a nominal account that contains the parent's proportionate share of the subsidiary's income or loss for the current period and is closed at the end of each annual accounting period.

T F 4. APB Opinion No. 18 requires that the parent use the equity method on its books to account for investments in consolidated as well as unconsolidated subsidiaries.

T F 5. If the parent owns only 80 percent of a subsidiary, the consolidated income statement should show consolidated sales equal to the parent's sales plus 80 percent of the subsidiary's sales.

T F 6. In the income statement division of consolidated working papers revenues, expenses, gains, and losses reported by an affiliate that resulted from transactions with another affiliate must be eliminated.

T F 7. According to one approach consolidated net income equals the affiliates' combined incomes after eliminations and after a deduction for the minority shareholders' interest in the subsidiary's reported net income.

T F 8. If the parent uses the equity method, its net income will equal consolidated net income.

T F 9. If the parent uses the equity method, ending consolidated retained earnings is equal to the parent's ending retained earnings plus the parent's share of the change in the subsidiary's retained earnings since acquisition.

T F 10. In consolidated working papers based on the equity method the first two elimination entries are designed to restore the investment account to the balance it had at the beginning of the period.

T F 11. If the parent uses the equity method, the entry eliminating
          the parent's share of the subsidiary's dividends debits
          Dividends Declared - Subsidiary and credits Investment in
          Subsidiary.

T F 12. After all elimination entries have been made on the
          consolidated working papers, the accounts Investment in
          Subsidiary and Equity in Subsidiary Earnings will have zero
          balances.

T F 13. The equity method is known as a one-line consolidation
          because the parent's income from its own operations plus its
          equity in the subsidiary's earnings equals consolidated net
          income.

T F 14. The difference between the parent's net income under the
          cost method and consolidated net income is the parent's
          share of the subsidiary's dividends declared.

T F 15. Consolidated retained earnings after acquisition is equal to
          the parent's retained earnings under the cost method plus
          the parent's share of the change in the subsidiary's
          retained earnings since acquisition.

Exercises

1. P Company acquired a 60 percent interest in S Company on January
1, 19x1, at a cost of $42,000. On this date S Company had common
stock of $10,000, paid-in capital of $20,000 and retained earnings of
$40,000.

During 19x1 S Company reported net income of $15,000 and declared and
paid cash dividends of $6,000.

Required:
a.   Prepare all entries on P Company's books relating to its
     investment in S for 19x1 using the equity method.

b.   Prepare all entries on P Company's books relating to its
     investment in S for 19x1 using the cost method.

2.   On January 1, 19x1, P Company purchased 7,200 shares of S Company
for $120,000 in cash.   On this date S Company's equity consisted of
common stock, par $10, of $90,000 and retained earnings of $60,000.

For 19x1 S Company reported net income of $20,000 and paid dividends
of $10,000.   For 19x2 S Company reported a net loss of $15,000.   It
paid no dividends in 19x2.

Required:
a.   Prepare the entries on P Company's books relating to its
     investment in S Company for 19x1 and 19x2 using the equity
     method.

19x1

19x2

b. Prepare the elimination entries for the consolidated working
    papers for 19x1 and 19x2.

19x1

19x2

3. On January 1, 19x1, P Company purchased 75 percent of the
outstanding voting stock of S Company at book value. For 19x1 S
Company reported net income of $40,000 and paid dividends of $20,000.

Required:
a. Assume that P Company uses the equity method and reported net
    income of $100,000 for 19x1.
    (1) Compute consolidated net income for 19x1 using the
         incremental approach.

(2) Compute consolidated net income for 19x1 using the residual approach.

b.   Assume that P Company uses the cost method and reported net income of $85,000 for 19x1.

   (1)   Compute consolidated net income for 19x1 using the incremental approach.

   (2) Compute consolidated net income for 19x1 using the residual approach.

4.   On January 1, 19x1, P Company acquired 60 percent of S Company for $120,000.   P will use the equity method to account for its investment.

On the day of acquisition S's equity consisted of common stock, par $1, of $10,000, paid-in capital of $40,000 and retained earnings of $150,000.   There have been no changes in S Company's outstanding common stock.

For 19x1 S Company reported net income of $40,000 and paid dividends of $25,000.   For 19x2 S Company reported net income of $20,000 and paid dividends of $15,000.

Required:
a.   Prepare the elimination entries for the consolidated working
      papers at the end of 19x1.

b.   Prepare the elimination entries for the consolidated working
      papers at the end of 19x2.

Solutions to Chapter 3 Exercises

True or False

1.	F	4.	F	7.	T	10.	T	13.	T
2.	T	5.	F	8.	T	11.	F	14.	F
3.	T	6.	T	9.	F	12.	T	15.	T

Exercises

1. a.   Investment in S Company   42,000

          Cash   42,000
       To record P's investment in S

       Cash   3,600
          Investment in S Company   3,600
       To record P's receipt of cash dividends

       Investment in S Company   9,000
          Equity in Subsidiary Earnings ..   9,000
       To record P's share of S's net income

  b.   Investment in S Company   42,000
          Cash   42,000
       To record P's investment in S

       Cash   3,600
          Dividend Income   3,600
       To report P's receipt of cash dividends

2. a.   19x1
       Investment in S Company 120,000
          Cash   120,000
       To record P's investment in S

       Investment in S Company   16,000
          Equity in Subsidiary Earnings ..   16,000
       To record P's share of S's net income

       Cash   8,000
          Investment in S Company   8,000
       To record P's receipt of cash dividend

       19x2
       Equity in Subsidiary Earnings   12,000
          Investment in S Company   12,000
       To record P's share of S's net loss

  b.   19x1
       Equity in Subsidiary Earnings   16,000
          Investment in S Company   16,000
       To eliminate P' share of S's income

```
           Investment in S Company ............     8,000
                Dividends Declared - S Company .               8,000
           To eliminate P's share of S's dividends


           Common stock - S Company (90,000 x .8)   72,000
           Retained earnings - S Company
             (60,000 x .8) ....................     48,000
                Investment in S Company ........             120,000
           To eliminate investment account


           19x2
           Investment in S Company ...........      12,000
                Equity in Subsidiary Earnings ..             12,000
           To eliminate P's share of S's net loss


           Common stock - S Company (90,000 x .8)   72,000
           Retained earnings - S Company
             (70,000 x .8) ....................     56,000
                Investment in S Company ........             108,000
           To eliminate investment account (120,000 +
           16,000 - 8,000 = 108,000 at 1/1/19x2)
```

3. a.   Incremental approach:
         P's reported net income $100,000
         Less P's share of S's net income (40,000 x .75) (30,000)
         P's net income from its own operations $70,000
         Add equity in subsidiary earnings (40,000 x .75) 30,000
         Consolidated net income $100,000

         Residual approach:
         P's reported net income $100,000
         S's reported net income   40,000
         Total reported net income $140,000
         Less P's share of S's net income included in
               P's net income (40,000 x .75) .... (30,000)
         Combined entity income $110,000
         Less minority interest (40,000 x .25) .... (10,000)
         Consolidated net income $100,000

    b.   Incremental approach:
         P's reported net income $85,000
         Less P's share of S's dividends (20,000 x .75) (15,000)
         P's net income from its own operations $70,000
         Add P's share of S's net income (40,000 x .75) 30,000
         Consolidated net income $100,000

```
Residual approach:
P's reported net income ..................... $85,000
S's reported net income .....................   40,000
Total reported net income ................... $125,000
Less P's share of S's dividends (20,000 x .75) (15,000)
Combined entity income ...................... $110,000
Less minority interest (40,000 x .25) ....... (10,000)
Consolidated net income ..................... $100,000
```

4. a.
```
Dividend income (25,000 x .6) .....      15,000
Minority interest (25,000 x .4) ...      10,000
      Dividends declared - S Company                  25,000
To eliminate S's dividends

Minority interest (40,000 x .4) ...      16,000
      Minority interest ............                  16,000
To allocate minority interest in S's
net income

Common stock - S Company ..........      10,000
Paid-in capital ...................      40,000
Retained earnings .................     150,000
      Investment in S Company ......                 120,000
      Minority interest ............                  80,000
To eliminate S's equity and the investment
account at acquisition and reclassify the
minority interest at beginning of 19x1
```

   b.
```
Dividend income (15,000 x .6) .....       9,000
Minority interest (15,000 x .4) ...       6,000
      Dividends declared - S Company                  15,000
To eliminate S's dividends

Minority interest (20,000 x .6) ...      12,000
      Minority interest ............                  12,000
To allocate minority interest in S's
net income

Common stock - S Company ..........      10,000
Paid-in capital - S Company .......      40,000
Retained earnings - S Company
  (150,000 x.6 + 165,000 x .4) ....     156,000
      Investment in S Company ......                 120,000
      Minority interest ............                  86,000
To eliminate P's share of S's equity at
acquisition and allocate minority interest's
share in S's equity at beginning of 19x2
```

Chapter 4
Additional Issues in Purchase Combinations

I.   Treatment of Differentials After Acquisition

    A.   At acquisition the differential between the parent's cost and its share of the subsidiary's equity is first determined and then allocated to specific assets and liabilities of the subsidiary for which differences exist between book and fair value. A remaining debit differential is classified as goodwill; a credit differential remaining after the specified reallocation to non-current assets is classified as a deferred credit.

    B.   After acquisition allocated differential amounts are given the same accounting treatment as the assets and liabilities to which they have been assigned. This adjustment is called differential amortization. The differential is amortized in the consolidated statements and on the parent's books under the equity method. Since the differential applies only to the portion of the subsidiary purchased by the parent, the total amortization is allocated to the parent. The allocated differentials are amortized over the remaining life of the asset or liability, as follows:

        1.   Amounts allocated to inventories are assigned to cost of goods sold during the period when the subsidiary's inventory is sold. For FIFO inventories this usually means the first year after acquisition, for LIFO inventories this means the period when the inventory is partly or totally liquidated.

        2.   Amounts allocated to assets with limited lives, such as buildings, equipment, natural resources, and intangibles, are amortized by the straight-line method over the remaining useful lives of these assets.

        3.   Amounts allocated to land are not amortized.

        4.   Amounts allocated to receivables and payables are amortized over the period of collection or payment.

        5.   Amounts allocated to goodwill or a deferred credit are amortized over their estimated useful lives or 40 years, whichever is shorter.

    C.   In the first year after acquisition differential amortization affects the parent's books under the equity method and the consolidated statement working papers.

1. Under the equity method the amortization is recorded on the parent's books with a debit to Equity in Subsidiary Earnings and a credit to the investment account if the amortization decreases a debit differential. The opposite entry is made if a credit differential is decreased.

   a. The effect of the amortization entries is to decrease the differential. Since changes in the subsidiary's equity, such as net income and dividends, are recorded on the parent's books, the balance in the investment account will always equal the parent's share of the subsidiary's equity plus or minus any remaining differential.

   b. The balance in the investment account can be computed at any time by multiplying the subsidiary's equity by the parent's ownership percentage and adding the unamortized differential.

   c. The parent's net income under the equity method will equal consolidated net income. For this reason the equity method is also referred to as a one-line consolidation.

2. The consolidated statement working papers are divided into three parts: the income statement, the retained earnings statement, and the balance sheet. The entries in the working papers are made to:

   a. Eliminate the subsidiary's income (loss) by:

      (1) debiting (crediting) the parent's Equity in Subsidiary Earnings with an offsetting entry to the investment account and

      (2) by allocating the minority interest in the subsidiary's earnings with a debit (credit) in the income statement and the offsetting entry in the balance sheet.

   b. Eliminate the dividends declared by the subsidiary with debits to the investment account for the parent's share and the minority interest in the balance sheet.

   c. Eliminate the subsidiary's equity as of the beginning of the year with credits to the parent's investment account and the minority interest for their respective shares at the beginning of the year. If the parent purchased its interest in the subsidiary at other than book value, this entry also sets up the differential at acquisition.

    d.   Allocate the differential as of the beginning of
         the year, in this case at acquisition.

    e.   Record the first-year amortization of the
         differential.

3.   Consolidated net income for any year can be computed
     using the incremental approach, as follows:

    a.   Parent's net income from its own operations,

    b.   Plus (minus) parent's share of subsidiary's net
         income (loss),

    c.   Minus (plus) current year's amortization of debit
         (credit) differential.

D. In the second and subsequent years after acquisition entries
   are again made on the parent's books under the equity method
   and in the consolidated working papers.

   1.   The entries made on the parent's book in subsequent
        years are similar to the ones made in the first year
        after acquisition. The differential amortization will
        change over time as amounts allocated to assets and
        liabilities at acquisition are fully amortized.

   2.   In the consolidated statement working papers the first
        two elimination entries in subsequent years are similar
        to the entries in the first year after acquisition.

       a.   The third entry, which eliminates the beginning
            balances of the subsidiary's equity and the
            parent's investment account and allocates the
            beginning minority interest, also sets up the
            differential as of the beginning of the year.

       b.   The next entry allocates the beginning-of-year
            differential.

           (1)   No allocation is made for amounts fully
                 amortized.

           (2)   The beginning balances allocated to assets
                 and liabilities are identical to the ending
                 balances in the prior year's consolidated
                 statement working papers.

       c.   The last entry records differential amortization
            for the current year.

E. The differential is gradually reduced on the parent's books
   under the equity method and on consecutive consolidated
   statement working papers until it becomes zero or pertains
   only to assets with unlimited lives, such as land. Once the

differential is fully amortized, the balance in the parent's investment account will equal its share of the subsidiary's equity. Therefore, subsequent entries eliminating the investment account will not allocate a differential.

F.   Amounts allocated to long-lived assets with contra accounts present a special problem. On the subsidiary's books the assets and their accumulated depreciation accounts are continued after acquisition. For consolidated purposes, however, the cost of such assets at acquisition is their net book value plus the allocated differential. In other words, there is no accumulated depreciation at acquisition. Therefore, adjustments must be made in the consolidated working papers, as follows:

1.   The asset account is credited for the difference between original cost and the replacement value at acquisition.

2.   The debit to the accumulated depreciation account decreases every year. At acquisition and one year later it is equal to the balance in the account at acquisition. After that the debit is reduced by the amortization of the amount allocated to the asset in previous years.

3.   The differential amortization is credited to the accumulated depreciation, instead of to the asset, account.

II. Realignment of Subsidiary's Shareholders' Equity

A.   The declaration of a stock dividend by the subsidiary requires special attention on the consolidated working papers in the year of declaration, because the parent only makes a memorandum entry.

1.   Because a stock dividend causes an increase in the subsidiary's paid-in capital account and in its Dividends Declared without a corresponding entry to the parent's investment account, an additional elimination entry is made reversing the entry recording the stock dividend declaration on the subsidiary's books. The investment elimination entry can then be made in a routine way, i. e. against the parent's share of the subsidiary's owners' equity balances as of the beginning of the period. No special eliminations are required in subsequent years because the entry closing the Dividends Declared account reduces the subsidiary's retained earnings and total book value is not changed by the stock dividend.

2.   Under the equity method a parent accumulates its share of a subsidiary's post-acquisition net income in its retained earnings account. Through consolidated net

income the parent's share of such post-acquisition earnings are also included in consolidated retained earnings. However, not all of these earnings are available for distribution to the parent's shareholders if the subsidiary has capitalized some post-acquisition income through a stock dividend. The parent can deal with this restriction by

   a. capitalizing the proportionate share of its retained earnings (and thus consolidated retained earnings), or

   b. disclosing the constraint on dividend availability either parenthetically or by footnote.

B. A change in the par or stated value of the subsidiary's capital stock causes no special elimination entry. However, the investment elimination entry is made against the end of the period balances in the contributed capital accounts.

C. Any appropriation of the subsidiary's retained earnings may simply be added to the parent's appropriated retained earnings. If the amount of the appropriation exceeds the subsidiary's retained earnings at acquisition, i. e. it includes some post-acquisition earnings, this creates a limitation on dividend availability and may warrant footnote disclosure.

III. Interim Purchases

A. A consolidation problem arises in the year a subsidiary is acquired in a purchase transaction if the acquisition happens during, rather than at the beginning of, the subsidiary's fiscal year. At issue are the subsidiary's revenues and expenses recorded before acquisition. The alternative methods for handling such preacquisition income are:

   1. The subsidiary's revenues and expenses for the entire year are consolidated with those of the parent. The parent's share of the subsidiary's preacquisition earnings is then deducted in the consolidated income statement. On consolidated statement working papers preacquisition earnings are set up in the investment elimination entry. This method is usually preferred since it facilitates comparisons of annual consolidated income statements.

   2. The subsidiary's revenues and expenses are assumed to have been closed to its retained earnings account at acquisition. Thus, only revenues and expenses recorded by the subsidiary after acquisition are consolidated with the annual revenues and expenses of the parent. The investment elimination entry is made against the

parent's interest in the net assets of the subsidiary at acquisition.

B.   Regardless of which of the above methods is used, the parent's share of the subsidiary's preacquisition net income does not become part of consolidated net income. A parent using the equity method records only its interest in subsidiary income earned after acquisition.

C.   If the annual income statement of the subsidiary is used in the consolidation, the elimination entries in the working papers for the year of acquisition are:

1.   The first entry eliminates the parent's share of post-acquisition net income and the minority interest's share of the year's net income.

2.   If no dividends were declared by the subsidiary prior to acquisition, the only change in the investment elimination entry is the addition of the debit to Purchased Preacquisition Earnings.

3.   If the subsidiary declared dividends prior to acquisition, the investment elimination entry will debit the subsidiary's retained earnings as of the beginning of the year and credit Dividends Declared for the total preacquisition dividends, thereby eliminating the subsidiary's retained earnings at acquisition, in addition to the debit to Purchased Preacquisition Earnings.

IV.   Income Tax Considerations

A.   If a parent does not include a subsidiary in a consolidated income tax return, it may have to pay income taxes in the future on its share of the subsidiary's undistributed earnings.

B.   Under APB Opinion No. 23 the parent is required to accrue deferred income taxes on undistributed earnings unless there is strong evidence that the earnings will be permanently invested or that eventual remittance will be in a tax-free liquidation.

C.   The parent's income tax expense resulting from its investment in the subsidiary consists of a current and a deferred portion, as follows:

1.   The parent's share of the subsidiary's income is decreased (increased) by the amortization of the debit (credit) differential, a non-deductible item for tax purposes. The resultant income, which will eventually be received in dividends, is then reduced by the dividends received deduction. These equity method earnings ultimately subject to taxation are then

46

multiplied by the tax rate to arrive at the income tax expense for the period.

2. The tax currently payable is based on the dividends received less the dividends received deduction multiplied by the tax rate.

3. The difference between the income tax expense and the tax currently payable is the deferred tax.

V. Consolidated Statement of Cash Flows

A. SFAS No. 95 requires a statement of cash flows as part of a full set of financial statements. The statement classifies cash flows into three categories: from operating activities, from investing activities, and from financing activities.

B. Cash flows from operating activities may be reported either by the direct or the indirect method, although the Statement prefers the direct method.

1. Under the direct method major classes of operating cash receipts and payments are reported. In addition, the Statement requires a reconciliation of net income with net cash flows from operating activities.

2. Under the indirect method net income is adjusted for operating items not affecting cash, such as depreciation, and changes in current assets and liabilities to arrive at net cash flows from operating activities.

C. In a consolidated statement of cash flows the reconciliation of consolidated net income with net cash flows has to include the minority interest in the subsidiary's earnings, since it is an expense not affecting cash. The changes in current assets and liabilities have to be computed on a consolidated basis. If the subsidiary was acquired during the year, the changes in working capital items must be net of any changes in these items resulting from the acquisition.

D. Because the acquisition of a subsidiary is an investing activity, the purchase price (net of subsidiary cash purchased) is reported as a cash outflow from investing. The portion of the purchase price paid in debt or stock is reported as a cash inflow from financing activities. Dividends paid to minority stockholders are reported as cash outflows from financing activities.

E. A consolidated statement of cash flows can be prepared directly from the consolidated financial statements in the same manner as preparing the statement for a single company.

F.   A consolidated statement of cash flows can also be prepared from the separate cash flow statements of the parent and subsidiary. In this case the dividends paid by the subsidiary to its parent must be eliminated from the parent's cash inflows from investing activities. The cash outflow from dividends paid will consist of the parent's dividends and the subsidiary's dividends paid to the minority interest.

G.   If the separate company reconciliations of net income with net cash inflows or outflows from operating activities are consolidated, the following adjustments are necessary:

1.   The entire amount of the subsidiary's net income is eliminated.

2.   Amortization of a debit (credit) differential has to be added to (subtracted from) net income.

3.   The equity method income subtracted from the parent's net income is eliminated.

4.   The minority interest in net income is added back since it represents an expense not requiring a cash outflow.

VI. Combined Financial Statements

A.   Combined financial statements may be prepared for two or more entities with a common owner or management.

B.   Since there is no parent-subsidiary relationship, no owners' equity accounts are eliminated.

C.   The combination of income statement and balance sheet accounts is similar to a consolidation in that intercompany transactions, such as receivables and payables, are eliminated.

VII. Appendix: Consolidated Working Papers Under the Cost Method

A.   Under the cost method the differential is not amortized on the parent's books but only in the working papers.

B.   The entries in the consolidated working papers are made to:

1.   Eliminate the parent's dividend income and the subsidiary's dividends declared and set up the minority interest in dividends.

2.   Record the minority interest in earnings in the income statement and the equity section of the balance sheet.

3.   Eliminate the investment account with a

a.   debit to the subsidiary's capital stock for 100%,

48

b. debit to the subsidiary's retained earnings at acquisition for the parent's percentage,

c. debit to the subsidiary's retained earnings as of the beginning of the year for the minority interest's percentage,

d. debit to the parent's or the subsidiary's beginning retained earnings for the cumulative differential amortization from acquisition to the beginning of the current year,

e. debit to the differential for the unamortized balance as of the beginning of the year (for the first year after acquisition this would be the differential at acquisition),

f. credit to the investment account for the balance in the account (i. e. original cost),

g. credit to the minority interest for its percentage of the subsidiary's equity as of the beginning of the year.

4. Allocate the differential to the appropriate accounts.

5. Amortize the differential for the current year.

C. The consolidated column in the working papers is the same whether the parent uses the cost or the equity method.

Test Your Understanding of Chapter 4

True or False

Instructions: Indicate your choice by circling either T, if you think the statement is true, or F, if you think the statement is false.

T F 1. Differential amounts that are allocated to specific assets and liabilities of the subsidiary are accounted for in a way consistent with the normal accounting practices used for these assets and liabilities.

T F 2. The part of a debit differential that is not allocated to identifiable net assets of the subsidiary is classified as goodwill and should be amortized over its estimated useful life or 40 years, whichever is longer.

T F 3. Differential amortization reduces the minority interest in subsidiary net income.

T F   4. In the third year after acquisition the investment elimination entry for a parent using the equity method establishes the balance of the unamortized differential as of the beginning of the third year.

T F   5. In the third year after acquisition the investment elimination entry for a parent using the cost method establishes the balance of the unamortized differential as of the beginning of the third year.

T F   6. For a parent using the equity method differential amortization affects its share of the subsidiary's net income.

T F   7. If the parent uses the cost method, the subsidiary should record the differential on its books.

T F   8. The consolidated working paper entry eliminating the investment account on the equity method sets up the differential as of the end of the current year.

T F   9. Consolidated net income is equal to the parent's net income under the equity method plus the parent's share of the subsidiary's net income less the current year's amortization of a debit differential.

T F   10. Consolidated retained earnings are the same as the parent's retained earnings under the equity method.

T F   11. The entry recording a stock dividend by a subsidiary must be reversed every year in the consolidated working papers.

T F   12. If a parent purchases a subsidiary at an interim date, consolidated net income includes the parent's interest in subsidiary net income for the entire year.

T F   13. Purchased preacquisition earnings resulting from an interim purchase are set up in the consolidated working papers by the investment elimination entry.

T F   14. The consolidated income statement of a parent and subsidiary who do not file a consolidated income tax return must always include deferred taxes.

T F   15. The dividends received from a subsidiary are included in a parent's cash flows from operating activities.

Consoli

Exercises

1. On January 1, 19x1, P Company purchased 70 percent of the outstanding voting stock of S Company for $90,000. On this date S Company's owners' equity consisted of Common Stock of $50,000, Additional Paid-in Capital of $30,000, and Retained Earnings of $20,000. Fair market values of the net assets of S Company equaled their book values with the following exceptions:

	Fair Value	Book Value
Inventory	$ 8,000	$ 4,000
Equipment (net)	30,000	24,000
Land	20,000	10,000
	$58,000	$38,000

The subsidiary's beginning inventory was sold during 19x1. The equipment is being depreciated by the straight-line method and has an estimated remaining useful life of two years. Any goodwill is to be amortized over five years. During 19x1 S Company reported net income of $20,000 and paid dividends of $10,000.

Required:
a. Prepare the entries on P Company's books under the equity method.

(handwritten annotations)

Paid 90,000

Got 70,000 (70% × (50K + 30K + 20K)

T.D.H 20,000

GW = 20,000 − 14,000
   = 6000

FMV > BV

Inv 4000 × 70% 2800

eq 6000   4200

Land 10,000   7000

14,000

Amt yl

Inv 2800

eq 2100 (2y)

Land 0

GW 1510 (5y)

6100

58K − 38K = 20,000 × 70%
   = 14,000

D.H.A

b. Prepare the elimination entries for the December 31, 19x1, consolidated statement working papers.

(1)

(2)

(3)

(4)

(5)

2.   On November 1, 19x1, P Company purchased 90 percent of the
outstanding voting stock of S Company for $153,000.   At January 1,
19x1, S Company's owners' equity consisted of Common Stock of $50,000
and Retained Earnings of $100,000.   On the date of acquisition fair
values of S Company's net assets equaled their book values.   S
Company's net income was earned evenly throughout the year.   The
separate 19x1 income statements of P and S are:

	P Company	S Company
Sales	$140,000	$90,000
Cost of Goods Sold	70,000	40,000
Gross Profit	$ 70,000	$50,000
Operating Expenses	30,000	26,000
Net Income	$ 40,000	$24,000

Required:
a.   Using the incremental approach, compute consolidated net income
     for 19x1.

b.   Prepare the consolidated income statement for 19x1 assuming P
     Company elects to include S Company's revenues and expenses for
     the entire year.

53

c. **Prepare the elimination entries for the 19x1 consolidated statement working papers. Assume P uses the equity method.**

(1)

(2)

Solutions to Chapter 4 Exercises

True or False

1.	T	4.	T	7.	F	10.	T	13.	T
2.	F	5.	T	8.	F	11.	F	14.	F
3.	F	6.	T	9.	F	12.	F	15.	F

Exercises

1. a. Entries on P Company's books:

To record investment:

Investment in S Company   90,000

   Cash   90,000

To record share of S's net income (20,000 x .7):

Investment in S Company   14,000

   Equity in S Company Earnings   14,000

To record receipt of dividends (10,000 x .7):

Cash   7,000

   Investment in S Company.......   7,000

To record differential amortization (2,800 + 2,100 + 1,200):

Equity in S Company Earnings   6,100

   Investment in S Company   6,100

  b. Working paper entries:

(1) To eliminate S's net income and set up minority interest:

Minority Interest (20,000 x .3) ...   6,000

Equity in S Company Earnings   14,000

   Investment in S Company   14,000

   Minority Interest   6,000

(2) To eliminate dividends declared by S:

Minority Interest (10,000 x .3) ...   3,000

Investment in S Company   7,000

   Dividends Declared - S Company   10,000

(3) To eliminate investment account:

Common Stock - S Company   50,000

Additional Paid-in Capital - S Co..   30,000

Retained Earnings - S Company   20,000

Differential   20,000

   Investment in S Company   90,000

   Minority Interest (100,000 x .3)   30,000

(4) To allocate debit differential:

Inventory [(8,000 - 4,000) x .7] ..   2,800

Equipment [(30,000 - 24,000) x .7]   4,200

Land [(20,000 - 10,000) x.7]   7,000

Goodwill   6,000

   Differential   20,000

(5)   To amortize differential:
         Cost of Goods Sold   2,800
         Depreciation Expense   2,100
         Amortization of Goodwill   1,200
             Inventory   2,800
             Equipment (4,200 : 2 years) ..   2,100
             Goodwill (6,000 : 5 years) ...   1,200

2.   a. P's net income from its own operations $40,000
         Add P's share of S's net income [(24,000
             x 2/12) x .9]   3,600
         Consolidated net income $43,600

     b. Sales (140,000 + 90,000) $230,000
         Cost of Goods Sold (70,000 + 40,000)   110,000
         Gross Profit $120,000
         Operating Expenses (30,000 + 26,000)   56,000
         Operating Income .... $ 64,000
         Less: Minority Interest (24,000 x .1) .$ 2,400
                Preacquisition earnings [(24,000
                x 10/12) x .9] 18,000   20,400
         Consolidated Net Income .... $ 43,600

     c. Working paper entries:

(1)   To eliminate S's net income and set up the minority
         interest:
         Minority Interest (24,000 x .1)   2,400
         Equity in S Company Earnings   3,600
             Investment in S Company   3,600
             Minority Interest   2,400

(2)   To eliminate investment account:
         Common Stock - S Company   50,000
         Retained Earnings - S Company 100,000
         Preacquisition Earnings   18,000
             Investment in S Company   153,000
             Minority Interest (150,000 x .1)   15,000

56

Chapter 5
Acquisitions, Mergers, and Consolidations;
The Purchase and Pooling of Interest Methods; and Consolidated EPS

Chapter Outline

I. Accounting for Acquisitions, Mergers, and Consolidations

   A. Acquisitions accounted for as purchases create a parent/subsidiary relationship. In a purchase acquisition the parent's share of the subsidiary's net assets are revalued at fair market value, and the subsidiary's retained earnings are not carried over to the consolidated statements.

      1. Entries on parent's books under the equity method:

         a. The acquisition of the subsidiary's stock in exchange for the parent's stock is recorded with a debit to the investment account and credits to the parent's capital stock and additional paid-in capital for the fair market value of the stock issued.

         b. The parent's share of the subsidiary's reported net income (loss) is debited (credited) to the investment account with an offsetting entry to an equity in subsidiary earnings account.

         c. The equity in subsidiary earnings is adjusted for the differential amortization.

      2. Elimination entries in the consolidated statement working paper:

         a. The first entry eliminates the equity in subsidiary earnings and its effect on the investment account.

         b. The next entry eliminates the subsidiary's equity accounts and the investment account and sets up the differential as of the beginning of the year.

         c. The third entry allocates the differential to the subsidiary's assets and liabilities.

         d. The last entry records the differential amortization for the current year.

      3. The balance in the investment account under the equity method can be computed as follows:

57

a. To the parent's initial purchase price is added the equity in subsidiary earnings net of differential amortization less the parent's share of subsidiary dividends.

b. To the parent's share of the equity of the subsidiary is added the unamortized balance of the differential.

4. The parent's equity in subsidiary earnings is added to the parent's retained earnings and thus becomes a part of consolidated retained earnings.

B. Mergers accounted for as purchases result in only one surviving company.

1. The acquiring company records the assets and liabilities of the acquired company and the stock issued to obtain them at their respective fair market values. The subsequent accounting for the enlarged acquiring company is the same as accounting for any one company.

2. Since only one company survives a merger, no consolidated statements are prepared.

C. Acquisitions accounted for as poolings of interest result in a parent/subsidiary relationship. In a pooling acquisition the parent's share of the subsidiary's net assets is recorded at the subsidiary's book value and the parent's share of the subsidiary's retained earnings is credited to the parent's retained earnings. By this entry the subsidiary's retained earnings become a part of consolidated retained earnings.

1. Entries on parent's books under the equity method:

pooling

a. The acquisition and stock issue is recorded with a debit to the investment account and credits to the capital stock account for the par value of the stock issued, to retained earnings for the parent's share of the subsidiary's retained earnings, and the difference to additional paid-in capital.

(1) If the credits to capital stock and retained earnings exceed the debit to the investment account, paid-in capital is debited for the difference.

(2) If the balance in the parent's paid-in capital account is not large enough to absorb such a debit, the credit to retained earnings is reduced and, if necessary, turned into a debit to the parent's retained earnings.

b. The parent's share of the subsidiary's net income (loss) is debited (credited) to the investment account with an offsetting entry to the equity in subsidiary earnings account.

c. Since the net assets of the subsidiary remain at their respective book values, there is no differential.

2. Elimination entries in the consolidated statement working paper:

a. The first entry eliminates the equity in subsidiary earnings and its effect on the investment account.

b. The second entry eliminates the equity of the subsidiary and the investment account as of the beginning of the year.

3. Since the equity of the subsidiary is added to the parent's equity in the acquisition entry, the consolidated balance sheet will look as if the two companies had always been a single entity.

D. Mergers accounted for as poolings of interests result in only one surviving company.

1. The acquiring company records the assets and liabilities of the acquired company and the stock issued to obtain them at their respective book values. The subsequent accounting for the enlarged acquiring company is the same as accounting for any one company.

2. Since only one company survives a merger, no consolidated statements are prepared.

E. Consolidations create a new entity which takes over the net assets of two or more predecessors. A consolidation may be accounted for as a purchase or as a pooling of interests.

1. If the consolidation is accounted for as a purchase, the assets and liabilities of each predecessor company are recorded at their fair market values. The fair market value of the stock issued by the new corporation is recorded as contributed capital.

2. If the consolidation is accounted for as a pooling of interests, the assets and liabilities of each predecessor company are recorded at their book values. The stock issued by the new corporation is credited at par value, retained earnings is credited for the sum of the retained earnings of the predecessor companies, and paid-in capital is credited for the difference.

F. A comparison between the effects of a purchase and a pooling is not possible, since these two methods are not alternatives for one another. However, it can be said that purchase accounting usually results in lower post-combination earnings since the fair values of net assets tend to exceed their book values. Therefore, the differential tends to be a debit and differential amortization will decrease earnings.

G. Trend analyses and projections of earnings are difficult after combinations because a decision has to be made as to what pre-combination earnings to use in the analysis.

1. Since a purchase combination assumes that the acquiring company purchased a group of assets at fair value, the pre-combination earnings used are generally those of the acquiring company only. In the first financial statements issued after the combination APB Opinion No. 16 requires footnote disclosure of the current and immediately preceding periods' results of operations based on a pro forma restatement as if the combination had taken place at the beginning of the preceding period.

2. In the case of combinations accounted for as poolings, pre-combination earnings are generally restated to give effect retroactively to the pooling.

II. Earnings Per Share Analysis

A. Traditional calculations divided net income available to common shareholders by the weighted average number of common shares outstanding. After a business combination which included convertible securities or common stock warrants, this computation could become misleading. APB Opinion No. 15 therefore changed the method of computing EPS.

B. Primary earnings per share are based on the concept of common stock equivalents which are added to common stock presently outstanding to determine the denominator in the calculation.

1. Convertible securities are common stock equivalents if, at the time of issuance, their effective yield is less than 66 2/3% of the average Aa corporate bond yield.

a. Conversion of these securities is assumed and net income is increased for interest or preferred dividends avoided due to conversion. For interest the calculation is net of tax.

b. Conversion is assumed only if the effect is dilutive, i. e. EPS are decreased.

2. Options and warrant are always considered to be common stock equivalents.

    a. Exercise of options and warrants is assumed at the option or warrant price.

        (1) If the number of shares issuable under options and warrants is 20 percent or less of the total number of shares outstanding at the end of the period, the "treasury stock" method is applied. Under this method the proceeds from the assumed exercise are used to purchase treasury stock at the average market price during the period.

        (2) If the 20 percent or less test is not met, the assumed proceeds are used:

            (a) first to purchase treasury stock at the average market price during the period not to exceed 20% of the outstanding shares, and then

            (b) to apply the balance to reduce short-term and long-term borrowings and invest any remaining funds in US government securities or commercial paper.

    b. If the average market price of shares outstanding is below the option or warrant price, these common stock equivalents are non-dilutive. Therefore, it is not assumed that they are exercised.

3. In the calculation of primary earnings per share both the denominator and the numerator have to be adjusted:

    a. The weighted average number of shares outstanding is increased by the shares of stock which would have to be issued when

        (1) convertible securities are converted and

        (2) options and warrants are exercised less the treasury shares assumed to be purchased.

    b. Net income is increased by the

        (1) interest expense, net of tax, avoided through the presumed conversion of convertible bonds,

        (2) interest expense, net of tax, avoided on interest-bearing bonds through their presumed retirement with the funds available from the presumed exercise of options and warrants, and

(3) interest income, net of tax, earned on securities acquired with funds available from the presumed exercise of options and warrants after the debt in (2) is presumed to be retired.

C. Fully diluted EPS is computed in a similar manner to primary EPS. It is, however, based on the assumption that all contingent issuances of stock have occurred.

1. Convertible securities are assumed to have been converted whether or not they are common stock equivalents. Appropriate adjustments to net income available to common stockholders are made.

2. The exercise of options and warrants is assumed with the anticipated proceeds used as in the computation of primary EPS with one exception: The price at which treasury stock is purchased is the higher of the average or end-of-period market price.

D. EPS calculations involving affiliates are complicated if the investee has issued convertible securities or options and warrants.

1. If a company's net income includes equity method earnings or the income of a consolidated subsidiary, its EPS calculations must consider potential dilution associated with the investee/subsidiary company's securities.

2. It is first desirable to calculate primary and fully diluted EPS for each investee/subsidiary company.

3. The basic steps for computing primary and fully diluted EPS for the investor/parent company are the same as those previously outlined for a single company. However, the EPS numerator excludes the investor/parent's unadjusted equity in the investee/subsidiary's reported earnings; but it is adjusted to include the investor/parent's aggregate interest in the investee/subsidiary's EPS (i. e. the product of the investee's particular EPS figure and the number of investee common shares and net equivalent common shares owned by the investor). The number of equivalent common shares must be determined consistent with the assumptions used to compute the investee's particular EPS measure. For example, if an investor owns warrants to acquire investee common shares, their assumed exercise results in a net change to the number of equivalent common shares owned by the investor. The size of the change depends on the assumed number of common shares obtained upon exercise and the number of subsidiary common shares it owns that are assumed

repurchased with the proceeds from the exercise of the warrants.

4. Outstanding securities of a <u>subsidiary</u> that may be exchanged for the <u>parent's</u> common shares will not affect subsidiary EPS. However, these securities must be considered when computing the parent's EPS. If their conversion is assumed in computing the parent's EPS, the subsidiary's deductions for payments to holders of these securities must be restored to earnings since no dividends or interest would be paid if they were converted. The restoration is made to the <u>parent's</u> income.

5. The fraction to compute the parent's primary EPS may be expressed as:

   a. P's net income from its own operations (excluding its share of the investee/s earnings) + N(S's primary EPS), divided by

   b. P's weighted average shares and common stock equivalents outstanding for primary EPS computations.

6. The fraction to compute the parent's fully diluted EPS may be expressed as:

   a. P's net income from its own operations + N(S's fully diluted EPS), divided by

   b. P's weighted average shares and common stock equivalents outstanding for fully diluted EPS computations.

   where N = the number of subsidiary common shares or equivalent common shares owned by the parent.

E. Changing conversion rates or exercise prices raise the question as to which rates or prices should be used when computing EPS.

   1. In general, for primary EPS calculations, the rate or price in effect during the current period should be used. (See textbook for exceptions.)

   2. For fully diluted EPS calculations the most attractive rate or price to the security holders should be used. This may be the most advantageous rate or price available during the ten years following the latest fiscal period.

F. Contingent stock issuances generally involve deferred payments of an indeterminate number of common shares based on future earnings or future market prices.

1. For primary EPS contingent stock issuances dependent on <u>future earnings levels</u> should be included in the denominator. The denominator should be adjusted for the number of common shares to be issued if current earnings are maintained. If the contingency is based on <u>future market prices of common stock</u>, the market price at the end of the period should be used to estimate the assumed number of shares to be issued.

2. Fully diluted EPS calculations should consider the highest reasonable number of common shares to be issued if a contingent issue is based on future earnings. This may result in the current period's income being increased to an earnings level consistent with estimated maximum dilution. The stock price at the end of the current period should be used if the contingency is based on future stock prices.

G. Restatement of prior period's earnings per share should be provided for comparative purposes if:

1. The number of outstanding common shares has changed due to stock dividends or splits;

2. Prior period adjustments are made to income;

3. A recent business combination is accounted for as a pooling of interests;

4. Prior periods' EPS figures include contingent stock issues and, at the end of the contingency period, the conditions for issuance have not been met;

5. Current stock prices or earnings levels indicate that previous assumptions regarding contingent issues should be modified.

Test Your Understanding of Chapter 5

True or False

Instructions: Indicate your choice by circling either T, if you think the statement is true, or F, if you think the statement is false.

T F 1. A business combination is always accounted for as a purchase if less than 90 percent of the acquired firm's outstanding voting stock is obtained by the parent company.

T F 2. A business combination is always accounted for as a pooling of interests if 90 percent or more of the acquired firm's outstanding voting stock is obtained by the parent company.

T F 3. A fundamental characteristic of a pooling of interests is the substantial continuation of operations and individual voting shareholders of both combining firms.

T F   4. The legal status of a business combination (i. e. merger, consolidation, or acquisition) has no effect on whether it is a purchase or a pooling.

T F   5. If an acquisition qualifies as a pooling of interests, the book values of the subsidiary's assets and liabilities are combined with those of the parent, regardless of the fair market value of the consideration given or received or the parent's ownership percentage.

T F   6. Contrary to a pooling of interests, net income of a combined entity accounted for as a purchase includes only income of the purchased company earned after the date of combination.

T F   7. Immediately after a pooling of interests, the retained earnings of the combined or consolidated entity equals the sum of the constituents' precombination retained earnings as long as the combined firm's legal of stated capital does not exceed their aggregate precombination paid-in capital.

T F   8. In general, the assets, income, and earnings per share reported after a purchase combination are larger than they would be after a pooling combination.

T F   9. For comparative purposes the constituents' pre-combination operating data are retroactively combined or consolidated for a pooling of interests but not for a purchase combination.

T F 10. If a company has outstanding warrants that may be exchanged for common stock, the EPS denominator is adjusted by the equivalent number of common shares issuable less the assumed number of common shares purchased for the treasury using the hypothetical proceeds from exercise of the warrants.

T F 11. The primary EPS numerator of a consolidated company excludes the parent's unadjusted equity in the subsidiary's reported earnings but does include the product of the subsidiary's primary EPS and the number of its common shares and net equivalent common shares owned by the parent.

T F 12. If a subsidiary has outstanding securities that may be exchanged for the parent's common stock, the parent's EPS numerator is increased by the amount of the payments (net of taxes) made by the subsidiary to holders of these securities,, and the denominator is appropriately adjusted so that it can be determined if these securities are dilutive.

T F 13. If a security has a conversion rate that changes over time, fully diluted EPS should be computed using the most advantageous rate for the security holders within the ten years following the end of the current period.

T F 14. EPS statistics for prior periods should not be restated under any circumstances.

65

T F 15. The parent's ownership percentage is not affected by the subsidiary's outstanding convertible securities which qualify as common stock equivalents, as long as the parent owns some of these convertible securities.

Exercises

1. On January 2, 19x1, B Company was merged into A Company. On this day A Company's stock was selling at $200 per share. Presented below are the simplified balance sheets of both firms. The book values of S Company's net assets equal their fair values except for land with a book value of $10,000 and a fair value of $15,000.

	A Company	B Company
Assets	$250,000	$100,000
Liabilities	$ 50,000	$ 30,000
Common stock, par $10 ...		10,000
Common stock, par $100 ..	100,000	
Other contributed capital	50,000	40,000
Retained earnings	50,000	20,000
	$250,000	$100,000

Required:

a. Assume that A Company exchanges 400 shares of its unissued stock for all of B Company's outstanding stock in a merger.

   (1) Prepare the entry on A Company's books to record the merger as a pooling of interests.

   (2) Prepare the entry on A Company's books to record the merger as a purchase.

b. Assume that A Company exchanges 600 shares of its unissued stock for all of B Company's outstanding stock in a merger.

(1) Prepare the entry on A Company's books to record the merger as a pooling of interests.

(2) Prepare the entry on A Company's books to record the merger as a purchase.

c. Assume that A Company exchanges 1,100 shares of its unissued stock for all of B Company's outstanding stock in a merger.

(1) Prepare the entry on A Company's books to record the merger as a pooling of interests.

(2) Prepare the entry on A Company's books to record the merger as a purchase.

d. Assume that A Company exchanges 400 shares of its unissued stock for 900 shares of B Company's outstanding stock.

(1) Prepare the entry on A Company's books to record the acquisition as a pooling of interests.

(2) Prepare the entry on A Company's books to record the acquisition as a purchase.

2. P Company owns 80 percent of S Company's outstanding common stock and 10 percent of S Company's outstanding warrants. During 19x1 P Company reported $11,600,000 of income from its own operations (excluding its equity in the subsidiary's earnings). P Company has a simple capital structure with 5,000,000 shares of common stock outstanding.

Selected financial information about S Company's 19x1 operations is as follows:

```
S Company's net income ......................        $5,000,000
Weighted average common shares outstanding
      during 19x1 ............................        1,968,000
Outstanding common shares at year-end .......        2,000,000
Outstanding warrants (each warrant may be
      exchanged for one share of its common
      stock at an exercise price of $8.125
      per share) ............................        1,000,000
Average market price of common stock ........           $10
End-of-period market price of common stock ..           $9
Outstanding 5% notes payable ................        $2,000,000
Return on US government securities ..........           6%
Tax rate ....................................          40%
```

Required:

a. Compute S Company's primary EPS.

b. Compute primary EPS for the consolidated entity of P and S.

Solutions to Chapter 5 Exercises

True or False

1.	T	4.	T	7.	T	10.	T	13.	T
2.	F	5.	T	8.	F	11.	T	14.	F
3.	T	6.	T	9.	T	12.	T	15.	F

Exercises

1. a. (1)

Assets 100,000
    Liabilities   30,000
    Common stock (400 sh. x $100 par).....   40,000
    Other contributed capital   10,000
    Retained earnings   20,000

1. a. (2)

Assets 110,000
    Liabilities   30,000
    Common stock   40,000
    Other contributed capital   40,000

1. b. (1)

Assets 100,000
Other contributed capital 10,000
    Liabilities   30,000
    Common stock (600 sh. x $100 par).....   60,000
    Retained earnings   20,000

1. b. (2)

Assets 150,000
    Liabilities   30,000
    Common stock   60,000
    Other contributed capital   60,000

1. c. (1)

Assets 100,000
Other contributed capital 50,000
    Liabilities   30,000
    Common stock (1,100 sh. x $100 par)...   110,000
    Retained earnings   10,000

1. c. (2)

Assets 250,000
    Liabilities   30,000
    Common stock   110,000
    Other contributed capital   110,000

1. d. (1)

```
Investment in B Company (.9 x $70,000) ....    63,000
    Common stock (400 sh. x $100 par).....              40,000
    Other contributed capital ............               5,000
    Retained earnings (.9 x $20,000)......              18,000
```

1. d. (2)

```
Investment in B Company (400 sh. x $200)...    80,000
    Common stock ........................               40,000
    Other contributed capital ............              40,000
```

2. a.

Numerator:
```
    Net income ...................................    $5,000,000
    Treasury method adjustments:
    Interest savings (net of taxes) from assumed
    retirement of notes payable (Note 3) ........        60,000
    Interest earned (net of taxes) on assumed
    investment in US securities (Note 4) ........        76,500
    Adjusted net income .........................    $5,136,500
```

Denominator:
```
    Weighted average outstanding shares ........     1,968,000
    Treasury stock method adjustments:
    Conversion of warrants .............1,000,000
    Repurchase of stock (Note 1) ....... (400,000)      600,000
    Adjusted weighted average shares outstanding    2,568,000
```

Primary EPS = $5,136,500 : 2,568,000 shares = $2.00

Note 1: Treasury stock purchased: 20% of shares outstanding at end
         of period = .2 x 2,000,000 shares = 400,000 shares

Note 2: Assumed proceeds from exercise of warrants
         (1,000,000 x $8.125) $8,125,000
         Less purchase of 400,000 shares of treasury
         stock at $10 per share (note 1).........   4,000,000
         Remaining proceeds $4,125,000
         Assumed retirement of debt   2,000,000
         Balance invested in US securities $2,125,000

Note 3: Interest saved on assumed retirement of
         debt: $2,000,000 x .05 .... $100,000
         Less income taxes at 40%   40,000
         Interest saved net of tax $60,000

Note 4: Interest income on US securities .06 x
         $2,125,000 .... $127,500
         Less income taxes at 40%   51,000
         Interest earned net of tax $76,500

                            71

2. b.

Numerator: P's net income from its own operations $11,600,000
            + S's primary EPS x P's shares and
            common stock equivalents (Note 5) =
            $2.00 x 1,660,000   3,320,000
            Adjusted numerator $14,920,000

Denominator: P's weighted average shares and common
              stock equivalents outstanding   5,000,000

Consolidated primary EPS: $14,920,000 : 5,000,000 shares = $2.98

Note 5:   P's shares of S stock   1,600,000
           Add P's share of net increase in S's
           outstanding stock equivalents from
           warrants less treasury stock purchased
           .1 x (1,000,000 - 400,000)   60,000
           P's shares of S's stock and common stock
           equivalents   1,660,000

Chapter 6
Consolidated Statements —
Unconfirmed Profits on Inventory Transfers

Chapter Outline

I. **Overview of the Merchandise Transfer Problem**

A. Consolidated financial statements present the summed results of the transactions of affiliated companies with non-affiliated companies. However, intercompany sales or transfers of merchandise are not transactions with non-affiliates. Therefore, the effects of such intercompany transactions are eliminated when consolidated statements are prepared.

move
le, purchase

1. The first elimination removes the total intercompany sales and the total intercompany purchases from the income statement section of the consolidated statement working paper.

move
er. company transaction

2. The second set of eliminations removes the unconfirmed portion of the profits made on intercompany sales until this merchandise is sold to non-affiliates. When the merchandise is subsequently sold to outsiders, the intercompany profit is considered realized and is then recognized.

   a. The unconfirmed profit in the ending inventory of the purchasing affiliate is eliminated from its cost of goods sold and ending inventory.

   b. When the beginning inventory is sold, the intercompany profit is recognized by reducing the purchasing affiliate's cost of goods sold, which contains the cost of the beginning inventory.

B. Intercompany merchandise transfers raise two questions:

1. What is the amount of the unconfirmed intercompany profit that should be eliminated? And

2. How should the eliminated profit be allocated between the majority shareholder (i. e. the parent) and the minority shareholders?

II. **Determination of Amount of Unconfirmed Profit to Eliminate**

A. <u>ARB No. 51</u> advocates the complete elimination of intercompany profits or losses.

B.   The unconfirmed portion of intercompany profits or losses is computed by multiplying the buyer's ending inventory of intercompany merchandise by the seller's gross profit rate.

III.   The Allocation of Unconfirmed Profit

A.   The two methods of allocating the unconfirmed profit are:

1.   Pro-rata allocation, in which the eliminated profit is allocated proportionately between majority and minority shareholders; or

2.   100-percent allocation, in which the eliminated profit is wholly allocated to the parent.

B.   The effect of the alternatives on consolidated net income depends on the identity of the seller and the existence of a minority interest.

1.   Downstream sales: When the parent is the seller, 100 percent of the profit elimination is allocated to the parent. Therefore, consolidated net income is reduced by 100 percent of the eliminated profit.

2.   Upstream sales:

a.   When the seller is a wholly-owned subsidiary, 100 percent of the profit elimination is ultimately allocated to the parent, since it is the only shareholder of the subsidiary. Therefore, consolidated net income is reduced by 100 percent of the eliminated profit.

b.   When the seller is a majority-owned subsidiary, the eliminated profit may be allocated:

(1)   100 percent to the parent. In this case consolidated net income is reduced by 100 percent of the eliminated profit.

(2)   proportionately to the parent and the minority interest in their respective ownership percentages. In this case consolidated net income is reduced only by the parent's percentage of the eliminated profit, and the minority interest in the subsidiary's net income is reduced by its percentage of the eliminated profit.

C.   Evaluation of the alternatives reveals that consolidated net income is higher under proportional allocation. The reason is that the minority interest's share of the subsidiary's net income is reduced by its percentage of the eliminated profit.

1. Pro-rata allocation is preferable because it totally eliminates the effects of intercompany transactions. The subsidiary's net income actually earned, i. e. its net income reduced by the unconfirmed profit, is allocated to the minority and majority interest.

2. Pro-rata allocation is supported by a 1981 AICPA Issues Paper.

IV. Reported and Confirmed Incomes of Affiliates

A. Using the incremental approach consolidated net income is defined as:

1. Under pro-rata allocation the parent company's confirmed net income from its own operations, plus (minus) its equity in the subsidiary's confirmed net income (loss), and minus (plus) the amortization of a debit (credit) differential.

2. Under 100-percent allocation the parent company's confirmed net income from its own operations, plus (minus) its equity in the subsidiary's net income (loss), minus (plus) the amortization of a debit (credit) differential, and minus (plus) the subsidiary's unconfirmed profit arising (becoming confirmed) during the period.

3. The parent's "net income from its own operations" excludes its equity in a subsidiary's earnings.

B. The unconfirmed profit is eliminated in the year when the intercompany merchandise is still in the ending inventory of the purchasing affiliate. It is recognized in the following year (assuming FIFO inventories), when the intercompany merchandise in the beginning inventory is sold to non-affiliates. Therefore, the reported net incomes for two subsequent years will equal the confirmed net incomes for these years, as long as there is no unconfirmed profit in the ending inventory of the second year. In other words, the recognition of the unconfirmed profit is deferred from the year of the intercompany sale to the year of the sale to a non-affiliate.

C. The consolidated profit on merchandise is the difference between the sales price to an independent customer and the purchase price from an independent supplier. The allocation of the total consolidated profit between the intercompany seller and buyer is determined by the intercompany transfer price.

V.   Parent Company Equity Method Entries for Unconfirmed Inventory
     Profits

     A.   Since the equity method is a "one-line consolidation,"
          unconfirmed profits should be treated the same under the
          equity method as they are in consolidated statements.

     B.   Parent's Entries in 19x1 - Upstream Sale

          1.   The parent recognizes its equity in the subsidiary's
               net income with the entry:

               Investment in S Company
                    Equity in Subsidiary Earnings

          2.   The parent eliminates its percentage of the
               subsidiary's unconfirmed profit with the entry:

               Equity in Subsidiary Earnings
                    Investment in S Company

          3.   The result of these two entries is that the parent
               recognizes its percentage of the subsidiary's confirmed
               net income.

          4.   If 100-percent allocation is used for a majority-owned
               subsidiary, the second entry above will be for 100
               percent of the unconfirmed profit.

     C.   Parent's Entries in 19x1 - Downstream Sale

          1.   The entry the parent makes to recognize its equity in
               the subsidiary's net income is the same, whether the
               intercompany sales are upstream or downstream.

          2.   The parent eliminates its percentage of its own
               unconfirmed profit with either of the following
               entries:

               a.   Equity in Subsidiary Earnings
                         Investment in S Company

               b.   Deferred Intercompany Profit
                         Deferred Credit for Intercompany Profit

          3.   The parent's net income and the consolidated income
               statement will be the same under either of the above
               entries since all these accounts are eliminated in the
               working paper.

          4.   In the parent's separate financial statements the
               deferred intercompany profit should be subtracted from
               gross profit, and the deferred credit for intercompany
               profit should be shown among the current liabilities.
               If the first entry, above, is made on the parent's

books, the accounts in the parent's separate financial statements should be adjusted to reflect the accounts used in the second entry.

D. Parent's Entries in 19x2 - Both Cases

   1. If the beginning inventory is sold to non-affiliated customers (FIFO assumption), the entry eliminating the unconfirmed profit in the previous year is reversed.

   2. If some of the beginning inventory is not sold, this unsold merchandise is added to unsold intercompany merchandise resulting from 19x2 sales. The entry eliminating the unconfirmed profit at the end of 19x2 is then made to include the unconfirmed profit from both 19x1 and 19x2.

VI. Unconfirmed Inventory Profits in the Consolidated Statement Working Paper

A. Two important variables in preparing a consolidated statement working paper are:

   1. Whether the intercompany sale is downstream or upstream, and

   2. Whether the unconfirmed profit is in the beginning or ending inventory of the purchasing affiliate.

B. Example used to illustrate entries on the consolidated statement working paper after entries on P Company's books under the equity method:

	19x1	19x2
Intercompany sales	20,000	30,000
Intercompany cost of goods sold	15,000	18,000
Gross profit rate	25%	40%
Ending inventory of intercompany merchandise - at buyer's cost	10,000	12,000
S's stockholders' equity at 1/1		
Capital stock	15,000	15,000
Retained earnings	50,000	66,000
Net income:		
P Company from own operations	50,000	60,000
S Company	16,000	22,000
Investment in S at 1/1 - 80% ..	52,000	

C. Downstream sale

   1. Parent company entries - 19x1

   Investment in S   12,800
      Equity in S earnings   12,800
   To record equity in S earnings (.8 x 16,000)

Equity in S earnings 2,500
     Investment in S   2,500
To eliminate unconfirmed profit (.25 x 10,000)

2. Consolidated statement working paper entries - 19x1

Minority interest expense 3,200
Equity in S earnings 10,300
    Investment in S   10,300
    Minority interest   3,200
To eliminate equity method income (12,800 - 2,500) and
record minority interest in S's net income (.2 x
16,000)

Sales - P 20,000
    Cost of goods sold - S ...   20,000
To eliminate intercompany sales

Cost of goods sold - S 2,500
    Inventory - S   2,500
To eliminate unconfirmed profit in S's ending inventory

Capital stock - S 15,000
Retained earnings - S 50,000
    Investment in S   52,000
    Minority interest   13,000
To eliminate beginning-of-year balances in S's
stockholders equity and P's investment account and
establish minority interest at beginning of year

3. Calculations of 19x1 consolidated net income

    a. Incremental approach
       P's 19x1 confirmed net income its
       own operations (50,000 -2,500) 47,500
       P's equity in S's 19x1 (confirmed)
       net income (.8 x 16,000) 12,800
       19x1 consolidated net income 60,300

    b. Modified residual approach
       P's 19x1 net income 60,300
       S's 19x1 net income 16,000
       Sum of affiliates' net incomes 76,300
       Less P's equity in S earnings ..... (10,300)
       Less unconfirmed profit .... (2,500)
       Combined entity income 63,500
       Less minority interest in S's
       net income (.2 x 16,000) .... (3,200)
       19x1 consolidated net income 60,300

4. The relationship between the investment account balance
and net assets of subsidiary is affected by unconfirmed
profits in ending inventories.

a.   The balance in the investment account will be the
     parent's percentage of the subsidiary's
     shareholders' equity less the parent's percentage
     of the unconfirmed profit in the ending inventory.

b.   The computation is:
     P's percentage of S's equity (.8 x
     81,000).............................   64,800
     Less P's percentage of unconfirmed
     profit at 12/31/19x1 (100% of 2,500)   (2,500)
     Investment in S at 12/31/19x1   62,300

c.   Because the unconfirmed profit in the ending
     inventory reduces the investment account, the
     entry eliminating the investment account in the
     following year must use the adjusted beginning-of-
     year balance.

5.   Parent company entries - 19x2

     Investment in S   17,600
          Equity in S earnings   17,600
     To record equity in S earnings (.8 x 22,000)

     Investment in S   2,500
          Equity in S earnings   2,500
     To record confirmation of profit in beginning inventory
     (.25 x 10,000)

     Equity in S earnings   4,800
          Investment in S   4,800
     To eliminate unconfirmed profit in 12/31/19x2 inventory
     (.4 x 12,000)

6.   Consolidated statement working paper entries - 19x2

     Minority interest expense   4,400
     Equity in S earnings   15,300
          Investment in S   15,300
          Minority interest   4,400
     To eliminate equity method income (17,600 + 2,500 -
     4,800) and record minority interest in S's net income
     (.2 x 22,000)

     Investment in S   2,500
          Cost of goods sold - S ...   2,500
     To record confirmation of profit in S's beginning
     inventory and adjust beginning-of-year balance in the
     investment account

     Sales - P   30,000
          Cost of goods sold - S ...   30,000
     To eliminate 19x2 intercompany sales

```
        Cost of goods sold - S ........        4,800
            Inventory - S ............               4,800
        To eliminate unconfirmed profit in S's ending inventory

        Capital stock - S .............        15,000
        Retained earnings - S .........        66,000
            Investment in S ..........               64,800
            Minority interest ........               16,200
        To eliminate adjusted beginning-of-year investment
        account balance against beginning-of-year equity of S
        and establish beginning-of-year minority interest
```

7. Calculation of 19x2 consolidated net income

   a. Incremental approach

```
        P's 19x2 confirmed net income from
        its own operations (60,000 + 2,500
        - 4,800) ..........................        57,700
        P's equity in S's (confirmed) 19x2
        net income (.8 x 22,000) .........         17,600
        19x2 consolidated net income ......         75,300
```

   b. Residual approach

```
        P's 19x2 net income ..............         75,300
        S's 19x2 net income ..............         22,000
        Sum of affiliates' net incomes ....        97,300
        Plus confirmation of profit in
        beginning inventory ..............          2,500
        Less unconfirmed profit in ending
        inventory ........................         (4,800)
        Less equity in S earnings .........        15,300)
        Combined entity income ...........         79,700
        Less minority interest in S's net
        income (.2 x 22,000) .............         (4,400)
        19x2 consolidated net income ......         75,300
```

8. The relationship between the investment account balance
   and the net assets of the subsidiary at the end of 19x2
   is again affected by the unconfirmed profit in the
   ending inventory of S.

D. Upstream sale

   1. Parent company entries - 19x1

```
        Investment in S  ..............        12,800
            Equity in S earnings .....                12,800
        To record equity in S earnings (.8 x 16,000)

        Equity in S earnings ..........         2,000
            Investment in S ..........                 2,000
        To eliminate P's percentage of unconfirmed profit (.8 x
        2,500)
```

2. Consolidated statement working paper entries - 19x1

Minority interest expense   2,700
Equity in S earnings   10,800
    Investment in S   10,800
    Minority interest   2,700
To eliminate equity method income (12,800 - 2,000) and
record minority interest in S's confirmed net income
[.2 x (16,000 - 2,500)]

Sales - S   20,000
    Cost of goods sold - P ...   20,000
To eliminate intercompany sales

Cost of goods sold - P   2,500
    Inventory - P   2,500
To eliminate unconfirmed profit in P's ending inventory

Capital stock   15,000
Retained earnings   50,000
    Investment in S   52,000
    Minority interest   13,000
To eliminate beginning-of-year balances in S's
stockholders equity and P's investment account and
establish minority interest at beginning of year

3. Calculations of 19x1 consolidated net income

    a. Incremental approach

        P's 19x1 (confirmed) net income
        from its own operations   50,000
        P's equity in S's 19x1 confirmed
        net income [.8 x (16,000 - 2,500) .   10,800
        19x1 consolidated net income   60,800

    b. Residual approach

        P's 19x1 net income   60,800
        S's 19x1 net income   16,000
        Sum of affiliates' net incomes   76,800
        Less equity in S earnings ....   (10,800)
        Less unconfirmed profit ....   (2,500)
        Combined entity income   63,500
        Less minority interest in S's
        confirmed net income [.2 x
        (16,000 - 2,500)] ....   (2,700)
        19x1 consolidated net income   60,800

4. The relationship between the investment account balance
and the net assets of the subsidiary is affected by
unconfirmed profits in ending inventories.

    a. The balance in the investment account will be the
       parent's percentage of the subsidiary's

81

shareholders' equity less the parent's percentage
of the unconfirmed profit in the ending inventory.

b. The computation is:
    P's percentage of S's equity
    [.8 x (15,000 + 50,000 + 16,000) ..   64,800
    Less P's percentage of unconfirmed
    profit at 12/31/19x1 (.8 of 2,500).   (2,000)
    Investment in S at 12/31/19x1   62,800

c. Because the unconfirmed profit in the ending
    inventory reduces the investment account, the
    entry eliminating the investment account in the
    following year must use the adjusted beginning-of-
    year balance.

5. The relationship between the minority interest and the
net assets of the subsidiary is affected in the
upstream case.

a. The minority interest in the ending balance sheet
    is the minority interest's percentage of the
    confirmed stockholders' equity.

b. The computation is:
    S's retained earnings at 12/31/19x1   66,000
    Less unconfirmed profit ....   (2,500)
    S's confirmed retained earnings ...   63,500
    S's capital stock   15,000
    S's confirmed equity   78,500
    Minority interest in 12/31/19x1
    confirmed equity of S - 20%   15,700

6. Parent company entries - 19x2

    Investment in S   17,600
        Equity in S earnings   17,600
    To record equity in S earnings (.8 x 22,000)

    Investment in S   2,000
        Equity in S earnings   2,000
    To record confirmation of profit in beginning inventory
    (.25 x 10,000 x .8)

    Equity in S earnings   3,840
        Investment in S   3,840
    To eliminate unconfirmed profit in 12/31/19x2 inventory
    (.4 x 12,000 x .8)

82

7. Consolidated statement working paper entries - 19x2

```
Minority interest expense .....        3,900
Equity in S earnings .........       15,760
     Investment in S .........              15,760
     Minority interest .......               3,900
To eliminate equity method income (17,600 + 2,000 -
3,840) and record minority interest in S's net income
[.2 x (22,000 - 2,500)]
```

(22000 + 2500 - 4800) × 0.8

```
Investment in S .............        2,000
Retained earnings - S ........         500
     Cost of goods sold - P ...              2,500
To record confirmation of profit in P's beginning
inventory and adjust beginning-of-year balances in the
investment account and S's retained earnings
```

```
Sales - S ....................      30,000
     Cost of goods sold - P ...             30,000
To eliminate 19x2 intercompany sales
```

```
Cost of goods sold - P ........      4,800
     Inventory - P ............              4,800
To eliminate unconfirmed profit in P's ending inventory
```

```
Capital stock - S ............      15,000
Retained earnings - S ........      65,500
     Investment in S .........              64,800
     Minority interest .......              15,700
To eliminate adjusted beginning-of-year investment
account balance against beginning-of-year equity of S
(beginning retained earnings balance of 66,000 less
minority interest in unconfirmed profit of 20% of
2,500) and establish beginning-of-year minority
interest (see computation in paragraph 5b, above)
```

8. Calculation of 19x2 consolidated net income

   a. Residual approach

```
P's 19x2 net income ...............      75,760
S's 19x2 net income ...............      22,000
Sum of affiliates' net incomes ....      97,760
Plus confirmation of profit in
beginning inventory ...............       2,500
Less unconfirmed profit in
ending inventory ..................      (4,800)
Less equity in S earnings .........     (15,760)
Combined entity income ............      79,700
Less minority interest in S's
confirmed net income [.2 x
(22,000 + 2,500 - 4,800)] .........      (3,940)
19x2 consolidated net income ......      75,760
```

83

b.   Incremental approach

P's 19x2 confirmed net income
from its own operations   60,000
P's equity in S's confirmed 19x2
net income [.8 x (22,000 + 2,500
- 4,800)].........................   15,760
19x2 consolidated net income   75,760

9.   The relationship between the investment account balance
and the net assets of the subsidiary is again affected
by unconfirmed profits in ending inventories.

a.   The balance in the investment account will be the
parent's percentage of the subsidiary's
shareholders' equity less the parent's percentage
of the unconfirmed profit in the ending inventory.

b.   The computation is:
P's percentage of S's equity
[.8 x (81,000 + 22,000)]   82,400
Less P's percentage of unconfirmed
profit at 12/31/19x2 (.8 of 4,800)   (3,840)
Investment in S at 12/31/19x2   78,560
(Or per 10.b., below: .8 x 98,200 = 78,560)

c.   Because the unconfirmed profit in the ending
inventory reduces the investment account, the
entry eliminating the investment account in the
following year must use the adjusted beginning-of-
year balance.

10. The relationship between the minority interest and the
net assets of the subsidiary is affected in the
upstream case.

a.   The minority interest in the ending balance sheet
is the minority interest's percentage of the
confirmed stockholders' equity.

b.   The computation is:
S's retained earnings at 12/31/19x2   88,000
Less unconfirmed profit ....   (4,800)
S's confirmed retained earnings ...   83,200
S's capital stock   15,000
S's confirmed equity   98,200
Minority interest in 12/31/19x2
confirmed equity of S - 20%   19,640

11. An analysis of consolidated net income for both cases reveals the following:

	19x1	19x2
Downstream case	60,300	75,300
Add minority interest in unconfirmed profit in ending inventory		
12/31/19x1 - .2 x 2,500	500	
12/31/19x2 - .2 x 4,800		960
Less minority interest in confirmed profit in beginning inventory		
1/1/19x2 - .2 x 2,500		(500)
Upstream case	60,800	75,760

12. The effect of 100-percent allocation in the upstream case is identical to the downstream case. In either case 100 percent of the unconfirmed profit is allocated to the parent.

13. Unconfirmed profit in both beginning and ending inventories has been illustrated in the 19x2 entries, above.

14. The effect of the parent carrying its investment account on cost or the modified equity method (which records the parent's equity in subsidiary net income, but does not record the effects of unconfirmed profits) is that no entries are made on the parent's books for unconfirmed or confirmed profits.

   a. The entry for unconfirmed profits in beginning inventory is modified by changing the debit to the investment account to a debit to the parent's beginning retained earnings. The reason is that the unconfirmed profit at the end of the previous year did not reduce either the parent's income or the parent's retained earnings. Therefore, the parent's retained earnings exceeds consolidated retained earnings by the parent's percentage of the previous year's unconfirmed profit. The debit to the parent's beginning retained earnings thus reduces it to the beginning balance of consolidated retained earnings.

   b. No other elimination entries are affected.

   c. The calculations of consolidated net income and minority interest are unchanged.

VII. Complicating Factors in the Elimination of Unconfirmed Profits

   A. Transportation costs on intercompany sales are valid costs to the consolidated entity.

85

1. If these costs are paid by the purchasing entity, they should be added to its cost of the merchandise. The computation of the seller's unconfirmed profit is not affected.

2. If these costs are paid by the selling entity, the seller's unconfirmed profit should be reduced by this selling expense. The result will be that the inventory will be shown in the consolidated balance sheet at the seller's cost plus its transportation cost.

B. Inventory market adjustments may be made by the purchasing affiliate to reduce its inventory to the lower of cost or market.

1. If the reduction to market is less than the selling affiliate's unconfirmed profit, it should be used to reduce the amount of unconfirmed profit to be eliminated. In other words, the unconfirmed profit eliminated should be the seller's gross profit less the buyer's markdown to market.

2. If the reduction to market is more than or equal to the seller's unconfirmed profit, no elimination of unconfirmed profit is required.

C. Income tax effects depend on whether the affiliates file a consolidated tax return or separate tax returns.

1. If a consolidated tax return is filed, no adjustments are necessary, since the unconfirmed profit on intercompany transactions is eliminated from consolidated taxable income.

2. If the affiliated companies file separate tax returns, the selling affiliate has to include its unconfirmed profit in its tax return and pay income taxes on it. A timing difference between book and taxable income is therefore created. For that reason the elimination entry is made for the unconfirmed profit net of tax.

Test Your Understanding of Chapter 6

True or False

Instructions: Indicate your choice by circling either T, if you think the statement is true, or F, if you think the statement is false.

T F 1. If merchandise sold by one affiliate to another remains in the purchasing affiliate's inventory, the seller's recorded profit should not be recognized from a consolidated perspective until the merchandise is sold to non-affiliates.

86

T F 2. The amount of intercompany profit to be eliminated from the ending inventory is usually based on the selling affiliate's net profit rate. By using this rate rather than the gross profit rate, operating expenses of the selling affiliate are effectively removed from consolidated inventory.

T F 3. A purpose of consolidated financial statements is to report the results of transactions that a single economic entity has experienced with both non-affiliates and affiliates.

T F 4. A parent sold merchandise costing $1,000 to a subsidiary for $1,500. In addition it paid $100 for transportation. $150 of the merchandise remains in the ending inventory of the subsidiary. The parent should make an elimination entry for $40 (10 percent of its gross profit less 10 percent of the transportation cost).

T F 5. Merchandise costing $100 was sold to an affiliate for $200 and remains in the buy company's ending inventory. The buyer values its inventory at the lower or cost or market and therefore marks this merchandise down to $180 at year-end. For this reason the intercompany inventory profit to be eliminated is $80.

T F 6. If unconfirmed intercompany profit results from the sales of a parent company or a wholly-owned subsidiary, the eliminated profit is wholly allocated to the parent company.

T F 7. If unconfirmed intercompany profit results from the sales of a partially owned subsidiary, the eliminated profit may be allocated either wholly to the parent or proportionately to the parent and the minority interest.

T F 8. Minority interest in a partially owned subsidiary's income is based on the subsidiary's reported income for the period, not its confirmed income.

T F 9. The reported income of an 80-percent owned subsidiary includes $500 of unconfirmed inventory profit. If the parent uses the equity method and proportionate allocation, it should defer $400 of the profit with a debit to the equity in subsidiary earnings account and a credit to the investment account.

T F 10. After intercompany profit resulting from either upstream or downstream sales has been deferred by the parent company, the balance in its investment account at the start of the subsequent period will correctly equal the parent's percentage interest in the subsidiary's stockholders' equity at that time (assuming no differential is involved).

T F 11. If unconfirmed profit resulting from downstream sales is a
          significant part of a parent's reported gross profit or is a
          significant part of a parent's equity in a subsidiary's
          reported income, an entry to defer the unconfirmed profit
          may (a) produce an offset account to reduce the parent's
          reported gross profit and (b) establish a deferred credit
          for intercompany profit.

T F 12. A parent company's ending inventory cost includes
          intercompany gross profit of $200 recorded by a 70 percent
          owned subsidiary. On the consolidated statement working
          papers $140 should be eliminated from the inventory.

T F 13. At the end of 19x1 the parent's inventory included $300 of
          unconfirmed profit of a 90 percent owned subsidiary. If the
          merchandise was sold in 19x2, the parent's cost of goods
          sold for 19x2 should be reduced by $300 in the consolidated
          statement working paper.

T F 14. Consolidated net income for a parent and its 80-percent
          subsidiary is $100,000, net of a $4,000 unconfirmed profit
          on a downstream sale. If the sale had been upstream and the
          parent uses proportionate allocation, consolidated net
          income would be $100,800.

T F 15. During 19x4 a 70 percent owned subsidiary sold merchandise
          costing $300 to its parent for $500. The merchandise has
          not been sold. At 12/31/19x4 the subsidiary's stockholders'
          equity on its books is $100,000. The minority interest in
          the consolidated balance sheet at 12/31/19x4 is $29,940.

Exercises

$0.3(100,000 - 200)$

1. On January 1, 19x1, P Company acquired 80 percent of S for $40,000
cash. On that date S Company's stockholders' equity consisted of
Capital Stock of $30,000 and Retained Earnings of $20,000.

During 19x1 S Company sold merchandise costing $12,000 to P Company
for $15,000. On December 31, 19x1, P's ending inventory included
$3,000 (P's cost) of the merchandise acquired from S. For 19x1 S
reported net income of $16,000; P's net income from its own operations
was $60,000. P and S file consolidated income tax returns.

GP Rate = 15000 - 1200/15000 = 20%

Required:
a. Prepare the 12/31/19x1 entries on P's books under the equity
    method.

88

b. Prepare the elimination entries for the 19x1 consolidated statement working paper.

(1)

(2)

(3)

(4)

c. Compute the 12/31/19x1 balance in the Investment in S account.

d. Compute consolidated net income for 19x1.

e. Compute the minority interest in the 19x1 consolidated income statement.

f.   Compute the minority interest in the 12/31/19x1 consolidated
      balance sheet.

NA

2.   Continuing with Exercise 1, assume that P's ending inventory of S
merchandise is sold in 19x2 to unaffiliated customers. Also in 19x2 S
sold merchandise costing $6,000 to P for $10,000. P's 12/31/19x2
inventory contained $5,000 of this merchandise. For 19x2 S and P
reported net income of $25,000 and $50,000 respectively.

Required:
a.   Prepare the entries on P's books under the equity method.

b.   Prepare the elimination entries for the 19x2 consolidated
      statement working paper.

(1)

(2)

(3)

(4)

(5)

c.   Compute the 12/31/19x2 balance in the Investment in S account.

d.   Compute consolidated net income for 19x2.

e.   Compute the minority interest in the 19x2 consolidated income statement.

f.   Compute the minority interest in the 12/31/19x2 consolidated balance sheet.

Solutions to Chapter 6 Exercises

True or False

1.	T	4.	T	7.	T	10.	F	13.	T
2.	F	5.	T	8.	F	11.	T	14.	T
3.	F	6.	T	9.	T	12.	F	15.	T

Exercises

1.   a.   Investment in S   12,800
             Equity in S earnings   12,800
          To record P's interest in S's reported income (.8 x 16,000)

          Equity in S earnings   480
             Investment in S   480
          To defer P's interest in the unconfirmed profit of S [.8 x (.2 x 3,000)]

   b.   (1)   Equity in S earnings   12,320
               Investment in S   12,320
             To eliminate P's equity in S's earnings

       (2)   Sales - S   15,000
               Purchases - P   15,000
             To eliminate intercompany sales

       (3)   Cost of goods sold - P   600
               Inventory - P   600
             To eliminate unconfirmed profit in ending inventory (.2 x 3,000)

       (4)   Capital stock - S   30,000
           Retained earnings - S   20,000
                Investment in S   40,000
                Minority interest   10,000
             To eliminate beginning-of-year balances in S's equity and P's investment account and establish minority interest at beginning of year

   c.   Cost of 80% of S   40,000
       Equity in S earnings (.8 x 16,000)   12,800
       Less P's percentage of unconfirmed profit
          in ending inventory (.8 x 600) ....   (480)
       12/31/19x1 balance in Investment in S   52,320

   d.   P's net income from its own operations   60,000
       P's equity in S earnings   12,320
       19x1 consolidated net income................   72,320

   e.   S's reported net income   16,000
       Less unconfirmed profit in ending
          inventory (.2 x 3,000)....................   (600)
       S's confirmed net income   15,400
       Minority interest - 20%   3,080

```
f.   S's retained earnings at 1/1/19x1 .........     20,000
     Add S's confirmed net income for 19x1 .....     15,400
     S's confirmed retained earnings at 12/31 ...    35,400
     S's capital stock .........................     30,000
     S's confirmed equity at 12/31/19x1 ........     65,400
     Minority interest - 20% ...................     13,080
```

2.   a.   Investment in S   20,000
               Equity in S earnings   20,000
          To record P's interest in S's income (.8 x 25,000)

          Investment in S   480
               Equity in S earnings   480
          To record P's interest in the confirmed profit (.8 x 600)

          Equity in S earnings   1,600
               Investment in S   1,600
          To defer P's interest in the unconfirmed profit of S [.8 x
          (.4 x 5,000)]

b.   (1) Equity in S earnings   18,880
               Investment in S   18,880
          To eliminate P's equity in S earnings (20,000 + 480 - 1,600)

     (2) Sales - S   10,000
               Purchases - P   10,000
          To eliminate intercompany sales

     (3) Investment in S   480
          Retained earnings - S *0.2x600* 120
               Cost of goods sold - P   600
          To record confirmation of profit in P's beginning inventory
          and adjust beginning-of-year balance in S's retained
          earnings and P's investment account

     (4) Cost of goods sold - P   2,000
               Inventory - P   2,000
          To eliminate unconfirmed profit in P's ending inventory (.4
          x 5,000)

     (5) Capital stock - S   30,000
          Retained earnings - S   35,880
               Investment in S   52,800
               Minority interest   13,080
          To eliminate adjusted beginning-of-year investment account
          balance against beginning-of-year equity of S (beginning
          retained earnings balance of 36,000 less minority interest
          in unconfirmed profit of 20% of 600) and establish
          beginning-of-year minority interest (see computation in 1.
          f., above)

c. Investment in S at 12/31/19x1   52,320
    Equity in S earnings   18,880
    Investment in S at 12/31/19x2   71,200

d. P's net income from its own operations   50,000
    Equity in S earnings   18,880
    19x2 consolidated net income   68,880

e. S's reported net income   25,000
    Add confirmed profit in beginning inventory..   600
    Less unconfirmed profit in ending inventory
        (.4 x 5,000) ....   (2,000)
    S's confirmed net income   23,600
    Minority interest - 20%   4,720

f. S's retained earnings at 12/31/19x2 per
        books (20,000 + 16,000 + 25,000)..........   61,000
    Less unconfirmed profit in 12/31/19x2
        inventory (.4 x 5,000) ....   (2,000)
    S's confirmed retained earnings at 12/31/19x2   59,000
    S's capital stock   30,000
    S's confirmed equity at 12/31/19x2   89,000
    Minority interest - 20%   17,800
    Parent's interest - 80% (see c, above)   71,200

Chapter 7
Consolidated Statements—Unconfirmed Profits:
Transfers of Plant and Equipment and Services

Chapter Outline

I. Unconfirmed Profit--Plant and Equipment

A. Overview of the problem

1. Recorded profit or loss from an intercompany sale of plant and equipment must be deferred from consolidated financial statements until confirmed from the perspective of the single economic entity.

2. For fixed assets held for use rather than resale, confirmation is accomplished through the recognition of depreciation expense by the purchasing affiliate. Ignoring salvage value, the purchaser's depreciable cost contains two components:

   a. The book value of the asset to the selling affiliate (which represents the consolidated entity's depreciable cost), and

   b. The intercompany profit or loss.

3. The purchaser's depreciation expense measures the portion of the asset's cost that has been consumed during the current period in the production of goods or services. The amount of the unconfirmed profit realized during the year equals the extra depreciation expense recorded from the consolidated viewpoint by the purchasing affiliate as a consequence of the intercompany sale. This treatment is based on the assumption that the use of an intercompany fixed asset is comparable to the resale of intercompany merchandise to unaffiliated customers, since both result in the consumption of the asset from the consolidated viewpoint.

4. If the depreciation of the asset acquired intercompany is expensed, the unconfirmed profit or loss is considered realized in the period in which the expense is recorded.

5. If the asset acquired intercompany is used in manufacturing and the depreciation is capitalized in the cost of goods manufactured, the unconfirmed profit or loss is not realized until the goods are sold to unaffiliated customers.

a.   Since the unconfirmed profit or loss in the
      beginning and ending inventories offset each
      other, the effect on income is immaterial if
      inventory levels are stable and can therefore
      usually be ignored.

b.   If the effect is material, i. e. if inventories
      increase or decrease substantially during the
      period, it should be recognized in the
      consolidated financial statements.

6.   Since the fixed asset acquired intercompany is
      depreciated over its remaining useful life, the
      intercompany profit or loss is considered realized over
      this same period.

7.   The allocation of the intercompany profit between
      parent and minority interest is similar to the
      allocation of intercompany profits in inventories.

a.   If the sale is downstream, 100 percent is
      allocated to the parent.

b.   If the sale is upstream from a 100-percent owned
      subsidiary, 100 percent is allocated to the
      parent.

c.   If the sale is upstream from a majority-owned
      subsidiary, the intercompany profit or loss is
      allocated to the parent and the minority interest
      in their ownership ratio.

B.   The upstream sale of plant and equipment results in a gain
      or loss on the sale on the books of the subsidiary and
      depreciation expense based on the intercompany sales price
      on the parent's books. Under the equity method and for
      consolidated statements the intercompany gain or loss is
      eliminated and the confirmed portion of the gain or loss is
      recognized.

1.   The analysis of the confirmation of the unconfirmed
      profit or loss reveals that the confirmed portion each
      year is equal to the profit or loss at the time of the
      intercompany sale divided by the remaining useful life
      of the asset. In other words, if the asset sold
      intercompany has a remaining useful life of 5 years, 20
      percent of the intercompany profit or loss is
      considered confirmed each year.

2.   The entries made by the parent under the equity method,
      in addition to the entry recording the parent's equity
      in the subsidiary's reported income for the year, are:

a.   In the year of the intercompany sale:

(1)   Equity in S earnings
             Investment in S
      To eliminate intercompany gain

(2)   Investment in S
             Equity in S earnings
      To eliminate intercompany loss

(3)   Investment in S
             Equity in S earnings
      To recognize P's percent of the current
      year's confirmed gain

(4)   Equity in S earnings
             Investment in S
      To recognize P's percent of the current
      year's confirmed loss

b.   In years subsequent to the intercompany sale:

(1)   Investment in S
             Equity in S earnings
      To recognize P's percent of the current
      year's confirmed gain

(2)   Equity in S earnings
             Investment in S
      To recognize P's percent of the current
      year's confirmed loss

c.   When the asset sold intercompany is fully
     depreciated, the sum of the entries made to
     recognize the portion of the gain or loss
     confirmed each year will equal the original gain
     or loss eliminated in the year of the intercompany
     sale.

3.   In addition to the elimination and confirmation of
     profit, the working paper entries must correct several
     misstatements that exist from the consolidated
     statement viewpoint. Besides eliminating the
     intercompany gain or loss, the entries must restore the
     original cost and accumulated depreciation at the time
     of the intercompany sale. The working paper entries
     are:

a.   In the year of the intercompany sale

(1)   Minority interest expense
      Equity in S earnings
            Investment in S
            Minority interest
      To eliminate equity in S earnings and
      establish the minority interest in the
      confirmed income of S

(2)   Gain on fixed asset sale
      Plant and equipment
            Accumulated depreciation
      To eliminate intercompany gain and restore
      original cost and accumulated depreciation at
      date of sale

(3)   Plant and equipment
            Accumulated depreciation
            Loss on fixed asset sale
      To eliminate intercompany loss and restore
      original cost and accumulated depreciation at
      date of sale

(4)   Accumulated depreciation
            Depreciation expense
      To record confirmation of intercompany profit
      by eliminating extra depreciation

(5)   Depreciation expense
            Accumulated depreciation
      To record confirmation of intercompany loss
      by increasing depreciation

(6)   Capital stock - S
      Retained earnings - S
            Investment in S
            Minority interest
      To eliminate beginning-of-year balances in
      investment in S's stockholders' equity and
      establish minority interest at beginning of
      year

b.   In years subsequent to the intercompany sale

(1)   Minority interest expense
      Equity in S earnings
            Investment in S
            Minority interest
      To eliminate equity in S earnings and
      establish the minority interest in confirmed
      income of S

(2)   Investment in S
       Retained earnings - S
       Plant and equipment
           Accumulated depreciation
       To eliminate unconfirmed profit remaining at
       beginning of year (as allocated to parent and
       minority interest), restore the original cost
       of the asset, and increase accumulated
       depreciation by balance at time of
       intercompany sale less confirmed portion of
       intercompany gain to beginning of year

(3)   Plant and equipment
           Accumulated depreciation
           Investment in S
           Retained earnings - S
       To eliminate unconfirmed loss remaining at
       beginning of year (as allocated to parent and
       minority interest), restore the original cost
       of the asset, and increase accumulated
       depreciation by balance at time of
       intercompany sale plus confirmed portion of
       intercompany loss to beginning of year

(4)   Accumulated depreciation
           Depreciation expense
       To record confirmation of intercompany gain
       by decreasing depreciation expense

(5)   Depreciation expense
           Accumulated depreciation
       To record confirmation of intercompany loss
       by increasing depreciation expense

(6)   Capital stock - S
       Retained earnings - S
           Investment in S
           Minority interest
       To eliminate adjusted beginning-of-year
       balances in investment account against
       remainder of beginning-of-year stockholders'
       equity of S and establish beginning-of-year
       confirmed minority interest

4.   Consolidated net income can be computed as follows:

a.   Using the incremental approach:
     P's net income from its own operations
     Plus P's equity in the confirmed net income of S

99

b. Using the residual approach:
P's net income
Plus S's net income
= Sum of affiliates' net income
Plus (minus) effects of working paper entries on sum of affiliates' net incomes:
Elimination of equity in S earnings
Elimination of unconfirmed loss (profit)
Confirmation of profit (loss)
= Combined entity income
Less minority interest in confirmed net income of S
= Consolidated net income

5. The relationship between the parent's investment account and its share of the net assets of the subsidiary is affected by intercompany gains and losses on fixed asset sales. The difference at any time is the parent's percentage of the unconfirmed portion of the intercompany gain or loss.

   a. In the case of an intercompany gain, the balance in the investment account is reduced by the parent's percentage of the unconfirmed portion of the intercompany gain.

   b. In the case of an intercompany loss, the balance in the investment account is increased by the parent's percentage of the unconfirmed portion of the intercompany loss.

6. The relationship between the minority interest as shown in the consolidated balance sheet and its share of the net assets of the subsidiary is affected only by upstream intercompany gains and losses on fixed asset sales. The difference at anytime is the minority interest's percentage of the unconfirmed portion of the intercompany gain or loss. For an intercompany gain (loss) the minority interest is decreased (increased) by the minority interest's percentage of the unconfirmed portion of the gain (loss).

II. Unconfirmed Profit--Related Topics

   A. Transfers of nondepreciable assets other than inventory and services

      1. Gains or losses on intercompany land sales are eliminated in the year of the sale and the cost of the land is adjusted each year.

         a. Under the equity method the parent decreases (increases) its equity in S's earnings by its percentage of the gain (loss) on the intercompany sale in the year of the sale. No entries are made

100

in subsequent years as long as the land is not sold. In the year in which the land is sold to an unaffiliated buyer, the entry made in the year of the intercompany sale is reversed.

b. In the working paper entries are necessary every year.

   (1) In the year of the intercompany sale the gain (loss) is eliminated with the offsetting credit (debit) to the land account.

   (2) In subsequent years the land account is credited (debited) for the full amount of the gain (loss) on the intercompany sale. The offsetting entry is to the parent's investment account and, if the sale was upstream from a majority-owned subsidiary, the subsidiary's beginning retained earnings.

   (3) In the year the land is sold to an unaffiliated buyer, the same entries are made to the investment account and, if the sale was upstream from a majority-owned subsidiary, the subsidiary's beginning retained earnings. However, instead of crediting (debiting) the land account for the original gain (loss), the credit (debit) is to the gain or loss on land sale account.

2. Intercompany sales of services fall into two groups:

a. If the services are capitalized by the intercompany buyer, as for instance in an intangible asset, the elimination entries are the same as they are for intercompany fixed assets.

b. If the services are consumed by the intercompany buyer in the period they are rendered by the seller, no entries are necessary in the parent's books under the equity method. In the working paper an entry is made crediting the seller's income account and debiting the buyer's expense account. Net income is not affected.

B. Transfer profits before affiliation

1. There are two alternative views regarding unrealized or unconfirmed profits on assets transferred between companies prior to their affiliation.

a. The dominant view is that the sale is a transaction between unaffiliated companies and no adjustments or eliminations are required, even if

101

the sale occurred while the two companies were negotiating their affiliation.

      b.   The other view holds that unconfirmed preaffiliation profits should be removed from the accounts for consolidation purposes at the date of stock acquisition and recognized when they are confirmed.

2.   If a subsidiary's assets acquired from its future parent are not stated at market value at the time of acquisition and the acquisition is accounted for as a purchase, these assets are revalued along with the subsidiary's assets acquired from others.

C.   Unconfirmed profit and interperiod income tax allocation

1.   If the parent and subsidiary do not file a consolidated income tax return, then each pays income taxes on its reported net income, including any unconfirmed intercompany profits. For financial statement purposes, however, the recognition of intercompany profits and losses is deferred from the period of the intercompany transfer to the period in which the profit or loss is considered realized. Therefore, intercompany profits and losses cause timing differences and require interperiod tax allocation.

2.   Since the intercompany profit is taxed at the time of the intercompany sale, the profit to be deferred should be net of tax.

3.   In the case of intercompany merchandise sales, the only change from the entries previously discussed is that the elimination and recognition of unconfirmed profits in inventories are made net of tax.

      a.   Under the equity method the entries on the parent's books deferring or confirming the intercompany profit are made net of tax. This means that the deferred or confirmed profit is multiplied by 1 minus the tax rate. In other words, if P's profit in S's ending inventory is $10,000 and P's tax rate is 40 percent, then the profit eliminated is $6,000 [10,000 x (1-.4)].

      b.   In the consolidated statement working paper the entries are:

          (1)   Cost of goods sold
                Inventory
            To eliminate unconfirmed profit from ending inventory

102

    (2)   Deferred income taxes
             Income tax expense
        To defer income tax expense on the
        unconfirmed profit in the ending inventory

    (3)   Investment in S
        Retained earnings - S
        Income tax expense
             Cost of goods sold
        To eliminate the unconfirmed profit in the
        beginning inventory from cost of goods sold,
        recognize income tax expense on the confirmed
        profit, and allocate the unconfirmed profit
        net of tax to the parent and the minority
        interest in their ownership ratio

4.   In the case of intercompany transfers of fixed assets, the only change from the entries previously discussed is that the elimination and recognition of intercompany gains and losses on fixed asset sales are made net of tax.

    a.   Under the equity method the entries on the parent's books deferring or confirming the intercompany profit (loss) are made net of tax. This means that the deferred or confirmed profit (loss) is multiplied by 1 minus the tax rate. In other words, if P's gain on an asset sale to S is $10,000 and P's tax rate is 40 percent, then the gain eliminated in the year of the intercompany sale is $6,000 [10,000 x (1-.4)]. If the asset has a 10-year life, then the gain recognized each year is $600 (6,000 : 10 years).

    b.   In the working paper the same entries are made as previously discussed. In addition, entries have to be made for the tax effect, as follows:

        (1)   Deferred income taxes
               Income tax expense
            To defer income tax expense on the
            unconfirmed gain on asset sale

        (2)   Income tax expense
               Deferred income taxes
            To defer income tax expense on the
            unconfirmed loss on asset sale

        (3)   Income tax expense
               Deferred income taxes
            To record income tax on the confirmed portion
            of the intercompany gain on asset sale

                (4)   Deferred income taxes
                        Income tax expense
                      To record income tax on the confirmed portion
                      of the intercompany loss on asset sale

        c.   The working paper entry adjusting the beginning
             balances of the investment account and S's
             retained earnings debits (credits) them for the
             unconfirmed profit (loss) as of the beginning of
             the year net of tax. The tax is debited
             (credited) to the deferred income tax account.
             The entries to the plant and equipment and
             accumulated depreciation accounts are not
             affected.

III. Appendix: Two Additional Unconfirmed Profit Elimination Methods

     A.   In the previous discussion 100 percent of the intercompany
          gain or loss was eliminated and allocated either 100 percent
          to the parent, if the sale is downstream or the subsidiary
          is wholly owned, or pro rata to the parent and the minority
          interest.

     B.   Under fractional elimination only the parent's percentage of
          the unconfirmed profit or loss on an upstream sale from a
          partially-owned subsidiary is eliminated. In this case
          consolidated net income and consolidated retained earnings
          are the same as under 100-percent elimination. The minority
          interest, however, is based on the subsidiary's reported
          income and equity. In addition, cost of goods sold and
          inventories are adjusted only for the parent's percentage of
          the unconfirmed profit.

     C.   Modified fractional elimination is supported by Accounting
          Interpretation No. 1 of APB Opinion No. 18. It sanctions
          eliminating only the parent's percentage of unconfirmed
          profits in downstream sales, instead of 100 percent. Under
          this method a different amount is obtained for consolidated
          net income and consolidated retained earnings.

                    Test Your Understanding of Chapter 7

True or False

Instructions: Indicate your choice by circling either T, if you think
the statement is true, or F, if you think the statement is false.

T F   1. Intercompany profit resulting from the sale of plant and
          equipment becomes confirmed through the depreciation process
          over the remaining life of the asset.

T F   2. To the purchasing affiliate a fixed asset's depreciable cost
          equals its cost to the selling affiliate plus (minus) any
          intercompany profit (loss).

                                104

T F 3. Depreciation expense measures the portion of the asset's cost consumed in generating goods and services in the current period, and this amount is assumed to be confirmed as the goods and services are sold to non-affiliates.

T F 4. If the selling affiliate is a parent company, equity method accounting requires the parent to defer 100 percent of its recorded gain or loss in the year of the intercompany sale.

T F 5. An objective of fixed asset elimination entries on the consolidated statement working paper is to adjust the asset and the accumulated depreciation accounts to the balances they would have had without an intercompany sale.

T F 6. If an 80-percent owned subsidiary sold fixed assets to an affiliate at a gain, an eliminating entry should reduce the purchasing affiliate's depreciation expense by 80 percent of the profit assumed confirmed during the period.

T F 7. In 19x6 a 60-percent owned subsidiary sold equipment to its parent. At the beginning of 19x8 the unconfirmed profit was $8,000. The consolidated working paper at 12/31/19x8 should include a debit to the investment account of $4,800.

T F 8. Under the incremental approach consolidated net income equals the parent's confirmed net income from its own operations plus (minus) its share of the subsidiary's confirmed net income (loss).

T F 9. A gain on land sale recognized by the selling affiliate should be confirmed in the consolidated statements over a period not to exceed 40 years.

T F 10. When land has been sold intercompany at a gain or loss, adjustments must be made in the parent's books and the consolidated statement working paper every year until the land is sold to an outsider by the purchasing affiliate.

T F 11. Profits or losses resulting from fixed asset sales prior to affiliation may be ignored.

T F 12. If affiliates file separate income tax returns, equity method adjustments to defer and to confirm intercompany profit are based on the parent's percentage interest in the intercompany profit net of income taxes on the profit.

T F 13. Prepaid taxes are established in the selling affiliate's general ledger for the amount of income taxes paid on the period's unconfirmed intercompany profit if consolidated financial statements are prepared for companies that file separate income tax returns.

T F 14. An elimination entry recognizes consolidated income tax
          expense based on intercompany profit when the profit becomes
          confirmed in periods subsequent to the period of the
          intercompany transfer or sale.

T F 15. Fractional elimination procedures are based on the premise
          that unconfirmed intercompany profits to be eliminated
          should equal the majority shareholder's interest in any
          unconfirmed profits.

cost = $100,000, BV = 70,000, FMV = 85,000

Exercises *upstream* *gain = 15,000, Acc Dep = 30,000*

1. P Company owns 80 percent of S Company's outstanding common stock.
On January 1, 19x1, S Company purchased a computer for $100,000. S
used straight-line depreciation, a 10-year life and no salvage value.
On December 30, 19x3, S sold the computer to P for $85,000. P will
use straight line depreciation, an estimated remaining useful life of
5 years and no salvage value. For 19x3 P and S Companies reported net
income of $200,000 and $100,000, respectively. For 19x4 P and S
reported net income of $220,000 and $120,000, respectively. The two
companies file a consolidated income tax return.

Required:
a. Prepare P's entries at 12/31/19x3 under the equity method.

b. Prepare the elimination entries on the 19x3 consolidated
    statement working paper.

(1)

(2)

c.   Compute consolidated net income using the incremental approach.

d.   Prepare P Company's entries for 19x4 under the equity method.

(85K→70K)/5 = 3000/y → 收回 $ confirm $3000.

e.   Prepare the elimination entries on the 19x4 consolidated statement working paper.

(1)

(2)

(3)

f.   Compute the minority interest in the 19x4 consolidated income
       statement.

2. Use the same information as in Exercise 1 but assume that the
companies file separate income tax returns. The income tax rate for
each company is 40 percent. S's net income for 19x3 and 19x4 was
$60,000 and $72,000, respectively.

Required:
a.   Prepare P Company's entries for 19x4 under the equity method.

b.   Prepare the elimination entries on the 19x4 consolidated
       statement working paper.

(1)

(2)

(3)

(4)

c.   **Prepare the elimination entry to adjust the computer and other related asset accounts for the unconfirmed profit as of January 1, 19x6.**

109

Solutions to Chapter 7 Exercises

True or False

1.	T	4.	T	7.	T	10.	F	13.	F
2.	T	5.	T	8.	T	11.	T	14.	T
3.	T	6.	F	9.	F	12.	T	15.	T

Exercises

1. a.   Investment in S   80,000
         Equity in S earnings   80,000
   To record P's share of S's net income

        Equity in S earnings   12,000
         Investment in S   12,000
   To defer P's interest in the intercompany gain (original cost of 100,000 - 30,000 accumulated depreciation = 70,000 book value - 85,000 sales price = gain of 15,000 x .8)

   b. (1) Minority interest expense   17,000
         Equity in S earnings   68,000
           Investment in S   68,000
           Minority interest   17,000
        To eliminate equity in S earnings (80,000 - 12,000) and establish minority interest in confirmed net income of S [.2 x (100,000 - 15,000)]

     (2) Gain on computer sale   15,000
        Computer   15,000
         Accumulated depreciation   30,000
        To eliminate gain on intercompany equipment sale

   c.   P's reported net income   200,000
       P's equity in S's confirmed net income
       [.8 x (100,000 - 15,000)]   68,000
       Consolidated net income   268,000

   d.   Investment in S   96,000
         Equity in S earnings   96,000
       To record P's share of S's net income

       Investment in S   2,400
         Equity in S earnings   2,400
       To recognize the confirmed profit for the year (12,000 : 5 years)

   e. (1) Minority interest expense   24,600
         Equity in S earnings   98,400
           Investment in S   98,400
           Minority interest   24,600
        To eliminate equity in S earnings (96,000 + 2,400) and establish minority interest [.2 x (120,000 + 3,000)]

(2)　Investment in S (.8 x 15,000) .....　　12,000
　　　Retained earnings (.2 x 15,000)....　　 3,000
　　　Computer ....　　15,000
　　　　　　Accumulated depreciation .....　　　　　　　30,000
　　　To adjust beginning balances of investment account and S's
　　　retained earnings and restore the computer's original cost
　　　and accumulated depreciation at time of intercompany sale

(3)　Accumulated depreciation ....　　 3,000
　　　　　Depreciation expense ....　　　　　　　 3,000
　　　To recognize confirmed profit for current year (15,000 : 5
　　　years) by decreasing depreciation expense

f.　　S's reported net income for 19x4 ....　　120,000
　　　Add confirmed profit (15,000 : 5 years)......　　 3,000
　　　S's confirmed net income for 19x4 ....　　123,000
　　　Minority interest:　.2 x 123,000 = 24,600

2.　a.　Investment in S ....　　48,000
　　　　　Equity in S earnings ....　　　　　　48,000
　　　To record P's share of S's net income (.8 x 60,000)

　　　Investment in S ....　　 1,440
　　　　　Equity in S earnings ....　　　　　　 1,440
　　　To record the confirmed profit for the period net of tax
　　　[2,400 x (1-.4)]

b.　(1)　Minority interest expense ....　　12,360
　　　　　Equity in S earnings ....　　49,440
　　　　　　　Investment in S ....　　　　　　49,440
　　　　　　　Minority interest ....　　　　　　12,360
　　　To eliminate equity in S earnings and establish minority
　　　interest in confirmed net income of S　(100,000 + 3,000 =
　　　103,000 income before tax - income tax of 41,200 = net
　　　income of 61,800 x .2)

(2)　Investment in S [12,000 x (1-.4)]..　　 7,200
　　　Retained earnings [3,000 x (1-.4)].　　 1,800
　　　Prepaid income tax (15,000 x .4)...　　 6,000
　　　Computer ....　　15,000
　　　　　Accumulated depreciation .....　　　　　　30,000
　　　To adjust the beginning balance of investment in S and S's
　　　retained earnings, set up prepaid tax on intercompany gain,
　　　and restore original cost and accumulated depreciation of
　　　computer

(3)　Accumulated depreciation ....　　 3,000
　　　　　Depreciation expense ....　　　　　　 3,000
　　　To recognize confirmed profit for current year by decreasing
　　　depreciation expense

(4)　Income tax expense ....　　 1,200
　　　　　Prepaid income tax ....　　　　　　 1,200
　　　To record income tax expense on confirmed profit (3,000 x
　　　.4)

c.

Investment in S (note 1)	4,320	
Retained earnings - S (note 2).....	1,080	
Prepaid income taxes (note 3)	3,600	
Computer	15,000	
Accumulated depreciation (note 4).....................		24,000

To adjustment beginning balances of investment in S, S's retained earnings and accumulated depreciation and restore original cost

Note 1:
Intercompany gain	15,000
Less income tax	6,000
Intercompany gain net of tax	9,000
Less portion recognized in 19x4 and 19x5 (2 x 1,800)	3,600
Unconfirmed gain at 1/1/19x6	5,400
P's share: .8 x 5,400 = 4,320	

Note 2: Minority interest's share of unconfirmed gain at 1/1/19x6: .2 x 5,400 = 1,080

Note 3:
Prepaid tax on gain (15,000 x .4) ..	6,000
Less tax expense recognized for 19x4 and 19x5 (2 x 1,200)	2,400
Prepaid tax at 1/1/19x6	3,600

Note 4: Consolidated accumulated depreciation at 1/1/19X6 should be:
19x1 - 19x3: 3 x (100,000 : 10) ..	30,000
19x4 - 19x5: 2 x (70,000 : 5).....	28,000
Correct balance at 1/1/19x6	58,000
Less balance on P's books [2 x (85,000 : 5 years)]	34,000
Adjustment needed	24,000

Chapter 8
Consolidated Statements—Preference Interests

Chapter Outline

I. Intercompany Bonds - General Comments

    A.   From the perspective of the consolidated entity, the purchase of a company's bonds by an affiliated company constitutes a constructive bond retirement. However, the bonds are not actually retired on the books of either affiliate since they remain outstanding and are accounted for in a routine way by each affiliate until they reach maturity.

    B.   Since the intercompany bonds are considered to be no longer outstanding, a gain or loss on their retirement is recorded for the consolidated financial statements, and the parent's share of the gain or loss is recorded under the equity method. Also, the intercompany bond investment and bond liability are eliminated in the consolidated statement working paper like other intercompany receivables and payables and do not appear in the consolidated statements.

    C.   If the purchasing affiliate's cost of the bond investment is less (greaster) than the issuing affiliate's carrying value of the bond liability, a net gain (loss) from bond retirement results for consolidation and equity method purposes.

    D.   The portion of the net gain or loss contributed by the purchasing affiliate equals the difference between the par value of the acquired bonds and the investment cost, i. e. the discount or premium on bond investment. The portion of the net gain or loss contributed by the issuing affiliate equals the unamortized premium or discount on the bonds that have been constructively retired.

    E.   In the period bonds are constructively retired, the parent company prepares equity method entries to record its interest in each affiliate's gain or loss. If the parent is either the purchasing or the issuing affiliate, it records 100 percent of the gain or loss it contributed.

II. Intercompany Bonds--Introductory Cases

    A.   In order to concentrate on the effects of the constructive bond retirement, it is assumed that P owns 100 percent of S and that the bonds are non-interest bearing.

    B.   When P acquires bonds issued by the subsidiary at a discount (premium), the difference between the purchase price and the par value of the bonds is the gain (loss) contributed by P.

1. The subsidiary makes no entries during the remaining life of the bonds since they are non-interest bearing and were issued at par. When they mature, S records the retirement with a debit to bonds payable and a credit to cash.

2. Under the equity method the parent makes entries when the bonds are acquired and each year until their maturity.

   a. The gain at the time of the bond investment is recorded with a debit to the investment account and a credit to P's equity in S earnings. (A loss is recorded with the opposite entry.)

   b. In the years after the bond investment P records the amortization of the discount (in the case of a gain) with debits to the discount account and credits to interest income. (A premium is amortized with debits to interest income and credits to the premium account.) These entries in effect record the gain on the constructive bond retirement for the second time.

   c. To avoid double recording of the gain under the equity method, P eliminates the annual discount amortization by debiting its equity in S earnings and crediting its investment in S account. (The annual premium amortization is eliminated with the opposite entry.)

   d. When the bonds are retired by S, P records the receipt of the cash with a debit and credits its Investment in S Bonds account.

3. The effects of the equity method entries related to bonds are:

   a. P's net income and consolidated net income are increased in the year of the bond investment, if the bonds were acquired at a discount, and decreased during the years when the discount is amortized.

   b. P's net income and consolidated net income are decreased in the year of the bond investment, if the bonds were acquired at a premium, and increased during the years when the premium is amortized.

   c. The entries amortizing the premium or discount do not affect either P's net income or consolidated net income.

114

d. The equity method entries relating to intercompany bond investments create a difference between P's share of S's stockholder's equity and its investment account.

4. In the consolidated statement working papers entries are necessary during the remaining life of the bonds.

   a. In the year of the bond investment the gain on the bond retirement is recorded with a debit to the discount and a credit to a gain account. (A loss is recorded with a debit to a loss and a credit to the premium account.)

   b. In each year the bonds held intercompany are eliminated with a debit to bonds payable and a credit to bond investment.

   c. In the years after the bond investment the beginning balance of the investment account must be adjusted for the gain recorded in this account under the equity method. This entry credits the investment account and debits interest income and the unamortized bond discount. (In the case of bonds acquired at a premium the investment account is debited to offset the loss recorded in that account initially and interest income and the unamortized premium are credited.) The unamortized discount or premium must be eliminated, since the related bonds are also eliminated (see b, above).

C. When the bonds purchased by P were issued at a discount or premium, the issuing company contributes to the gain or loss the difference between their carrying and their par value. The net gain or loss on intercompany bond retirement is the difference between the price paid by the purchasing affiliate and the carrying value of the issuing affiliate.

1. Under the equity method P records 100 percent of the premium or discount on the purchase price as a loss or gain. In addition it records its share of the gain or loss contributed by the subsidiary.

2. In the consolidated statement working paper the beginning balance of the investment account must be adjusted both for the gain or loss contributed by P and for the gain or loss contributed by S. The entry for the gain contributed by P is as described in 4.c, above. In addition the unamortized discount on S's balance sheet is eliminated with a credit, interest expense is credited for the current year's discount amortization, and the investment account is debited for the initial loss recorded by P under the equity method.

115

3. Each year the intercompany bond holdings are eliminated with a debit to the bonds payable and a credit to the bond investment.

III. Additional Comments on Allocating Gains and Losses From Intercompany Bond Acquisitions

A. The consolidated gain or loss on bond retirement equals the sum of any unamortized discounts or premiums recorded on the affiliates' books on the date of the bond acquisition.

B. If the parent is involved in the intercompany bond acquisition, its share of the gain or loss consists of two parts: 100 percent of the parent's unamortized premium or discount and the parent's percentage of the subsidiary's unamortized premium or discount.

C. If both the issuing and the acquiring company are subsidiaries of P, then P's share of the gain or loss consists of each subsidiary's gain or loss multiplied by the parent's ownership percentage of that subsidiary. In other words, if P owns 90 percent of A and 70 percent of B, P's share of the gain or loss is 90 percent of the unamortized premium or discount on A's books and 70 percent of the unamortized premium or discount on B's books.

D. Since GAAP are silent on the issue of allocating the gains or losses on intercompany bond retirements, it is also possible to allocate 100 percent of the gain or loss to P.

IV. Intercompany Bonds--Advanced Cases

A. Accounting for intercompany bond retirements becomes more complicated if the subsidiary is only partially owned and if the bonds are issued and acquired at a price other than par. Another complication exists if the bonds are acquired during the year. In the following discussion it is first assumed that the bonds are acquired at the end of the year and, later, that they are acquired during the year.

1. The entries on the issuing company's books (in this case the subsidiary) are discussed in intermediate accounting. They consist of an entry to record the issuance, periodic entries to amortize the premium or discount with an offsetting entry to interest expense, and finally the entry to retire the bonds. These entries are not affected by the acquisition of the bonds by an affiliated company.

2. In the year of the bond acquisition the following entries are necessary:

a. The acquiring company (in this case the parent) records the bond investment in the usual way. The gain or loss on the bond retirement consists of

116

two parts, if the bonds are issued and acquired at other than par, and two entries should be made.

Parent purchase

(1) P records 100 percent of the premium (discount) it recorded when the bonds were acquired with a debit (credit) to its equity in S earnings and a credit (debit) to the investment account. (Note: A premium paid at acquisition results in a loss, since the price at acquisition exceeds par value. Conversely, a discount at acquisition results in a gain.)

S' sale.

(2) P records its percentage of the subsidiary's unamortized premium (discount) with a debit (credit) to the investment account and a credit (debit) to its equity in S earnings. (Note: A premium obtained at issuance results in a gain, since it exceeds par value. Conversely, a discount at issuance results in a loss.)

b. In the consolidated statement working paper the following entries are affected:

(1) The minority interest is established at its percentage of the confirmed income of the subsidiary, which includes the gain or loss on bond retirement contributed by the subsidiary.

(2) The net gain or loss is recorded with two entries:

(a) The premium on the bond investment is eliminated with a credit to the premium and a debit to net gain or net loss. The opposite entry is made if the bonds were acquired at a discount.

(b) The premium on the bond issuance is eliminated with a debit to the premium and a credit to net gain or loss. The opposite entry is made if the bonds were issued at a discount.

(3) The par value of the bonds held intercompany is eliminated with a debit to bonds payable and a credit to bond investment.

(4) Bond interest receivable and payable are eliminated with a debit to the payable and a credit to the receivable.

117

3. In years after the intercompany bond investment each company makes the usual entries on its books to record interest income and expense, including the amortization of the premium or discount paid or received and any accrued interest receivable and payable. In addition, the intercompany gain or loss must be adjusted on P's books under the equity method and in the consolidated statement working paper.

   a. On P's books two entries are again necessary.

      (1) The effect on income of the entry P made to record premium or discount amortization is reversed with an entry to the investment account and P's equity in S earnings. In other words, if the amortization of a premium paid at acquisition decreases bond interest income, the offsetting entry increases P's equity in S earnings.

      (2) When P records its share of the reported net income of S, it includes in that entry the premium or discount amortization made by S on its books. The effect of this entry must also be reversed with an entry to the investment account and P's equity in S earnings. In other words, if S amortizes a premium received at issuance by decreasing interest expense, P must decrease its equity in S earnings with a debit to that account and a credit to the investment account.

   b. In the consolidated statement working paper the following entries are affected:

      (1) The minority interest is established at the minority interest's percentage of the confirmed net income of S, i. e. excluding premium or discount amortization on S's books.

      (2) The beginning balance in the investment account is adjusted for the beginning balance of the gain or loss contributed by both P and S.

         (a) The gain (loss) contributed by P is eliminated with a debit (credit) to the investment account with the offsetting entry to the year-end balance of the premium (discount) on bond acquisition and interest income for the current year's amortization.

118

(b) The gain (loss) contributed by S is eliminated with credits (debits) to the investment account and the beginning balance in S's retained earnings for P's and the minority interest's pro rata share of the gain (loss). The offsetting entry eliminates the year-end balance of the premium (discount) and the current period's premium (discount) amortization from interest expense.

(3) The par value of the bonds held intercompany is eliminated with a debit to bonds payable and a credit to bond investment.

(4) Bond interest receivable and payable are eliminated with a debit to the payable and a credit to the receivable.

(5) Bond interest income and expense are eliminated with a debit to the income and a credit to the expense.

B. Calculations of consolidated net income are affected by intercompany bond investments. Using the incremental approach, consolidated net income consists of:

1. In the year of the intercompany bond investment:

   a. P's confirmed net income from its own operations, which includes the gain or loss on the intercompany bond retirement contributed by P, plus

   b. P's percentage of the confirmed net income of S, which includes the gain or loss on the intercompany bond retirement contributed by S.

2. In years after the intercompany bond investment:

   a. P's confirmed net income from its own operations, which excludes the amortization of the premium paid or the discount received on the bond investment, plus

   b. P's percentage of the confirmed net income of S, which excludes the amortization of the premium or discount on bond issuance.

C. The relationship between the investment account balance and the net assets of the subsidiary is also affected by intercompany bond investments. The balance in the investment account at any date is equal to:

1. P's share of the confirmed stockholders' equity of S, which includes the balance of the gain or loss contributed by S which has not yet been recorded on S's books through premium or discount amortization, plus or minus

2. The balance of the gain or loss contributed by P which has not yet been recorded on P's books through premium or discount amortization.

D. The relationship between the minority interest and the net assets of the subsidiary is affected by intercompany bond investments if S either issued or purchased the bonds at a price other than par. The minority interest is equal to its share of the confirmed stockholders' equity of S, which includes the balance of the gain or loss contributed by S which has not yet been recorded on S's books through premium or discount amortization.

E. The general case outlined above is adapted when the situation is changed.

1. If the affiliate company acquires only a portion of the outstanding bonds, then the elimination entries are for the portion of the bonds acquired intercompany. In other words, only a portion of the bonds payable, the bond interest expense, and the interest payable is eliminated.

2. When the bonds are acquired during the year and at dates other than interest payment dates, the principles outlined above still apply. The gain or loss contributed by each company is the difference between par value and carrying value on the day of the bond investment, and discount and premium amortization are recorded for the remainder of the year.

3. When the intercompany bond holding is between two subsidiaries, the entries on P's books under the equity method must be adjusted accordingly. In other words, in the year of the bond investment P records its percentage of the gain or loss contributed by each company and in subsequent years it records its percentage of the premium and discount amortization.

F. When the bond investment is made during the year, the gain or loss contributed by the investing and the issuing company is computed on the day the bonds are acquired and amortization of the premium or discount on both the bond investment and the bond liability is computed from acquisition for consolidated statement purposes. In other words, entries made in two different years in the previous example are now made in the year of the bond investment.

1. Under the equity method P records its share of the gain or loss of the investing and issuing companies. The portion of the gain or loss recorded through premium or discount amortization is then reversed with entries to the investment and the equity in S earnings accounts.

2. In the consolidated statement working paper the gain or loss on the day of the bond investment is recorded and the effects of the premium or discount amortization are eliminated.

3. The minority interest in the income statement is based on the confirmed net income of S, which includes the gain or loss contributed by S minus the portion of the gain or loss recorded through discount or premium amortization since the day of the bond investment.

4. The elimination entries for the par value of the bonds, interest payable and receivable, and interest income and expense are the same as outlined above.

V. Preferred Stock--General Comments

A. If a subsidiary has outstanding preferred stock, its net income and retained earnings have to be allocated between the common and the preferred stock.

B. If the parent owns some of the preferred stock, it should account for it using the cost method. The parent's holding of preferred stock is eliminated against the pro rata share of the subsidiary's outstanding preferred stock.

VI. Allocating Subsidiary Earnings

A. The allocation of a subsidiary's net income and retained earnings between its preferred and common stock depends on the characteristics of the preferred stock.

1. If the preferred stock is noncumulative and nonparticipating, no allocation of retained earnings is necessary. The subsidiary's net income is not affected if no preferred dividends are declared. Any preferred dividends declared reduce the net income available to the common stock.

2. If the preferred stock is cumulative and nonparticipating, the subsidiary's retained earnings up to any arrearage is allocated to the preferred stock, with any excess allocated to the common stock. Net income is reduced by the current year's dividends due on the preferred, whether or not they were declared. If net income is insufficient to absorb the preferred dividends, a loss is allocated to the common stock.

3. If the preferred stock is noncumulative and fully participating, the subsidiary's retained earnings are allocated pro rata between the preferred and the common stock. If dividends are declared, the net income is allocated pro rata between the preferred and common stock.

4. If the preferred stock is cumulative and fully participating, the subsidiary's retained earnings up to any arrearage is allocated to the preferred stock with any remainder shared pro rata between the preferred and the common stock. If there is no arrearage, the subsidiary's retained earnings are allocated pro rata between the preferred and the common stock. Whether or not dividends are declared, the subsidiary's net income is shared pro rata between the preferred and common stock. If net income is less than the preferred dividend requirement, a loss is allocated to the common stock.

B. When P owns some of the subsidiary's outstanding noncumulative, nonparticipating preferred stock in addition to a majority of the common stock, retained earnings does not have to be allocated. The subsidiary's net income is reduced by any dividends declared during the year.

1. The entries on P's books regarding its common stock holdings are made in the usual manner, with the exception that net income available to the common stock is reduced by preferred dividends declared.

2. Any dividends declared on the preferred stock are recorded as dividend income under the cost method.

3. In the consolidated statement working paper several entries are affected by the existence of the preferred stock.

    a. The preferred dividends declared are eliminated with debits to the parent's preferred dividend income and minority interest expense.

    b. The entry eliminating P's equity in S earnings establishes the minority interest in the subsidiary's net income available to common stock.

    c. The subsidiary's preferred stock is eliminated with credits to the parent's preferred stock investment and the minority interest if the preferred was acquired at book value.

    d. The common stockholders' equity is eliminated in the usual manner.

4. Consolidated net income, using the incremental approach, consists of:

    a. P's net income from its own operations, plus

    b. P's share of the preferred dividends declared, plus

    c. P's share of the subsidiary's net income available to common stock.

C. When P owns some of the subsidiary's outstanding cumulative, nonparticipating preferred stock in addition to a majority of the common stock, retained earnings have to be allocated if preferred dividends are in arrears. The subsidiary's net income is reduced by any preferred dividends due for the year.

1. The entries on P's books regarding its common stock holdings are made in the usual manner, with the exception that net income available to the common stock is reduced by preferred dividends due, whether declared or not.

2. Any dividends declared on the preferred stock are recorded as dividend income under the cost method.

3. In the consolidated statement working paper several entries are affected by the existence of the preferred stock.

    a. The preferred dividends declared are eliminated with debits to the parent's preferred dividend income and minority interest expense.

    b. The entry eliminating P's equity in S earnings establishes the minority interest in the subsidiary's net income available to common stock.

    c. The subsidiary's preferred stock is eliminated with credits to the parent's preferred stock investment and the minority interest if the preferred was acquired at book value.

        (1) If the preferred stock was acquired below its book value, the elimination entry includes a credit to other contributed capital.

        (2) If the preferred stock was acquired above its book value, the subsidiary's other contributed capital is debited. If the balance in this account is insufficient to absorb the debit, the parent's paid-in capital or, if insufficient, retained earnings is debited.

          d.   The common stockholders' equity is eliminated in the usual manner.

      4.   Consolidated net income, using the incremental approach, consists of:

          a.   P's net income from its own operations, plus

          b.   P's share of the preferred dividends due, whether or not declared, plus

          c.   P's share of the subsidiary's net income available to common stock.

      5.   The parent's net income under the equity method will equal consolidated net income if the preferred dividends were declared. If they were not declared, the parent should accrue the dividends due with a debit to dividends receivable and a credit to dividend income. The accrual of the preferred dividends is warranted because the parent controls the subsidiary and can compel S to pay the preferred dividend.

Test Your Understanding of Chapter 8

True or False

Instructions: Indicate your choice by circling either T, if you think the statement is true, or F, if you think the statement is false.

T F 1. The purchase of an affiliate's bonds by another affiliate constitutes constructive retirement of the bonds from a consolidated perspective.

T F 2. A net gain or loss from the constructive retirement of bonds is computed by subtracting from the carrying value of the bonds on the books of the issuing (borrowing) company the purchasing affiliate's investment cost, including payment for accrued interest.

T F 3. Generally accepted accounting principles permit a net gain or loss from the purchase of intercompany bonds to be either wholly assigned to the purchasing company, to the issuing affiliate, or allocated between the two affiliates.

T F 4. Assuming a net gain or loss is allocated between affiliates, the issuing company and the purchasing company both record on their books their respective gain or loss in the period the intercompany bond investment occurred.

124

T F   5. The equity method requires a parent company to adjust its investment in subsidiary stock account and equity in subsidiary earnings account for the parent's interest in the entire amount of the gain or loss from constructive bond retirement allocated to each affiliate.

T F   6. Allocation of a net gain or loss from constructive bond retirement between the involved affiliates is based on the assumption that the purchase was effected at the bond's par value. Thus, a purchasing affiliate's premium on bond investment equals the amount of its loss from constructive bond retirement.

T F   7. A net gain or loss from the purchase of intercompany bonds is not confirmed for consolidation purposes until the involved affiliates amortize their respective premiums or discounts associated with the constructively retired bonds.

T F   8. Because annual amortization of an issuing affiliate's premium on constructively retired bonds has the effect of reporting a part of its gain in reported net income, the parent company is required under the equity method to offset its interest in the effect the amortization has on the subsidiary's income.

T F   9. In years following the year in which intercompany bonds are constructively retired, elimination entries are necessary to remove from consolidation all asset, liability, revenue, and expense accounts associated with the bonds.

T F   10. In years following the year in which intercompany bonds are constructively retired, an elimination entry adjusts the parent's investment in subsidiary stock account for its interest in each affiliate's unamortized premium or discount on the constructively retired bonds as of the beginning of the current year.

T F   11. Minority interest in combined net income for each period in which the subsidiary's constructively retired bonds remain outstanding is the product of the minority ownership percentage and the subsidiary's reported net income.

T F   12. On January 1, 19x1, S Company's capital structure includes cumulative, nonparticipating, 10 percent preferred stock (par $100) of $100,000, premium on preferred stock of $50,000, common stock of $200,000, and retained earnings of $5,000. Preferred dividends are in arrears for two years. P owns 20 percent of S Company's preferred and 90 percent of its common stock. S earned $60,000 in 19x1 and paid a $30,000 dividend on the preferred and a $20,000 dividend on the common. If P reported income from its own operations of $50,000, 19x1 consolidated net income is $97,000.

125

T F 13. Assume the same information presented in question 12 and that P paid $35,000 for the preferred stock on January 1, 19x1. In this case the preferred stock investment elimination entry at year-end would produce a debit differential of $1,000.

T F 14. If a parent buys less than 20 percent of a subsidiary's preferred stock, it must use the cost method to account for this investment.

T F 15. A debit differential resulting from a parent's purchase of subsidiary preferred stock is eliminated on the consolidated statement working paper by allocating the differential to the undervalued assets of the subsidiary.

Exercises

1. On 1/1/19x1 S issued 10% bonds with a face value of $50,000 at 98. The bonds pay interest on 6/30 and 12/31 and are due on 12/31/19x10.

On 1/1/19x4 P acquired 80 percent of S stock for $80,000. On this day the stockholders' equity of S consisted of common stock of $20,000 and retained earnings of $80,000.

On 12/31/19x8 P acquired S bonds with a par value of $30,000 at 103. Both P and S use straight-line amortization for discounts and premiums.

At 1/1/19x8 the balance in the retained earnings of S was $150,000. For 19x8 P and S reported net income from their own operations of $40,000 and $20,000, respectively. They paid no dividends in 19x8.

Required:
a. Prepare the entries for 19x8 relating to the bonds and the investment account on the books of P.

b. **Prepare the elimination entries on the consolidated statement working paper for 19x8.**

(1)

(2)

(3)

(4)

(5)

c. **Compute consolidated net income for 19x8.**

d. **Compute the minority interest in the consolidated balance sheet at 12/31/19x8.**

127

e.   Compute the balance in the investment account at 12/31/19x8.

2.   Use the information provided in Exercise 1 and assume that P and S
reported net income from their own operations of $50,000 and $25,000,
respectively, for 19x9.   They paid no dividends.

Required:
a.   Prepare the entries for 19x9 relating to the bonds on the books
      of S.

b.   Prepare the entries for 19x9 relating to the bonds and the
      investment account on the books of P.

c. Prepare the elimination entries on the consolidated statement
    working paper for 19x9.

(1)

(2)

(3)

(4)

(5)

(6)

d.   Compute consolidated net income for 19x9.

e.   Compute the minority interest in the consolidated balance sheet at 12/31/19x9.

f.   Compute the balance in the investment account at 12/31/19x9.

Solutions to Chapter 8 Exercises

True or False

1.	T	4.	F	7.	F	10.	T	13.	T
2.	F	5.	T	8.	T	11.	F	14.	F
3.	T	6.	T	9.	T	12.	T	15.	F

Exercises

1.   a.

```
12/31   Investment in S bonds .............      30,000
        Premium on bond investment .........        900
            Cash ...........................              30,900
        To record purchase of S bonds
```

```
12/31   Investment in S stock .............      16,000
            Equity in S earnings ..........              16,000
        To record P's share of S's reported net income (.8 x 20,000)
```

```
12/31   Equity in S earnings ..............       900
            Investment in S stock .........               900
        To record loss contributed by P to intercompany bond
        retirement
```

P paid more

```
12/31   Equity in S earnings ..............             96
            Investment in S stock .........                  96
        To record P's percentage of loss contributed by S (carrying
        value of bonds on 12/31/19x8 = 49,800 x .6 = 29,880 carrying
        value of bonds retired less 30,000 par value = loss of 120 x
        .8 = 96)
```

b.   (1)

```
        Minority interest expense .........      3,976
        Equity in S earnings ..............     15,004
            Investment in S stock .........              15,004
            Minority interest .............               3,976
        To eliminate equity in S earnings and establish minority
        interest in confirmed net income of S [.2 x (20,000 - 120)]
```

= 900 + 0.8x(20000 - 120)

(2)

```
        Common stock - S ..................     20,000
        Retained earnings - S .............    150,000
            Investment in S Company .......             136,000
            Minority interest .............              34,000
        To eliminate S's stockholders' equity and P's investment
        account and set up minority interest as of the beginning of
        the year
```

170K x 0.8   *170K x 0.2*

(3)

```
        Loss on bond retirement ...........        900
            Premium on bond investment ....                 900
        To record loss on intercompany bond retirement contributed
        by P
```

    (4)   Loss on bond retirement   120
              Bond discount   120
          To record loss on intercompany bond retirement contributed
          by S (12/31/19x8 balance of bond discount = $200 x 60%
          purchased by P = $120)

    (5)   Bonds payable   30,000
              Investment in S bonds   30,000
          To eliminate intercompany bond holding

c.   P's net income from its own operations $40,000
         P's share of S's reported net income (.8
           x 20,000)   16,000
         Less loss on intercompany bond retirement
           contributed by P ....   (900)
         Less P's share of loss on intercompany bond
           retirement contributed by S (.8 x 120) ....   (96)
         Consolidated net income $55,004

d.   Common stock .... $ 20,000
         Retained earnings at 1/1/19x8   150,000
         Reported net income for 19x8   20,000
         Loss on intercompany bond retirement
           contributed by S ....   (120)
         S's confirmed stockholders' equity at
           12/31/19x8 .... $189,880
         Minority interest in net assets of S
           at 12/31/19x8 - 20% $37,976

e.   P's share of confirmed net assets of
           S at 12/31/19x8 (.8 x 189,880) $151,904
         Less loss on intercompany bond retirement
           contributed by P ....   (900)
         Balance in P's Investment in S account
           at 12/31/19x8 .... $151,004

2.   a.
6/30   Bond interest expense   2,550
             Bond discount   50
             Cash   2,500
         To record semi-annual payment of bond interest

12/31   Bond interest expense   2,550
             Bond discount   50
             Cash   2,500
         To record semi-annual payment of bond interest

b. 6/30 Cash   1,500
             Bond interest income   1,500
         To record receipt of interest from S

12/31   Cash   1,500
             Bond interest income   1,500
         To record receipt of interest from S

132

```
12/31    Bond interest income ...............        450
            Premium on bond investment.....                   450
         To record premium amortization (900 : 2 years)

12/31    Investment in S stock .............     20,000
            Equity in S earnings ..........                20,000
         To record P's share of S's reported net income (.8 x 25,000)

12/31    Investment in S stock .............        450
            Equity in S earnings ..........                   450
         To eliminate decrease in income due to premium amortization

12/31    Investment in S stock .............         48
            Equity in S earnings ..........                    48
         To eliminate P's percentage of decrease in S's income due to
         discount amortization of the 60% of bonds held by P [.8 x
         (100 x .6)]

c.  (1)  Minority interest expense .........      5,012
         Equity in S earnings ..............     20,498
            Investment in S stock .........                20,498
            Minority interest .............                 5,012
         To eliminate equity in S earnings and establish minority
         interest in confirmed net income of S [.2 x (25,000 + 60)]

    (2)  Investment in S stock .............      900
            Bond interest income ..........                   450
            Premium on bond investment ....                   450
         To adjust beginning-of-year balance in investment account
         for loss on intercompany bond retirement recorded in 19x8,
         to eliminate 19x9 amortization of bond premium, and to
         eliminate year-end balance in premium account

    (3)  Investment in S stock (.8 x 120)....       96
         Retained earnings - S (.2 x 120)....       24
            Discount on bonds payable .....                    60
            Bond interest expense ........                     60
         To adjust beginning-of-year balances of investment account
         for P's share and S's retained earnings for minority
         interest's share of the loss on intercompany bond retirement
         contributed by S, to eliminate year-end balance of discount
         on bonds payable for portion held intercompany (.6 x 100),
         and to eliminate discount amortization relating to bonds
         held intercompany (.6 x 100)

    (4)  Common stock - S ...................     20,000
         Retained earnings - S .............    169,976
            Investment in S stock .........               152,000
            Minority interest .............                37,976
         To eliminate adjusted beginning-of-year balances of S's
         retained earnings (170,000 - 24) and P's investment account
         (151,004 + 900 + 96) and set up beginning-of-year minority
         interest (see solution to exercise 1.d. and 1.e., above)
```

(5) Bonds payable 30,000
       Investment in S bonds   30,000
    To eliminate intercompany bond holding

(6) Bond interest income 3,000
       Bond interest expense   3,000
    To eliminate intercompany bond interest income and expense
    (30,000 x 10%)

d.   P's net income from its own operations $50,000
     P's share of S's reported net income (.8
      x 25,000) 20,000
     Plus premium amortization for 19x9 450
     Plus P's share of discount amortization
      relating to intercompany bond holding
      [.8 x (100 x .6)] 48
     Consolidated net income $70,498

e.   Common stock .... $ 20,000
     Retained earnings at 1/1/19x9 170,000
     Reported net income for 19x9 25,000
     Loss on intercompany bond retirement
      contributed by S (120) less portion
      recorded in 19x9 (60) .... (60)
     S's confirmed stockholders' equity at
      12/31/19x9 .... $214,940
     Minority interest in net assets of S
      at 12/31/19x9 - 20% $42,988

     Or: Balance at 12/31/19x8 (per 1.d.) $37,976
     Add minority interest in confirmed net
      income of S [entry (1)] 5,012
     Minority interest at 12/31/19x9 .... $42,988

f.   P's share of confirmed net assets of
     S at 12/31/19x9 (.8 x 214,940) $171,952
     Less loss on intercompany bond retirement
      contributed by P (900) less portion
      recorded in 19x9 (450) .... (450)
     Balance in P's Investment in S account
      at 12/31/19x9 .... $171,502

     Or: Balance at 12/31/19x8 (per 1.e.) $151,004
     Add equity in S earnings for 19x9 (20,000
      +450 + 48) 20,498
     Balance at 12/31/19x9 .... $171,502

Chapter 9
Consolidated Statements –
Changes in Parent Companies' Ownership Percents

Chapter Outline

I.   Increases in Parent's Ownership Percentage

    A.   A parent's percentage of ownership in a subsidiary increases in the following situations:

        1.   The parent acquires additional shares of the subsidiary's stock in the open market.

        2.   The subsidiary issues additional shares and the parent acquires more than its proportionate share of the newly issued shares, e. g. a parent who owns 80% of a subsidiary acquires 100% of the newly issued shares.

        3.   The subsidiary acquires its own stock mostly or only from the minority interest, e. g. the subsidiary buys half of the shares owned by the minority interest and none of the shares owned by the parent.

    B.   A parent may achieve control through one stock acquisition or through several purchases of blocks of subsidiary stock.

        1.   If control is achieved with one stock purchase, only one analysis of the parent's interest in the subsidiary's stockholders' equity and consequent determination of the differential is necessary.

        2.   However, if control is acquired through several block purchases, two methods of analysis are possible under current accounting policy:

            a.   A step-by-step analysis determines the parent's share of the subsidiary's stockholders' equity and the allocation of the differential for each block of stock purchased. This is the more accurate method. It is feasible as long as the number of block purchases is limited and is the method used in this chapter.

            b.   A date-of-control analysis assumes that all shares were acquired on the day control is achieved. The differential and its allocation are only computed on this day. Changes in the stockholders' equity of the subsidiary over the period when the parent was increasing its interest in the subsidiary are ignored. This method is more convenient than the step-by-step method; however, it should be used only when its effects are immaterial. This method is explained in the appendix.

C. If control is achieved through several block purchases, each acquisition is analyzed under the step-by-step method.

1. If the acquisition was at the beginning of the year, the allocation of the purchase price and amortization of the differential are identical to the procedures illustrated in Chapter 4, except that more than one block of stock is involved.

a. For each purchase the parent's interest in the subsidiary's stockholders' equity is subtracted from the purchase price to arrive at the differential.

b. Each differential is allocated to differences between fair and book value of the subsidiary's identifiable assets and liabilities, with the remainder allocated to goodwill.

c. For each allocated amount the remaining useful life of the asset or liability is determined and the annual amortization is computed.

d. The amounts allocated to each asset and liability are totalled, as are the amounts of amortization. Since the parent's interest increases with each purchase, the amounts of allocation and amortization also increase.

e. For each year the parent recognizes its percentage of the subsidiary's earnings. Since the parent's interest increases with each purchase, it will recognize an increasing percentage of the subsidiary's earnings.

f. The working paper entries are identical to those illustrated in Chapter 4 with one exception: The entry eliminating the subsidiary's stockholders' equity as of the beginning of the year does not eliminate the balance in the investment account as of the beginning of the year. It eliminates instead the balance right after the block purchase was made, which occurred at the start of the first business day of the year.

g. Consolidated net income, using the incremental approach, is calculated as follows:

(1) P Company's net income from its own operations

        (2)   Plus P Company's percentage (after the block purchase) multiplied by S Company's net income

        (3)   Plus or minus differential amortization

2.   If the acquisition was at an interim date, the subsidiary's stockholders' equity as of the purchase date has to be calculated. Usually this involves only the retained earnings account which is increased by income earned and decreased by losses incurred and dividends declared between the beginning of the year and the purchase date.

    a.   The calculation and allocation of the differential is identical to the procedures used for purchases at the beginning of the year.

    b.   A difference exists in the first year's amortization of allocated amounts. Since the purchase occurred during the year, the amortization is computed only for the remainder of the year.

    c.   The parent's equity in the subsidiary's earnings is recognized only for the portion of the income earned after the interim purchase date.

    d.   The subsidiary income allocable to the shares purchased by the parent during the year is termed Purchased Preacquisition Earnings and recorded in the working paper entry eliminating the subsidiary's stockholders' equity accounts, as explained in Chapter 4.

    e.   The minority interest is computed by multiplying the subsidiary's net income for the entire year by the minority interest's percentage at the end of the year.

    f.   Consolidated net income, using the incremental approach, is calculated as follows:

        (1)   P Company's net income from its own operations

        (2)   Plus P Company's percentage before the current year's block purchase multiplied by S Company's net income from the beginning of the year to the day of the block purchase

        (3)   Plus P Company's percentage after the current year's block purchase multiplied by S Company's net income from the day of the block purchase to the end of the year

(4) Plus or minus differential amortization

(a) for the period from the beginning of the year to the day of the purchase, and

(b) for the period from the day of the purchase to the end of the year

D. A parent's ownership interest will also increase if the subsidiary issues additional stock and the parent purchases more than its proportionate share of the newly issued stock. Such an ownership percent increasing subsidiary stock transaction produces two changes: The parent's investment account and the subsidiary's stockholders' equity are increased. Exactly the same changes occur if the subsidiary sells the newly issued shares in the open market and the parent buys more than its proportionate share in the open market at the issue price.

1. In the differential calculation both of the above changes must be considered:

a. The stockholder's equity of the subsidiary before the stock issue is multiplied by the parent's percentage before the stock purchase; and

b. The stockholders' equity of the subsidiary after the stock issue is multiplied by the parent's percentage after the stock purchase.

c. The increase in the parent's share of the subsidiary's stockholders' equity is subtracted from the parent's purchase price. The difference is the differential. The amount of the differential will be:

(1) zero if the shares were issued at book value;

(2) a debit if the shares were issued above book value;

(3) a credit if the shares were issued below book value.

d. A debit differential is allocated and amortized in the same manner as previously illustrated. The treatment of a credit differential arising from a sale of stock by a subsidiary to its parent is not covered by current accounting policy.

2. If the stock issue occurred at the beginning of the year, the parent's percentage is increased for the entire year.

a. The entry on the parent's books recognizing its equity in the subsidiary's earnings is made at the higher percentage and differential amortization is recorded for the entire year.

b. The working paper entries will be identical to those illustrated in Chapter 4 with one exception: The entry eliminating the stockholders' equity of the subsidiary eliminates the capital stock and other contributed capital balances after the stock issue and the investment account after the stock purchase.

c. Consolidated net income, using the incremental approach, is calculated as follows:

   (1) P Company's net income from its own operations

   (2) Plus P Company's percentage after the stock purchase multiplied by S Company's net income

   (3) Plus or minus differential amortization

3. If the stock issue occurred during the year, the above procedures have to be combined with the interim purchase techniques of Chapter 4.

   a. The subsidiary's stockholders' equity both before and after the stock issue has to be adjusted for changes in retained earnings since the beginning of the year.

   b. The parent's equity in subsidiary earnings will consist of:

      (1) The subsidiary's net income earned before the stock issue multiplied by the parent's percentage before the stock purchase, plus

      (2) The subsidiary's net income earned after the stock issue multiplied by the parent's percentage after the stock purchase.

   c. The minority interest is computed by multiplying the income for the entire year by the minority interest's percentage at the end of the year.

   d. Purchased preacquisition earnings are computed by multiplying the income earned by the subsidiary before the stock issue by the difference in the parent's percentage before and after the stock purchase.

139

e. Differential amortization is computed for the entire year for the differential existing at the beginning of the year and for the remainder of the year for the differential arising from the interim stock purchase.

f. Consolidated net income, using the incremental approach, is calculated as follows:

   (1) P Company's net income from its own operations

   (2) Plus P Company's percentage before the current year's stock purchase multiplied by S Company's net income from the beginning of the year to the day of the stock issue

   (3) Plus P Company's percentage after the current year's stock purchase multiplied by S Company's net income from the day of the stock issue to the end of the year

   (4) Plus or minus differential amortization

       (a) for the period from the beginning of the year to the day of the purchase, and

       (b) for the period from the day of the purchase to the end of the year

4. The procedures discussed above apply also if the minority interest acquires some, but less than its proportionate share, of the newly issued stock.

5. If the new stock is issued proportionately to the parent and the minority interest, as is the case if the stockholders exercise their preemptive rights, the parent's percentage will not change. In addition, no differential will exist because the parent's purchase price exactly equals its proportionate share of the increase in the subsidiary's stockholders' equity.

E. The parent's percentage of ownership will also increase if the subsidiary acquires its own stock from the minority interest. The purchase of treasury stock decreases the number of outstanding shares. Since the number of shares owned by the parent remains the same, it now owns a larger percentage of the outstanding shares.

1. The effect on the parent's interest in the subsidiary's stockholders' equity depends on the price paid by the subsidiary for its own stock.

   a. If the subsidiary purchases its own stock at book value, the amount of the parent's interest in the

140

subsidiary's stockholders' equity will not change.

b. If the subsidiary purchases its own stock above book value, the amount of the parent's interest in the subsidiary's stockholders equity will decrease, because the book value of the remaining outstanding shares is decreased. This decrease is treated the same as a debit differential.

c. If the subsidiary purchases its own stock below book value, the amount of the parent's interest in the subsidiary's stockholders' equity will increase, because the book value of the remaining outstanding shares is increased. This increase constitutes a credit differential. Current accounting policy is silent on the treatment of such credit differentials.

2. If the treasury stock acquisition by the subsidiary occurred at the beginning of the year, the parent's higher percentage is used for the entire year. The computation of the parent's equity in subsidiary earnings and consolidated net income are the same as illustrated above for increases in the parent's percentage of ownership as of the beginning of a year.

3. If the treasury stock acquisition by the subsidiary occurred during the year, the interim procedures outlined above apply again.

a. To compute the parent's equity in subsidiary earnings, the subsidiary's net income is allocated to the period before and after the treasury stock acquisition. Each portion of the income is then multiplied by the parent's appropriate ownership percentage. And the differential existing for each portion of the year is amortized for that period.

b. The minority interest is computed by multiplying the subsidiary's net income for the entire year by the minority interest percentage at the end of the year.

c. Purchased preacquisition earnings are computed by multiplying the income earned by the subsidiary before the treasury stock acquisition by the difference in the parent's percentage before and after the stock acquisition.

d. The working paper entries are changed in two respects:

(1) An additional entry is made offsetting the treasury stock account against the

141

proportionate amount of capital stock and other contributed capital, with any difference debited to retained earnings.

(2) The entry eliminating the subsidiary's stockholders' equity eliminates the balances after the preceding entry is made.

e. Consolidated net income, using the incremental approach, is calculated as follows:

(1) P Company's net income from its own operations

(2) Plus P Company's percentage before the treasury stock acquisition multiplied by S Company's net income from the beginning of the year to the day of the stock purchase

(3) Plus P Company's percentage after the treasury stock acquisition multiplied by S Company's net income from the day of the stock purchase to the end of the year

(4) Plus or minus differential amortization

(a) for the period from the beginning of the year to the day of the purchase, and

(b) for the period from the day of the purchase to the end of the year

f. The procedures outlined above apply also if the subsidiary acquires shares from both the minority interest and the parent, as long as the parent sells less than its proportionate share.

g. If the subsidiary acquires its own stock proportionately from both the minority interest and the parent, the parent's percentage and the differential do not change.

II. Decreases in Parent's Ownership Percentage

A. A parent's percentage of ownership in a subsidiary decreases in the following situations:

1. The parent sells shares of the subsidiary's stock in the open market.

2. The subsidiary issues additional shares and the parent acquires less than its proportionate share of the newly issued shares, e. g. a parent who owns 80% of a subsidiary acquires only 50% of the newly issued shares.

3. The subsidiary acquires its own stock mostly or only from the parent, e. g. the subsidiary buys some of the shares owned by the parent and none of the shares owned by the minority interest.

B. The parent's sale of subsidiary shares to a nonaffiliate is accounted for like other disposals of asset. First, the entries necessary under the equity method are made to the date of the sale. Then the carrying value of the shares sold is subtracted from the sales price to determine the gain or loss on the sale. The carrying value may be determined using one of the following three methods:

1. Specific identification. This method is acceptable for federal income tax purposes.

2. First-in, first-out. This method is also acceptable for federal income tax purposes.

3. Weighted average. This method is not acceptable for federal income tax purposes. It is nevertheless used because the shares held in the subsidiary are interchangeable.

C. When the parent sells some of its subsidiary shares, the entries it makes under the equity method are affected.

1. Net income earned by the subsidiary is allocated to the periods before and after the stock sale by the parent.

    a. The income earned before the sale of stock is multiplied by the parent's old percentage.

    b. The income earned after the sale of stock is multiplied by the parent's new, reduced percentage.

2. Differential amortization is also affected by the stock sale.

    a. For the period before the stock sale the annual amortization is multiplied by the fraction of the year until the date of the sale, e. g. if the sale occurs on October 1, the annual amortization is multiplied by 3/4 of a year.

    b. For the period after the stock sale the annual amortization is multiplied by the fraction of its stock ownership which the parent is retaining, e g. if the parent owned 8,000 shares of S and sold 1,000, it now owns 7,000 shares, or 87.5% (7,000 : 8,000) of its previous ownership. This calculation is necessary, because some of the differential is sold along with the sold shares. The differential amortization so calculated becomes the new annual amount. For the year of the stock sale it is multiplied by the fraction of the year remaining after the date of the stock sale.

c. If it is assumed that the annual amortization for 8,000 shares of S stock is $10,000 and that P sells 1,000 shares of the stock on October 1, then the differential amortization for the first 9 months is $10,000 x 3/4 year, or $7,500. For future years it is $10,000 x .875 (the percentage of the stock P keeps out of its total interest in S), or $8,750. For the remaining three months in the year of the stock sale it is $8,750 x 1/4 year, or $2,187.50.

3. Consolidated net income for the year of the stock sale is computed as follows:

a. P Company's net income from its own operations (excluding the gain or loss on the stock sale)

b. Plus (minus) the gain (loss) on the stock sale

c. Plus P Company's equity in subsidiary earnings

    (1) Income earned by the subsidiary until the date of the sale is multiplied by the parent's old percentage

    (2) Income earned by the subsidiary after the date of the sale is multiplied by the parent's new, reduced percentage

d. Plus or minus differential amortization

    (1) Annual amortization is multiplied by the fraction of the year until the stock sale

    (2) Annual amortization is first multiplied by the fraction of stock the parent keeps and then by the fraction of the year after the stock sale

4. The working paper entries are affected by the stock sale as follows:

a. The entry that eliminates the parent's equity in subsidiary earnings and establishes the minority interest is affected in two ways:

    (1) The parent's equity in subsidiary earnings is debited for the subsidiary's net income multiplied by the parent's percentage ownership at year-end less the annual

144

differential amortization pertaining to the stock the parent still owns. In other words, the amount eliminated is computed using the year-end percentage of ownership and the year-end differential amortization. The balance remaining in the equity in subsidiary earnings account is carried to the consolidated column.

(2) The minority interest expense is computed by multiplying the subsidiary's net income by the minority interest's percentage ownership at year-end.

b. The entry eliminating the subsidiary's stockholders' equity eliminates the balances as of the beginning of the year but uses the ownership percentages as of the end of the year.

(1) The differential is the actual beginning balance multiplied by the fraction of subsidiary stock which the parent retained, e.g. if the differential was $10,000 at the beginning of the year when the parent owned 8,000 shares, and at the end of the year the parent owns only 7,000 shares, then the beginning differential for the 7,000 shares is $10,000 x 7,000/8,000, or $8,750.

(2) The investment account is credited for the subsidiary's beginning stockholders' equity multiplied by the parent's ending percentage.

(3) The minority interest is credited for the subsidiary's beginning stockholders' equity multiplied by the minority interest's ending percentage.

c. The entries allocating the differential and recording the current year's amortization are based on the amount computed in b.(1), above. In other words, the entries use the year-end percentages for the whole year.

5. The entries affecting the minority interest must be based on its year-end percentage ownership, because the consolidated balance sheet is prepared as of the end of the year.

6. When the parent's equity in subsidiary earnings (before differential amortization) and the minority interest expense are added, the total will exceed the subsidiary's net income for the year. The reason is that the parent uses its actual ownership percentages for each fraction of the year, while the minority

145

interest uses the year-end percentage. The excess of income represents the amount of income earned by the shares the parent sold before the shares were sold. This income became part of the carrying value of the shares sold; therefore the parent actually received this income as part of the sales price. At the end of the year, however, the minority interest is entitled to this income, since it now owns the shares sold by the parent.

7. The sale of subsidiary stock does not cause any complications in subsequent years.

D. The parent's percentage of ownership in the subsidiary also decreases when the subsidiary issues additional shares and the parent acquires less than its proportionate share of the newly issued shares, e. g. a parent who owns 90% of a subsidiary acquires only 20% of the newly issued shares. Such an ownership percent decreasing subsidiary stock transaction increases the subsidiary's stockholders' equity without a proportionate increase in the parent's interest.

1. If the parent acquires its proportionate interest of shares newly issued by the subsidiary, its percentage ownership remains the same and the increase in its share of the subsidiary's stockholders' equity is exactly equal to its purchase price, no matter whether the shares are issued at, above, or below book value by the subsidiary. If a parent does not acquire its proportionate interest of such newly issued shares, its percentage ownership will decrease and its share of the subsidiary's stockholders equity may change. If the shares are issued by the subsidiary above the book value of the outstanding shares, the parent's interest in the subsidiary's stockholders' equity will increase. This increase constitutes a gain, since the same effect can be produced through a properly structured parent company sale of subsidiary shares to nonaffiliates, as illustrated in the appendix. If the subsidiary issues new shares below the book value of its outstanding shares, the parent's interest will decrease and a loss results. If the subsidiary issues new shares at the book value of its outstanding shares, the parent's interest in the subsidiary's stockholders' equity will remain the same, even though its percentage of ownership decreases.

2. The change in the parent's interest in the subsidiary's stockholders' equity is computed as follows:

a. The subsidiary's stockholders' equity immediately prior to the new stock issue is multiplied by the parent's percentage of ownership before the stock issue.

146

b. The subsidiary's stockholders' equity immediately after the new stock issues is multiplied by the parent's percentage of ownership after the stock issue.

c. If the parent's interest after the stock issue is larger than its interest before the stock issue, it realizes an increase.

d. If the parent's interest before the stock issue is larger than its interest after the stock issue, it realizes a decrease.

e. If no differential exists at the time of the new stock issue, the above increase (decrease) is debited (credited) to the investment account and credited to a gain account (debited to a loss account).

3. If a differential exists when the subsidiary's new stock issue reduces the parent's percentage of ownership, the differential should be decreased. This is done by multiplying the original differential by the ratio of the post-sale and pre-sale ownership percentages of the parent. For example, if the original differential is $100,000 when the parent owns 80%, it is $75,000 if the parent's ownership drops to 60% (100,000 x 60%/80%).

a. The decrease in the differential is subtracted from the increase in the parent's interest in the subsidiary's stockholders' equity.

(1) If the decrease is less than the increase, a gain results.

(2) If the decrease is more than the increase, a loss results.

b. The decrease in the differential is added to the decrease in the parent's interest in the subsidiary stockholders' equity, thereby increasing the loss.

c. A gain (loss) is recorded on the parent's books with a debit (credit) to the investment account and a credit to a gain (debit to a loss) account.

4. If the new stock is issued by the subsidiary at the beginning of the year, the parent's new, reduced percentage of ownership applies to the entire year.

a. The entries on the parent's books under the equity method are made using the new, reduced percentage and the reduced amount of differential. In addition, the gain or loss on the subsidiary's stock transaction is recorded.

b. The working paper entries use the new, larger percentage for the minority interest and the subsidiary's stockholders' equity after the stock issue. The credit to the investment account is adjusted for the recorded gain or loss on the subsidiary's stock transaction.

c. Consolidated net income, using the incremental approach, is computed as follows:

   (1) P Company's net income from its own operations (excluding the gain or loss on the subsidiary's stock transaction)

   (2) Plus (minus) the gain (loss) on the subsidiary's stock transaction

   (3) Plus P Company's equity in subsidiary earnings computed at the new, reduced percentage

   (4) Plus or minus amortization of the reduced differential

5. If the new stock is issued by the subsidiary during the year, the effects are similar to a parent's sale of some of its subsidiary stock during the year (see II.C, above).

   a. On the parent's books the entries under the equity method must be made again for the two fractions of the year at different percentages. And the differential amortization must again be reduced for the period after the subsidiary's stock issue.

   b. The working paper entries use the year-end ownership percentage for the minority interest expense and the parent's equity in subsidiary earnings, the year-end differential for the allocation and amortization, and the beginning stockholders' equity accounts of the subsidiary adjusted for the new stock issue. The difference remaining in the parent's equity in subsidiary earnings is again carried to the consolidated column.

   c. Consolidated net income is computed as in the case of a stock sale by the parent (see II.C.3., above).

E. The parent's percentage of ownership in the subsidiary also decreases when the subsidiary acquires treasury shares and the parent sells more than its proportionate share to the subsidiary, e. g. a subsidiary buys 10% of its outstanding stock for its treasury only from its parent. Such an ownership percent decreasing subsidiary stock transaction decreases the subsidiary's stockholders' equity and decreases the parent's interest more than proportionately. This case is similar to the previous case and requires similar treatment.

1. The change in the parent's interest in the subsidiary's stockholders' equity is again computed by multiplying the subsidiary's equity before and after the treasury stock acquisition by the parent's before and after percentages of ownership.

2. The differential and differential amortization are again reduced to reflect the parent's reduced ownership percentage.

3. The gain or loss accruing to the parent is again a combination of the change in its interest in the subsidiary's stockholders' equity and the decrease in the differential.

4. The working paper entries are again made using the year-end percentages and the beginning stockholder's equity and investment accounts adjusted for the treasury stock acquisition.

5. Consolidated net income is again computed by allocating the subsidiary's net income to the periods before and after the treasury stock acquisition and multiplying each portion of income by the appropriate percentage and by adjusting the differential amortization for the decrease in the differential following the treasury stock acquisition.

III. Confirmed Profits on Upstream Sales and Subsidiary's Contributions to Gains and Losses from Intercompany Bond Holdings

A. When unconfirmed profits arising from an upstream sale become confirmed during a period when the parent's ownership percentage changes, the profits becoming confirmed can be divided into two groups:

1. Profits becoming confirmed before the change in percentage, and

2. Profits becoming confirmed after the change in percentage.

B. Two procedures can be used for calculating the parent's equity in subsidiary earnings:

1. The subsidiary's confirmed net income before and after the change is used in computing the parent's equity before and after the change. Computations of the parent's interest in the subsidiary's stockholders' equity use the confirmed retained earnings on the day of the change. This approach is consistent with the concept of pro rata allocation and therefore preferable.

2. The subsidiary's actual net income and retained earnings on the day of the change are used.

C. Gain and losses on intercompany bond holdings contributed by the subsidiary should be treated in a manner similar to confirmed profits on upstream sales.

IV. Appendix: Date-of-Control Analysis and Equivalence of Sales of Subsidiary Shares to Nonaffiliates and Other Ownership Percent Decreasing Transactions

A. Date-of-Control Analysis: Calculation, Allocation, and Amortization of Differentials

1. Under this approach the cost of all stock purchases and the percentages acquired until control is achieved are added together. The differential is computed as of the day control is obtained.

   a. The subsidiary's stockholders' equity is multiplied by the parent's percentage as of the day of control and subtracted from the total purchase price.

   b. The differential is allocated on the basis of the fair and book values of the subsidiary's net assets on the day of control.

   c. The allocated differential is amortized starting on the day of control.

2. Stock purchases after the day of control use the step-by-step approach of computing and allocating the differential.

B. Equivalence of Properly Structured Sales of Subsidiary Shares to Nonaffiliates and Other Ownership Percent Decreasing Transactions

1. A new stock issue by a subsidiary in which the parent acquires less than its proportionate share can be likened to a proportionate stock issue by the subsidiary and a subsequent sale of the acquired shares by the parent to nonaffiliates. The entries on the parent's books will be slightly different, because the purchase and sale of the shares have to be recorded.

150

However, the working paper entries and consolidated net income will be identical to those described in section II.C., above.

2. Since a gain or loss would be recorded by the parent on the sale of the stock to nonaffiliates, the recognition of a gain or loss on a subsidiary's ownership percent decreasing transaction can be defended using the principle of substance over form.

Test Your Understanding of Chapter 9

True or False

Instructions: Indicate your choice by circling either T, if you think the statement is true, or F, if you think the statement is false.

T F 1. Either a parent company or its subsidiary may participate in a transaction that changes the parent's percentage interest in the subsidiary's net assets.

T F 2. A parent company makes three purchases of a subsidiary's common stock: 10 percent, 20 percent, and 50 percent. In this case the parent is justified to measure the differential as of the day control was achieved, rather than for each block.

T F 3. Over several years a parent company makes many small purchases of a subsidiary's common stock until it is able to buy a block of 50 percent and thereby achieve control. In this case it may be convenient for the parent to measure the differential as of the day control was achieved.

T F 4. If the step-by-step analysis is used for a number of block purchases of subsidiary stock, then the fair and book values of the subsidiary's net assets have to be determined as of each purchase date.

T F 5. If a parent company sells a portion of its investment in a subsidiary during the year, it may use the carrying value as of the last balance sheet date to determine the gain or loss on the sale.

T F 6. If a parent company sells a portion of its investment in a subsidiary during the year, the subsidiary's net income should be allocated to the period before and after the stock sale. Each portion of the income should then be multiplied by the parent's and minority interest's respective percentages of ownership to determine their shares of the income.

T F 7. A parent may increase its ownership percentage in a subsidiary by having the subsidiary acquire treasury shares in the open market.

151

T   F   8. When a parent sells a portion of its investment in a subsidiary at an interim date, the unamortized differential should be updated to the date of the sale before it is allocated wholly or in part to the sold shares.

T   F   9. If a parent sells a portion of its investment in a subsidiary at an interim date, the elimination entry to reverse the year's equity in subsidiary earnings will leave a balance in this account to be reported on the consolidated income statement. The balance should equal equity in subsidiary earnings applicable to the sold shares for the fraction of the year they were held.

T   F 10. P Company owns 80 percent of S Company when S decides to purchase 5 percent of its own stock above book value in the open market. As a result P's percentage ownership and its interest in S's stockholders' equity increase.

T   F 11. P Company owns 70,000 of S Company's 100,000 outstanding shares. If S issues 50,000 new shares above book value and P exercises its preemptive right, its interest in the subsidiary's stockholders' equity and its percentage interest will both increase.

T   F 12. If a subsidiary issues new shares on the open market below book value, the parent will report a loss from the transaction.

T   F 13. If a subsidiary purchases treasury stock in the open market, the parent's percentage ownership will increase. Therefore it will report a gain on the transaction, no matter at which price the treasury stock was purchased.

T   F 14. P owns 80,000 of S Company's 100,000 outstanding shares. The stockholders' equity of S is $200,000. If S sells an additional 20,000 shares for a total of $100,000, P should report a gain of $40,000.

T   F 15. If a parent sells some of the shares it owns in a subsidiary back to the subsidiary, the parent's gain or loss equals the difference between its proceeds and the sum of (a) the decrease in its monetary interest in the subsidiary's net assets and (b) the proportionate part of any preexisting unamortized differential applicable to the sold interest.

Exercises

1. On January 1, 19x1, S Company had outstanding capital stock (par $10) of $20,000 and retained earnings of $30,000. P Company made the following purchases of S Company stock in the open market:

        January 1, 19x1 .... 400 shares, cost $15,000
        July 1, 19x1 .... 500 shares, cost $25,500
        December 1, 19x1 .... 900 shares, cost $44,400

During 19x1 S Company's net income was $24,000 earned evenly
throughout the year. All differentials are assigned to goodwill and
are to be amortized over 10 years.

Required:
a. Prepare the 19x1 entries on P's books to record its equity in
    subsidiary earnings and any differential amortization.

b. Prepare the elimination entries on the consolidated statement
    working paper at December 31, 19x1.

(1)

(2)

(3)

(4)

2. On January 1, 19x1, P Company acquired 9,000 of S Company's 10,000 outstanding shares for $396,000. On that day the stockholders' equity of S consisted of $200,000 of common stock and $220,000 of retained earnings. Any differential is to be assigned to goodwill and amortized over 10 years.

On July 1, 19x1, P sold 1,000 shares of S stock at $60 per share. S's net income, earned evenly throughout the year, was $120,000 for 19x1. S declared a dividend of $30,000 on 5/1, which was paid on 6/1/19x1. P's 19x1 net income from its own operations was $200,000.

Required:
a.   Prepare the 19x1 entries on P's books relating to its investment in S.

1/1

5/1

6/1

6/30

. **Prepare the elimination entries on the consolidated statement working paper at December 31, 19x1.**

1)

2)

3)

4)

5)

c. Compute consolidated net income, using the incremental approach.

d. Compute the correct balance remaining in equity in S earnings after the elimination entries.

3. On January 1, 19x1, S Company had outstanding capital stock (par $10) of $10,000 and retained earnings of $40,000. P Company owned 80% of S Company's shares. The balance in P's investment account on that day was $48,000. Any differential is allocable to goodwill.

On 1/1/19x1 S Company issued an additional 200 shares of stock at $200 per share. All of these shares were purchased by nonaffiliates.

Required:
a. Prepare P's journal entry to record its interest in the subsidiary's stock transaction.

b. Prepare the investment elimination entry if a consolidated balance sheet is prepared immediately after the transaction.

156

Solutions to Chapter 9 Exercises

True or False

1.	T	4.	T	7.	T	10.	F	13.	F
2.	F	5.	F	8.	F	11.	F	14.	T
3.	T	6.	F	9.	T	12.	T	15.	T

Exercises

1. a.   Investment in S 8,700
           Equity in S earnings   8,700
      To record equity in S earnings, consisting of:
      $24,000 x 20% = $4,800
      + $24,000 x 1/2 year x 25% =   3,000
      + $24,000 x 1/12 year x 45% =   900

      Equity in S earnings 1,100
           Investment in S   1,100
      To record goodwill amortization, consisting of:
      (1) $5,000 : 10 years = $500
      (2) $10,000 : 10 years x 1/2 yr =   500
      (3) $12,000 : 10 yrs x 1/12 yr =   100

Supporting Calculations:

	20%	25%	45%
Cost	$15,000	$25,500	$44,400
Less book value:			
Common stock	$ 4,000	$ 5,000	$ 9,000
Retained earnings	6,000	7,500	13,500
Preacquisition earnings ...	-0-	3,000*	9,900**
Total book value	$10,000	$15,500	$32,400
Differential	$ 5,000	$10,000	$12,000

* .25 x (24,000/12 x 6 months) = $3,000
**.45 x (24,000/12 x 11 months)= $9,900

   b.
   (1) Minority interest expense 2,400
        Equity in S earnings.............. 7,600
          Investment in S..............   7,600
          Minority interest (24,000 x .1)   2,400
      To eliminate equity in S earnings and set up minority
      interest

```
(2)  Common stock - S .................    20,000
     Retained earnings - S ............    30,000
     Purchased preacquisition earnings .   12,900
     Differential (5,000 + 10,000 + 12,000)  27,000
          Investment in S (15,000 +
             25,500 + 44,400) ..........              84,900
          Minority interest (50,000 x .1)              5,000
     To eliminate beginning balances of S's stockholders' equity,
     record preacquisition earnings, set up differential,
     eliminate cost of block purchases in the investment account,
     and establish minority interest at year-end percentage

(3)  Goodwill............................    27,000
          Differential..................              27,000
     To allocate differential

(4)  Amortization of goodwill..........      1,100
          Goodwill .....................               1,100
     To amortize goodwill

2.  a.
1/1       Investment in S ..................   396,000
               Cash..........................            396,000
          To record purchase of 90% of S stock

5/1       Dividend receivable (30,000 x .9)..   27,000
               Investment in S ..............             27,000
          To record declaration of dividends by S

6/1       Cash ..............................    27,000
               Dividend receivable ..........             27,000
          To record receipt of dividends from S

6/30      Investment in S (120,000 x 1/2 year
               x .9) ...........................   54,000
               Equity in S earnings .........             54,000
          To record equity in S earnings as of 6/30

6/30      Equity in S earnings (18,000 :
               10 yrs x 1/2 yr) ...............      900
               Investment in S ..............                900
          To record goodwill amortization:
          Purchase price          $396,000
          - $420,000 x .9          378,000
          Goodwill               $ 18,000

6/30      Cash (1,000 x 60) ................     60,000
               Investment in S ..............             46,900
               Gain on sale of S stock ......             13,100
          To record sale of 1,000 shares of S stock (Basis = 396,000 -
          27,000 + 54,000 - 900 = 422,100 x 1.000/9,000)

12/31     Investment in S (120,000 x 1/2 yr x .8)  48,000
               Equity in S earnings ........             48,000
          To record equity in earnings from 7/1 to 12/31
```

Equity in S earnings (16,000 :
           10 yrs x 1/2 yr)   800
               Investment in S   800
       To record goodwill amortization from 7/1 to 12/31:
       Goodwill retained : 18,000 x 8/9 = 16,000

b. (1) Minority interest expense   24,000
         Equity in S earnings [(120,000 x
           .8) - 1,600).....................   94,400
             Investment in S   94,400
             Minority interest (120,000 x .2)   24,000
         To eliminate year-end percentage of equity in earnings less
         goodwill amortization and set up minority interest at year-
         end percentage

    (2) Minority interest (30,000 x .2)   6,000
         Investment in S (30,000 x .8)   24,000
             Dividends declared - S   30,000
         To eliminate dividends declared at year-end percentages

    (3) Common stock - S   200,000
         Retained earnings - S   220,000
         Differential (18,000 x 8/9)   16,000
             Investment in S (396,000 x 8/9)   352,000
             Minority interest (420,000 x .2)   84,000
         To eliminate beginning balances of S's stockholders' equity,
         set up differential retained, eliminate retained portion of
         beginning balance of investment account, and establish
         minority interest at year-end percentage

    (4) Goodwill   16,000
             Differential   16,000
         To allocate differential

    (5) Amortization of goodwill   1,600
             Goodwill   1,600
         To amortize goodwill

c. P's net income from its own operations $200,000
    Gain on sale of S stock   13,100
    Equity in S earnings:
        1/1 - 6/30 - 120,000 x 1/2 yr x .9   54,000
        6/30 - 12/31 - 120,000 x 1/2 yr x .8   48,000
    Less goodwill amortization:
        1/1 - 6/30 - 18,000 : 10 yrs x 1/2 yr ....   (900)
        6/30 - 12/31 - 16,000 : 10 yrs x 1/2 yr ....   (800)
    Consolidated net income $313,400

d. Equity in S earnings - per P's books (54,000 - 900
                + 48,000 - 800) $100,300
        Less equity in S earnings eliminated   94,400
        Balance remaining .... $ 5,900
        Consisting of income earned by sold shares ....
                120,000 x 1/2 year x .1 .... $6,000
        Less amortization of goodwill pertaining to sold .
                1,000 shares (18,000 x 1/9 = 2,000 : 10 yrs
                x 1/2 yr)..   (100)
        Equity in earnings of sold 1,000 shares $5,900

3. a. Investment in S   18,670
            Gain from subsidiary stock
                transaction   18,670

Calculation of gain:
P's equity in S's stockholders' equity:
        Before transaction - .8 x 50,000 .... $40,000
        After transaction - .667 x (50,000 + 40,000)......   60,000
Increase in P's equity in S's stockholders' equity..... $20,000
Less differential applicable to sold interest (.8 -
        .667 = .133) 8,000* x .133/.8 ....   (1,330)
Net gain on transaction $18,670

*Differential before transaction:
Balance in investment account $48,000
Less P's share of S's net assets (50,000 x .8)   40,000
Differential at 1/1/19x1 .... $ 8,000

b. (1) Common stock - S [10,000 + (200 x 10)   12,000
        Other contributed capital - S
                [200 x (200 - 10)]   38,000
        Retained earnings - S   40,000
        Differential (8,000 - 1,330)   6,670
            Investment in S (48,000 + 18,670)   66,670
            Minority interest [.333 x
                (12,000 + 38,000 + 40,000)].   30,000

160

Chapter Outline

I. Multilevel Affiliations

A. In a multilevel affiliation at least one company in addition to the parent will be an investor company and own stock in an investee company. In addition, each company will use the equity method to account for its investment. Analyses of complex affiliation structures are often simplified by being depicted in an affiliation diagram.

B. In a simple affiliation structure the parent owns a controlling interest in its subsidiary which, in turn, owns a controlling interest in its investee. Each investor company must determine and allocate the differential at the acquisition of its investee.

   1. Since the income of each investor company includes its share of the income of its investee, the allocation of income has to start with the company at the lower level of the affiliation structure and work upward. In other words, if A controls B which, in turn, controls C, then the entries under the equity method should be done as follows:

      a. First B should recognize its equity in the earnings of C, including any differential amortization, then

      b. A should recognize its equity in the earnings of B, including any differential amortization.

   2. In the consolidated statement working papers the elimination entries are made as described in previous chapters.

   3. The minority interest in each investee company is computed by multiplying its recorded net income by the minority interest's percentage of ownership. In the case of B, above, the recorded income includes, of course, its equity in the earnings of C, net of any differential amortization.

   4. Consolidated net income consists of the parent's net income from its own operations plus (minus) its share of the recorded net income (loss) of its subsidiary, plus (minus) any differential amortization.

161

C. In a complex multilevel affiliation at least one investee is controlled jointly by two or more investors.

1. Examples of such affiliation structures are:

   a. A owns 80 percent of B and 40 percent of C. In addition, B owns 30 percent of C. In this case A and B together control C.

   b. A owns 80 percent of B and 70 percent of C. B owns 40 percent of D, and C owns 30 percent of D. In this case B and C together control D.

2. In these complex multilevel affiliations income allocation should again start at the lowest level of the affiliation structure and proceed upward. In the above examples this would be done as follows:

   a. A and B recognize their share of C's net income, including any differential amortization; then A recognizes its share of B's equity basis income and amortizes the differential applying to its investment in B.

   b. B and C recognize their share of D's net income and amortize the differentials applying to their respective investments. Then A recognizes its share of the equity basis income of both B and C and amortizes the differentials applying to these investments.

3. The elimination entries in the consolidated statement working papers are prepared as described in previous chapters.

4. The minority interest is again computed by multiplying the investee's income and net assets on the equity basis by the minority interest's percentage of ownership.

5. Consolidated net income consists again of the parent's income from its own operations plus (minus) its share of the equity basis net income (loss) of its subsidiary or subsidiaries, plus or minus any differential amortization.

6. In complex multilevel affiliations investments under 20 percent also use the equity method, since control is exercised through the combined holdings of two or more investors.

D. Chain or indirect control may be less than 50 percent. For example, if A owns 70 percent of B which, in turn owns 70 percent of C, then A's indirect ownership of C is 49 percent (.7 x .7). In this case consolidated statements are still

162

warranted, since each investor controls its investee through majority ownership.

E. Intercompany profits in multilevel affiliations are eliminated as described in previous chapters. For each investor company in the affiliated group the confirmed net income on the equity basis is computed before any allocation is made to its majority and minority interests. Consolidated net income and the minority interest are, of course, affected by the method chosen for the elimination and allocation of upstream intercompany profits.

   1. If 100 percent of upstream intercompany profits are eliminated and allocated pro rata to the majority and minority interest, then the minority interest will be based on the confirmed net income under the equity method.

   2. If 100 percent of upstream intercompany profits are eliminated and wholly allocated to the majority interest, then the minority interest will be based on the net income under the equity method.

   3. If only the parent's percentage of upstream intercompany profits is eliminated and wholly allocated to the majority interest, then the minority interest will be based on the net income under the equity method.

II. Bilateral Stockholdings - Traditional Allocation Method

A. In a bilateral affiliation at least two companies own stock in each other. In this reciprocal relationship the parent may or may not be one of the companies involved.

B. If the parent is not involved in a reciprocal relationship, the affiliation structure may be: P owns 60 percent of S which, in turn, owns 80 percent of T; and T owns 10 percent of S. In this case the equity basis net income cannot be determined for either T or S until the other company's equity basis net income is determined.

   1. The reciprocal allocation of income can be done by using either successive iterations or simultaneous equations.

      a. If the successive iterations method is used, a progression of successive estimates is made. At each step the equity pickup uses the estimate of the affiliate's equity basis net income from the preceding step. The sequence of steps continues until the solution values stabilize.

      b. If the simultaneous equation or algebraic method is used, an equation is set up for each company in the reciprocal relationship. For each company its equity basis net income equals its income from its own operations plus its share of the equity basis net income of its investee. If, in the above example, S and T have net income from their own operations of $30,000 and $10,000, respectively, the two equations are:

(1)   S = 30,000 + .8T

(2)   T = 10,000 + .1S

  where S = equity basis net income of S and
  T = equity basis net income of T

(3)   The solution is:
  Solving for S by substitution:
  S = 30,000 + .8(10,000 + .1S)
  S = 30,000 + 8,000 + .08S
  .92S = 38,000
  S = 41,304
  and T = 10,000 + .1(41,304) = 14,130

2.   After the equity basis net income for the companies in the reciprocal relationship has been calculated, the income allocations to the majority and minority interests can be made.

a.   Consolidated net income is equal to P's net income from its own operations plus its share of the equity basis net income of its subsidiary. In the above example, if P's net income from its own operations is $100,000, then consolidated net income is 100,000 + .6(41,304) = 124,783.

b.   The minority interest in each company involved in a reciprocal relationship is its equity basis net income multiplied by the percentage of stock owned by outsiders. In the above example:

(1)   the minority interest in S is 30 percent (100 percent less 60 percent owned by P and 10 percent owned by T) multiplied by its equity basis net income of 41,304 = 12,391.

(2)   the minority interest in T is 20 percent (100 percent less 80 percent owned by S) multiplied by its equity basis net income of 14,130 = 2,826.

c.   Consolidated net income plus the minority interest in the net income of each affiliated company must equal the total net income each company earned from its own operations. In the above example:

        (1)   Consolidated net income $124,783
               Minority interest in S   12,391
               Minority interest in T   2,826
               Total income allocated $140,000

        (2)   P's net income from its own
                  operations $100,000
               S's net income from its own
                  operations   30,000
               T's net income from its own
                  operations   10,000
               Total income to be allocated $140,000

3.   The algebraic solution can become cumbersome when many
      affiliates are involved in the reciprocal relationship
      and many simultaneous equations have to be solved.   In
      such cases matrix algebra may be the most practical way
      to solve the system of equations.

C.   If the parent is involved in the reciprocal relationship,
      the affiliation structure may be: P owns 80 percent of S
      and 90 percent of T, and T owns 10 percent of P.   In this
      case the equity basis net income cannot be determined for
      either P or T until the other company's equity basis net
      income has been determined.   This can again be done with
      successive iterations or with simultaneous equations.

      1.   Using the above net incomes from their own operations
            of $100,000, $30,000, and $10,000 for P, S, and T,
            respectively,

            a.   The equations are:
                  P = 100,000 + .8S + .9T
                  S = 30,000
                  T = 10,000 + .1P

            b.   The solution is:
                  Solving for P by substitution:
                  P = 100,000 + .8(30,000) + .9(10,000 + .1P)
                  P = 100,000 + 24,000 + 9,000 + .09P
                  .91P = 133,000
                  P = 146,154
                  and T = 10,000 + .1(146,154) = 24,615

      2.   After the equity basis net income for the companies in
            the reciprocal relationship has been calculated,   the
            income allocations to the majority and minority
            interests can be made.

            a.   When the parent is involved in a reciprocal
                  relationship, consolidated net income is
                  calculated by multiplying the parent's equity
                  basis net income by the percentage of P stock
                  owned by outsiders.   In the above example
                  consolidated net income is 146,154 multiplied by

                                  165

90 percent (100 percent less the 10 percent owned by T) = 131,539.

b. The minority interest in each subsidiary involved in the reciprocal relationship is determined by multiplying its equity basis net income by the percentage of its stock held by outsiders. The minority interest in other subsidiaries is determined by multiplying its net income from its own operations by the percentage of its stock held by outsiders. In the above example:

(1) the minority interest in S = 30,000 x .2 = 6,000.

(2) the minority interest in T = 24,615 x .1 = 2,461.

c. Consolidated net income plus the minority interest in the net income of each affiliated company must equal the total net income each company earned from its own operations. In the above example:

Consolidated net income	$131,539
Minority interest in S	6,000
Minority interest in T	2,461
Total income allocated	$140,000

D. Intercompany profits on asset transfers are handled in the consolidated statement working papers as discussed in previous chapters. Such profits, whether confirmed or unconfirmed, are allocated like net income.

1. Two methods can be used to determine the allocation of intercompany profits on asset transfers:

a. The intercompany profit is allocated using simultaneous equations in the same manner as net income is allocated. This method can be used for 100 percent pro rata or fractional elimination. In this case the intercompany profit allocable to each company is subtracted (if the profit is unconfirmed) from its equity basis net income.

b. If 100 percent pro rata elimination is used, the unconfirmed intercompany profit can be subtracted from each company's net income from its own operations before the equations are set up. The equations are then solved as discussed above.

2. Each of the above methods can be used when the parent is involved in the reciprocal relationship and when it is not so involved.

E. Differential amortization can be handled in the same two ways as discussed above for the allocation of intercompany profits.

F. Recording the equity in affiliates' earnings creates problems when bilateral relationships exist.

1. If the parent is involved in a reciprocal relationship the question is whether the parent should record its equity basis net income, as determined by the simultaneous equations, or the majority interest in its equity basis net income.

    a. If the parent records its equity basis net income, then consolidated net income will not equal the parent company's net income, as required by APB Opinion No. 18.

    b. If the parent records the majority interest in its equity basis net income, then consolidated net income will equal the parent company's net income, as required by APB Opinion No. 18.

2. No matter which income is recorded, a difference will still exist between the parent's stockholders' equity and consolidated stockholders' equity, since the subsidiary's interest in the parent's equity is eliminated in the consolidated statement working papers. To achieve this equality the subsidiary's ownership of the parent's equity would have to be eliminated on the parent's books, and such an entry is difficult to justify.

3. If the parent is not involved in the reciprocal relationship, its financial statements will be in accordance with APB Opinion No. 18. However, the problem still exists for subsidiaries involved in reciprocal relationships who publish their financial statements for their outside stockholders.

4. No general solution to the problem created by reciprocal relationships in adhering to APB Opinion No. 18 exists; therefore, each case must be solved individually.

G. Matrix applications for complex affiliations are appropriate when the number of affiliates involved is large. The only practical drawback to using matrix algebra is that the matrix has to be inverted. However, if the intercompany shareholdings do not change, the inverse of the coefficient matrix remains constant, thereby alleviating the arithmetic complexities.

167

III. Bilateral Stockholdings - Treasury Stock Method

   A.   Some accountants view the purchase of parent company shares
        by a subsidiary as similar to the parent's acquisition of
        treasury stock. In other words, the subsidiary is seen as
        acting on behalf of the parent; therefore, the shares should
        be treated as if the parent had reacquired them.

   B.   In this view the parent company shares should be subtracted
        from the parent's contributed capital and retained earnings
        in the consolidated statement working papers. Therefore, no
        differential at acquisition is computed. Under the
        traditional method, discussed above, the subsidiary's
        investment in the parent's stock is also eliminated, but a
        differential is determined, allocated, and then amortized.

   C.   Under the treasury stock method the investment account is
        kept on the cost basis. As a result, none of the parent's
        income is allocated to the stock held by the subsidiary.
        Some accountants advocate that dividends paid by the parent
        be excluded from subsidiary income, since dividends are not
        paid on treasury stock. However, most accountants include
        the parent's dividends in the subsidiary's reported net
        income when computing the minority interest.

   D.   The traditional and the treasury stock methods result in
        different consolidated financial statements.

        1.   In the consolidated income statement the major
             difference is in the minority interest expense. It is
             due to the use of the cost or equity method of
             accounting for the subsidiary's investment in the
             parent. The amount of the difference depends on the
             parent's dividend policy: the higher the dividend
             payout, the smaller the difference between cost and
             equity basis net income.

        2.   In the consolidated balance sheet the parent's stock
             held by the subsidiary is eliminated under both
             methods. The major difference is the differential
             which is established and allocated only under the
             traditional method.

                   Test Your Understanding of Chapter 10

True or False

Instructions: Indicate your choice by circling either T, if you think
the statement is true, or F, if you think the statement is false.

T F   1. Consolidated net income for a multilevel affiliation does
          not include the confirmed income of a second level (or
          lower) subsidiary unless the dominant parent directly owns
          stock in such a subsidiary.

T F   2. At least one company other than the dominant parent company in a multilevel affiliation is an investor company using the equity method.

T F   3. Proper equity method accounting for a multilevel affiliation requires equity basis net income(s) to be determined first for the lowest level investor company (companies) and then for each successively higher investor company in the multilevel hierarchy until the dominant parent company eventually records its interest in the equity basis earnings of each of its direct subsidiaries or investees.

T F   4. P Company owns 85 percent of S Company's stock and 60 percent of T Company's stock, and T Company owns 5 percent of S Company's stock. In this case T should use the cost method to account for its investment in S, even if significant influence over S's operations is exerted by T as a result of indirect and direct ownership.

T F   5. The minority ownership in S Company in the affiliation described in Statement No. 4, above, is 15 percent.

T F   6. Differential amortization of a parent company in a reciprocal ownership relationship with a partially owned subsidiary is allocated between majority and minority shareholders.

T F   7. Minority interest calculations in a multilevel affiliation are based on the subsidiaries' recorded incomes and net assets, provided they are based on the equity method.

T F   8. The confirmed intercompany profit of a partially owned subsidiary that is also an investor company in a multilevel affiliation is properly allocated between majority and minority shareholders if the parent's interest in subsidiary net income is determined from the subsidiary's income from its own operations (i. e. excluding equity method adjustments).

T F   9. If two affiliates are related through reciprocal stock ownership, the first step in apportioning their incomes from their own operations between majority and minority shareholders is to calculate their respective equity basis net incomes.

T F 10. P Company owns 80 percent of S Company's stock which, in turn, owns 10 percent of P Company's stock. If P uses the equity method, it should adjust its accounting records to reflect 90 percent of its equity basis net income. This adjustment results in equality between the parent's recorded net income and consolidated net income as prescribed by APB Opinion No. 18.

T F 11. If an algebraic approach is used to compute equity basis net income for each bilaterally related affiliate, at least two linear equations require solution.

T F 12. P Company owns 60 percent of S Company's stock which, in turn, owns 10 percent of P Company. P and S report net incomes from their own operations of $100,000 and $50,000 respectively. Consolidated net income is 100,000 + .6(50,000 + .05P).

T F 13. Proper allocation of a bilaterally related affiliate's differential amortization may be achieved by first deducting this amount from its operating income and then using this adjusted operating income in the equations set up to determine the equity basis net incomes of the affiliates.

T F 14. Under the traditional method of treating reciprocal relationships, a subsidiary's investment in its parent is eliminated against the parent's stockholders' equity accounts in the consolidated statement working papers.

T F 15. Under the treasury stock method of treating reciprocal relationships, simultaneous equations must still be used to determine the parent's equity basis net income.

Exercises

1. On January 1, 19x1, P Company purchased 70 percent of S Company's outstanding stock. On the same day S Company acquired 60 percent of T Company's outstanding stock. The debit differentials on these acquisitions amounted to $20,000 and $10,000, respectively, which are wholly attributable to goodwill to be amortized over 10 years. For 19x1 the companies report the following net income from their own operations:

$$
\begin{array}{lcr}
\text{P Company} & - & \$40,000 \\
\text{S Company} & - & 30,000 \\
\text{T Company} & - & 20,000 \\
\end{array}
$$

Required:
a. Prepare the year-end entries made by P and S on their books under the equity method.

Entries on S Company's books

Entries on P Company's books

b. Compute consolidated net income.

c. Assume that S Company's net income includes unconfirmed
    intercompany profit of $10,000. Compute consolidated net income.
    Use pro rata allocation of intercompany profits.

2. In 19x1 the PSUT Group had the following multilevel and bilateral
structure:

    P owned 70 percent of S
    S owned 80 percent of U
    U owned 10 percent of S
    S also owned 90 percent of T
    T owned 10 percent of S

There were no differentials and no intercompany profits. For the year
the companies reported the following incomes from their own
operations:

    P Company - $50,000
    S Company -   45,000
    U Company -   25,000
    T Company -   20,000

Required:
a. Using the traditional method, compute S Company's equity basis
    net income for 19x1.

b. **Prepare the entries on S Company's books to record its equity in
    the earnings of U and T Companies.**

c. Compute consolidated net income and allocate the net incomes of
    the affiliates to minority shareholders. Verify that the total
    equals the combined incomes of the companies.

3. A Company owns 60 percent of B Company which, in turn, owns 5 percent of A Company. In 19x1 A and B reported net incomes from their own operations of $36,500 and 20,000 respectively. There are no differentials associated with these investments.

Required:
a. Use the traditional method to compute consolidated net income and the minority interest in B Company for 19x1.

b. Use the treasury stock method to compute consolidated net income and the minority interest in B Company for 19x1.

Solutions to Chapter 10 Exercises

True or False

1.	F	4.	F	7.	T	10.	T	13.	T
2.	T	5.	F	8.	F	11.	T	14.	T
3.	T	6.	T	9.	T	12.	F	15.	F

Exercises

1. a.   Entries on S Company's books:

    Investment in T Company   12,000
        Equity in T earnings (.6 x 20,000).   12,000
    To record S Company's share of T Company's income

    Equity in T earnings (10,000 : 10 yrs)..   1,000
        Investment in T Company   1,000
    To record goodwill amortization

        Entries on P Company's books:

    Investment in S Company   28,700
        Equity in S earnings   28,700
    To record P Company's share of S Company's net income [.7 x
    (30,000 + 12,000 - 1,000)]

    Equity in S earnings (20,000 : 10 years)   2,000
        Investment in S Company   2,000
    To record goodwill amortization

    b. P Company's net income from its own operations ... $40,000
        Add P's share of S's net income (.7 x 41,000)   28,700
        Less goodwill amortization ....   (2,000)
        Consolidated net income $66,700

    c. S Company's net income from its own operations ... $30,000
        Less unconfirmed intercompany profit ....   (10,000)
        Add S Company's share of T Company's net
            income (.6 x 20,000)   12,000
        Less goodwill amortization ....   (1,000)
        S Company's equity basis net income.............. $31,000

        P Company's net income from its own operations ... $40,000
        Add P Company's share of S Company's confirmed
            net income (.7 x 31,000)   21,700
        Less goodwill amortization ....   (2,000)
        Consolidated net income........................... $59,700

2.   a.

Let S = S Company's equity basis net income
    U = U Company's equity basis net income
    T = T Company's equity basis net income
Then:
    S = 45,000 + .8U + .9T
    U = 25,000 + .1S
    T = 20,000 + .1S
By substitution:
    S = 45,000 + .8(25,000 + .1S) + .9(20,000 + .1S)
    S = 45,000 + 20,000 + .08S + 18,000 + .09S
    S = 83,000 + .17S
  .83S = 83,000
    S = 100,000
    U = 25,000 + .1(100,000) = 35,000
    T = 20,000 + .1(100,000) = 30,000

b.   Entries on S Company's books:

     Investment in U Company   28,000
         Equity in U earnings (.8 x 35,000).   28,000
     To record equity in U Company's equity basis net income

     Investment in T Company   27,000
         Equity in T earnings (.9 x 30,000).   27,000
     To record equity in T Company's equity basis net income

c.   P Company's net income from its own operations ... $ 50,000
     Add P's equity in S Company's equity basis net
         income (.7 x 100,000)   70,000
     Consolidated net income $120,000
     Minority interest:
         S Company (.1 x 100,000) $10,000
         U Company (.2 x 35,000)   7,000
         T Company (.1 x 30,000)   3,000
     Total minority interest   20,000
     Total income allocated $140,000

     Net income - P Company .... $ 50,000
     Net income - S Company   45,000
     Net income - U Company   25,000
     Net income - T Company   20,000
     Total income to be allocated $140,000

3. a.   Traditional allocation method

Let A = A Company's equity basis net income
    B = B Company's equity basis net income
Then:
    A = 36,500 + .6B
    B = 20,000 + .05A
By substitution:
    A = 36,500 + .6(20,000 + .05A)
    A = 36,500 + 12,000 + .03A
 .97A = 48,500
    A = 50,000
    B = 20,000 + .05(50,000) = 22,500

        Consolidated net income: .95 x 50,000 ...... $47,500
        Minority interest in B: .4 x 22,500   9,000
        Total income allocated $56,500

b.   Treasury stock method

        Consolidated net income: 36,500 + .6(20,000) $48,500
        Minority interest in B: .4 x 20,000   8,000
        Total income allocated $56,500

Chapter 11
Branch Accounting,
Segmental and Interim Reporting

Chapter Outline

I. Branch Accounting

   A. Agencies and branches

   1. Business expansion is often accomplished by creating agencies or branches of a company to establish new sales outlets.

   2. Generally, an agency carries only display items and accepts sales orders to be filled by the home office. Since an agency is essentially little more than an extension of existing sales territories, no new accounting problems arise.

   3. A branch typically carries a full line of inventory, initiates and fills sales orders, makes collections, and functions as an autonomous business unit. However, company policy will determine the specific operations of an agency or branch.

   B. Branch accounts

   1. Branch books contain accounts for assets, liabilities, revenues, expenses, and a proprietary account, entitled Home Office Current. The Home Office Current Account is used to close the nominal accounts. The specific accounts used by a branch depend upon their frequency of use, relevance to branch operations, and company policy.

   2. The Home Office Current account basically represents the home office's claim to the net assets of the branch. It is reciprocal to the account Branch Current (or Investment in Branch or Branch Account) on the home office's books. For a company with several branches it is usually desirable to open a separate current account for each branch.

   3. The branch fixed assets are sometimes recorded on the home office books, although the related depreciation expense is recorded on the branch books. Branch expenses incurred by the home office are usually recorded on the branch books with an offsetting credit to the Home Office account. If expenses applicable to one or more branches are not formally assigned to, and recorded by, the branches, they are usually charged

177

against the branch net income or loss on the home
office books.

C. Illustrative entries

   1. Transactions affecting both the home office and the
      branch must be recorded on both sets of books.

      a. Typical entries on the branch books:

         (1) Cash
                 Home Office Current
             To record cash remittance from home office

         (2) Shipments from Home Office
                 Home Office Current
             To record receipt of merchandise from home
             office

         (3) Expenses
                 Cash
             To record cash payments for expenses

         (4) Purchases
                 Accounts Payable
             To record merchandise purchases from outside
             suppliers

         (5) Accounts Receivable
                 Sales
             To record credit sales

         (6) Cash
                 Accounts Receivable
             To record collection of accounts

         (7) Home Office Current
                 Cash
             To record cash remittance to home office

         (8) Sales
             Ending Inventory
                 Purchases
                 Shipments from Home Office
                 Expenses
                 Income Summary
             Income Summary
                 Home Office Current
             To close nominal accounts and credit home
             office for net income of branch

178

b. Reciprocal entries on home office books for above branch entries:

  (1) Branch Current
          Cash
       To record cash remittance to branch

  (2) Branch Current
          Shipments to Branch
       To record merchandise shipment to branch

  (3) No entry

  (4) No entry

  (5) No entry

  (6) No entry

  (7) Cash
          Branch Current
       To record cash remittance from branch

  (8) Branch Current
          Branch Net Income
       To record branch net income

2. The reciprocal shipments accounts are used to maintain accounting control of intracompany merchandise shipments.

  a. The Shipments to Branch account on the home office books is a contra account to Purchases or Cost of Goods Manufactured. It is kept at cost and closed at the end of the accounting period.

  b. The Shipments from Home Office account on the branch books is equivalent to a Purchases account. It is kept at the intracompany billing price and closed at the end of the accounting period.

D. Combined financial statements

1. Combined statements of the home office and branch reflect the transactions of the entire business entity with outsiders.

2. The effects of transactions between the home office and branches (or between branches) are eliminated. Reciprocal branch and home office accounts are eliminated in the appropriate columns of a combined statement working paper. Once the Branch Current and Home Office Current accounts are eliminated against each other, the branch's assets, liabilities, revenues, and expenses can be combined with those of the home

179

office (after other appropriate eliminations have been made).

3. The three-divisional form of a combined statement working paper uses the account balances before closing. In this working paper the beginning balance of retained earnings for each branch is always zero, since the branch does not accumulate its profits, but instead closes its nominal accounts to the home office account. The end-of-period retained earnings balance of each branch equals the branch's net income and is brought forward to the balance sheet section where it is added to the home office's retained earnings to equal combined retained earnings.

E. Branch billing in excess of cost

1. The home office may elect to bill the branch at a price in excess of cost, e.g. the retail price or at a percentage markup on cost. The branch may not be given the cost of merchandise, therefore the income reported on the branch books excludes the home office's markup. An adjusting entry for the realized intracompany profit is required on the home office books.

2. The home office account Intracompany Inventory Profit is initially credited for the markup above cost when merchandise is shipped to the branch. It is adjusted at the end of the period to reflect the unconfirmed markup on the home office merchandise still in the branch's ending inventory.

3. In the combined statement working paper the balance in the Intracompany Inventory Profit account consists of the unconfirmed profit in the beginning inventory plus the markup on this period's shipments. It is eliminated in two entries:

    a. The unconfirmed profit in the beginning inventory is credited to the beginning inventory in the cost of goods sold section of the income statement.

    b. The markup on the current period's shipments is credited to Shipments from Home Office along with their cost.

4. The branch's inventory at the end of the period is stated at transfer prices on its books. To reduce this ending inventory to cost, the unconfirmed intracompany profit at the end of the period is debited to the ending inventory in the cost of goods sold section and credited to the ending inventory in the balance sheet.

5. In the home office's balance sheet the balance in the Intracompany Inventory Profit account should be deducted from the Branch Current account.

6. If the branch does not know the cost of the merchandise it receives from the home office, the net income on its books is necessarily based on the transfer prices charged by the home office. On the home office books the branch net income, as reported by the branch, is adjusted for the confirmed portion of the Intracompany Inventory Profit. This is done with a debit to the Intracompany Inventory Profit account and a credit to the Branch Net Income account.

F. Reconciling adjustments

1. If the reciprocal intracompany account balances are not the same, equality must be established before the accounts are eliminated in the combined statement working paper.

2. Three frequent causes of differences between Branch Current and Home Office account balances are:

    a. End-of-period billings by the home office for the branch's share of expenses are recorded on the home office but not yet on the branch's books;

    b. In transit cash remittances between the branch and home office are unrecorded by the receiving entity; and

    c. In transit shipments of merchandise between the branch and home office are unrecorded by the receiving entity.

3. These adjustments may be entered on the combined statement working paper in the same manner as the elimination entries; they are, however, usually identified by a different system of indexing.

G. Transshipments of merchandise

1. If it is necessary for a branch to ship merchandise it received from the home office to another branch, the branches must record the transaction so their account balances are reciprocal to the recorded effects on the home office books.

a. The shipping branch reduces its Home Office Current account (at cost plus total freight) and Shipments from Home Office (at cost).

    Home Office Current
          Freight-in
          Shipments from Home Office
          Cash

b. The receiving branch increases its Home Office Current account (at cost plus normal freight) and Shipments from Home Office (at cost).

    Shipments from Home Office
    Freight-in
          Home Office Current

c. The home office debits Shipments to Branch (the shipping branch) and credits Shipments to Branch (the receiving branch) for the cost of the merchandise. The home office also debits the Branch Current account of the receiving branch for the amount of the merchandise plus normal freight had the shipment come directly from the home office. It credits the Branch Current account of the shipping branch for the merchandise cost plus the total freight cost incurred by the home office and the shipping branch.

    Shipments to Branch (shipping)
          Shipments to Branch (receiving)

    Branch Current (receiving)
    Excess freight on branch transshipment
          Branch Current (shipping)

2. Freight on assets transferred by the home office to a branch is properly included as an element of asset cost to the receiving branch. However, the difference between total freight cost and normal freight is absorbed by the home office as Excess Freight on Branch Transshipment.

H. Other accounting systems

1. The home office may choose to centralize the accounting for all branch operations on its own books. This may result in the creation of a separate set of accounts to identify branch operations, or the branch's operations may be recorded as part of home office operations. In the latter case the system is similar to accounting for agencies.

2. The home office may also choose to have two sets of branch records: one kept by the branch and one kept by

the home office. This system has the disadvantage of duplicating work and the advantage that the home office may have more detailed knowledge of the branch's operations.

II. Segmental Reporting

A. The need for segmental reports

1. Corporate growth and diversification have made it difficult for users of consolidated financial statements to develop a reasonable understanding of a company's risks, returns, and opportunities. Complex business activities have created a need for detailed information about the diverse operations of a business.

2. Revenues, expenses, and assets of different businesses are often combined and reported on consolidated statements. As a result, users may not have adequate information to assess the success or failure of each business or operation. Consequently, supplemental statements are prepared to fill this need.

3. Segmental reports provide disaggregated information about the significant business segments, major customers, and domestic and foreign operations of a reporting entity.

4. Guidelines for preparing segmental reports are contained in FASB Standard No. 14.

B. Identifying significant segments of a firm

1. Three alternatives have been considered for identifying business segments:

a. By geographical divisions--particularly helpful for evaluating domestic and foreign operations.

b. By product lines or industry divisions--useful for reporting differences in profitability, risk, and growth opportunities for the product lines or industry groups.

c. By divisions that conform to the internal structure of managerial control--facilitates the accurate accumulation of data at the least cost.

2. FASB Statement No. 14 requires information on the following three items:

a. The enterprise's foreign operations and export sales,
b. Its major customers, and
c. Its operations in different industries.

3. Foreign operations are identified as operations that are located in foreign countries and that generate revenue from sales to unaffiliated customers. Foreign geographical areas may consist of one or more countries. Information should be presented separately for each significant geographical area and in the aggregate for those geographical areas which are not individually significant. If export sales of domestic operations are significant in amount, they should be reported in the aggregate and by appropriate geographical areas.

    a. Significance is defined as follows:

        (1) A geographical area is considered significant if its revenues from unaffiliated customers or its identifiable assets are 10 percent or more of the related consolidated amounts.

        (2) Export sales are considered significant if they amount to 10 percent or more of the company's consolidated sales.

    b. For domestic operations and for each foreign geographical area, the following information must be reported:

        (1) Sales to unaffiliated customers,

        (2) Intra-enterprise sales and transfers between geographical areas,

        (3) Operating profit (loss), and

        (4) Identifiable assets.

4. A major customer is one to whom sales equal 10 percent or more of the company's total sales. The fact and revenue to each major customer must be reported. Customers need not be individually identified. but the industry segment(s) making the sales must be identified. Separate entities under common control are regarded as one customer, such as the federal government, a state government, or a foreign government.

5. In identifying industry segments the nature of the products produced, the nature of the production processes involved, and the markets and marketing methods employed to sell the products should be considered. Sales by industry segments should be primarily to unaffiliated customers.

a. For industrial segments the following information
    must be reported:

    (1) Sales to unaffiliated customers,

    (2) Intra-enterprise sales and transfers between
        industrial segments,

    (3) Operating profit (loss),

    (4) Identifiable assets, and

    (5) Depreciation, amortization, and additions to
        property, plant, and equipment.

b. A reportable industry segment must meet one of the
    following tests:

    (1) Its revenue is 10 percent or more of all
        revenue, including intersegment sales or
        transfers.

    (2) The absolute amount of its operating profit
        (loss) is 10 percent or more of the greater,
        in absolute amount, of:

        (a) The total operating profit of all
            profitable segments, or

        (b) The total operating loss of all
            unprofitable segments.

    (3) Its identifiable assets are 10 percent or
        more of the combined identifiable assets of
        all industry segments.

c. If a segment meets one of these tests in the
    current period but has not done so in prior
    periods and is not expected to do so in the
    future, it does not have to be reported.

d. If a normally significant segment fails all tests
    in a single year, it is treated as a reportable
    segment.

e. If a single segment accounts for more than 90
    percent of the firm's revenue, operating profit
    (loss), and identifiable assets and no other
    segment meets any of the above 10 percent tests,
    reports for that segment do not have to be
    presented separately.

f. If the total sales of reportable segments do not
    amount to 75 percent of sales to unaffiliated
    customers, additional industry segments should be

185

identified as reportable segments until the 75 percent test is met.

    C.   Intersegmental transfer pricing

        1.   An ideal basis for setting transfer prices would be independent market prices.

        2.   As a practical matter the FASB has determined that the transfer prices used should be those which are used by the company to price the intersegment sales or transfers.

    D.   Allocating common costs and measuring segmental profitability

        1.   Measuring segmental profitability is difficult because, among other reasons, some costs are common to two or more reporting segments. Consequently, an allocation process is often needed, but it should not be arbitrary.

        2.   The FASB has concluded that the following nine specific items should not be allocated to the segments for calculating their operating profit or loss:

            a.   Revenue earned at the corporate level,
            b.   General corporate expenses,
            c.   Interest expense,
            d.   Income taxes,
            e.   Equity in the income (loss) of an unconsolidated subsidiary,
            f.   Gain (loss) from discontinued operations,
            g.   Extraordinary items,
            h.   Minority interests, and
            i.   Cumulative effect of a change in an accounting principle.

    E.   Identifying segmental assets

        1.   Many assets are easily identified with a specific segment, especially those used exclusively by one segment. If two or more segments use the same assets, a reasonable basis must be used for allocating the books values of those assets among the segments.

        2.   Cash, marketable securities, investments accounted for by the equity method, and assets that are primarily used at the corporate level (e. g. central offices) should not be allocated to industry segments.

III. Interim Reporting

    A.   Interim reporting refers to financial reporting for periods of less than a year, e. g. monthly or quarterly periods.

Public companies must report quarterly results of operations.

1.   Quarterly reports normally include revenues, provisions for income taxes, net income, earnings per share, extraordinary items, discontinued operations, and the cumulative effect of a change in accounting principle.

2.   These items are normally reported for the current quarter of the current and the previous year. In addition, year-to-date amounts are reported for the current and prior year(s).

B.   The two viewpoints from which to resolve interim reporting issues see the interim period either as a "stand alone" accounting period or as an integral part of an annual accounting period.

1.   The results of the "stand alone" approach are best seen for income taxes. If taxes are progressive, then each quarter's income tax would be computed using the lowest rates, since each quarter's income is viewed as standing alone.

2.   The integral approach forecasts the average tax rate which will apply to annual pretax earnings and then applies this rate to the income of each quarter.

C.   FASB Statement No. 3 views interim periods as integral portions of the annual accounting period.

D.   Income tax issues arise not only from differences in rates but also from differences between accounting and taxable income.

1.   The expected average annual tax rate is computed by dividing the expected income tax expense on the annual income statement by the expected annual pretax accounting income. Their quotient is a rate of financial accounting income tax expense per dollar of pretax financial accounting income.

2.   Operating losses create special problems:

a.   If a quarterly loss is expected to be offset by income in later quarters, so that positive income results for the year, the tax benefit is reported in the loss period. This tax benefit is calculated by multiplying the loss by the expected average annual rate.

b.   If a quarterly loss is not expected to be offset by income in later quarters, the tax benefit is not assured and should therefore not be reported in the loss period.

187

c.   If quarterly income is expected to be offset by a loss for the year, the expected average annual rate is used. This rate is computed by dividing the expected tax benefit for the year by the expected operating loss, giving due consideration to the firm's carryback or carryforward position. The same method is used for loss quarters in a year in which an annual loss is expected.

E.   **Costs associated with sales depend for their treatment on the firm's expectations for the year.**

1.   The liquidation of a LIFO layer during a quarter is ignored if the liquidated layer is expected to be replaced by year-end. Cost of goods sold for the interim period is based on the expected replacement cost of the liquidated layer.

2.   If the firm uses the lower of cost or market rule, a price reduction below cost is handled as follows:

a.   If the price decline is considered permanent, the loss is recognized in the interim period. If prices recover, a gain is reported in the period in which the recovery occurs.

b.   If the price decline is considered temporary, the loss is ignored in the interim period.

3.   Interim period purchase price, volume, or capacity cost variances that are expected to be absorbed by the end of the year are ignored. If such variances are not expected to be absorbed by the end of the year, they are recorded in the quarter in which they occur.

F.   **Other costs, special items, and earnings per share also create problems.**

1.   Annual period costs must be allocated to interim periods on a logical basis.

2.   Material extraordinary items and discontinued operations are reported separately in interim reports.

3.   Earnings per share computations are affected by share prices and the number of outstanding shares. Therefore quarterly EPS may not add up to annual EPS.

G.   **Accounting changes can also be a source of problems.**

1.   They do not present a special problem if they are made in the first quarter because the cumulative effect is the same at the beginning of the first quarter and the beginning of the year. If the change is made in a later quarter, the preceding quarter(s) used the old

method. In this case year-to-date data should be restated as if the change occurred in the first quarter.

2. The effect of a change in an accounting estimate is accounted for in the quarter in which the change is made. Accordingly the quarter in which a change is made will contain a positive or negative "catch up" adjustment. The amount of the adjustment will be the cumulative difference between the amount previously reported and the year-to-date amount.

Test your Understanding of Chapter 11

True or False

Instructions: Indicate your choice by circling either T, if you think the statement is true, or F, if you think the statement is false.

T F 1. The balance in the account Branch Current represents the claim of the home office to the net assets of the branch and is reciprocal to the account Home Office Current on the branch's books.

T F 2. The reciprocal accounts Shipments from Home Office and Shipments to Branch always have equivalent balances at any given point in time.

T F 3. Combined statement of the home office and branch are needed to reflect the effects of transactions of the total business entity with outside interests.

T F 4. The effects of transactions between the home office and branches or between branches must be eliminated in the preparation of combined financial statements to avoid an overstatement of values.

T F 5. The account Intracompany Inventory Profit appears on branch books if the home office bills the branch for more than cost.

T F 6. The post-closing balance in Intracompany Inventory Profit represents the unconfirmed profit in the branch's ending inventory.

T F 7. Selected information about a business segment must be reported if it passes the revenue test, the operating profit (loss) test, and the identifiable net assets test.

T F 8. If no industry segments pass a 10 percent test, a segmental report need not be prepared.

T F 9. In the determination of a segment's operating profit or loss income taxes are ignored.

189

T F 10. A geographical area is deemed to be significant it its total revenues or its identifiable assets are 10 percent or more of the related total amounts.

T F 11. The fire department and the police department of a city are considered to be one major customer.

T F 12. If the operating profit or loss of reportable industry segments does not equal at least 75 percent of the combined profit or loss, more segments must be added to achieve the 75 percent requirement.

T F 13. The FASB considers each interim period as an integral part of the annual accounting period.

T F 14. The expected annual average rate is computed by dividing the expected income tax expense for the year by the expected taxable income.

T F 15. The temporary liquidation of a LIFO layer during the fourth quarter may be ignored.

Exercises

1. On April 17, 19x2, the Leisure Wear Company opened a branch in a beach resort. On the Home Office books journalize the following transactions which occurred during the first year of the Beach Branch's operations.

a.   Leisure Wear Company transferred $5,000 to its Beach Branch.

b.   Merchandise costing the home office $20,000 was shipped to the branch; the branch was billed $25,000.

c.   Equipment for the branch was purchased by the home office for $10,000. Fixed asset accounts are maintained by the home office.

1. Following home office instructions, the Beach Branch shipped
    $2,500 of merchandise to the Mountain Branch and paid $100
    freight. Normal freight charges on shipments of this size from
    the home office to the Mountain Branch are $75.

2. The Beach Branch remitted $8,000 to the home office.

3. The home office informed the branch that depreciation on its
    fixed assets amounted to $1,000 for the year.

4. The Beach Branch reported an ending inventory of $5,000 (all
    obtained from the home office) and net income of $12,000.

. Use the information from Exercise 1 and journalize the
transactions on the books of the Beach Branch.

b.

c.

d.

e.

f.

g.

3. The Diversified Company has four major segments. Financial data for the segments are presented below:

	Segments			
	A	B	C	D
Sales revenue	$ 5,000	$25,000	$ 8,000	$ 62,000
Operating expenses	7,000	15,000	26,000	32,000
Operating profit (loss)	$(2,000)	$10,000	$(18,000)	$ 30,000
Identifiable assets	$10,000	$30,000	$10,000	$100,000

Included in the sales of segment D are sales of $12,000 to segment B. Segment B subsequently sold all of this merchandise to nonaffiliates. General administrative expenses are $8,000 and income taxes are $5,000.

Required: Determine which segments are reportable.

4. Acme Company expects to realize the following income during the current year:

Net income from operations	$150,000
Rental income	30,000
Municipal (tax-free) interest	20,000
Total pretax accounting income	$200,000

Acme's tax rate is 25 percent on the first $25,000 of taxable income and 50 percent on any excess over $25,000.

Actual pretax accounting income for the year was as follows:

First quarter $ 40,000 (including $5,000 of municipal interest)
Second quarter   30,000 (including $5,000 of municipal interest)
Third quarter   30,000 (including $5,000 of municipal interest)
Fourth quarter   100,000
                $200,000

Because Acme was short of cash in September, it sold the municipal bonds. Therefore it received no interest in the last quarter.

Required:
a. Compute the expected average annual tax rate.

b. Compute the income tax expense and net income for each of the four quarters and for the year.

193

Solutions to Chapter 11 Exercises

True or False

1.	T	4.	T	7.	F	10.	F	13.	T
2.	F	5.	F	8.	F	11.	T	14.	F
3.	T	6.	T	9.	T	12.	F	15.	F

Exercises

1. Home Office Books

a. Beach Branch Current   5,000
        Cash   5,000
    To record cash transfer to Beach Branch

b. Beach Branch Current   25,000
        Shipments to Beach Branch   20,000
        Intracompany Inventory Profit   5,000
    To record shipments to Beach Branch

c. Equipment   10,000
        Cash   10,000
    To record purchase of equipment for Beach Branch

d. Shipments to Beach Branch   2,500
        Shipments to Mountain Branch   2,500
    Mountain Branch Current   2,575
    Excess Freight on Transshipment   25
        Beach Branch Current   2,600
    To record shipment by Beach Branch to Mountain Branch. Freight
    paid by Beach Branch was $100; normal freight to Mountain Branch
    is $75

e. Cash   8,000
        Beach Branch Current   8,000
    To record receipt of cash from Beach Branch

f. Beach Branch Current   1,000
        Accumulated Depreciation   1,000
    To record Beach Branch's depreciation

g. Beach Branch Current   12,000
        Beach Branch Net Income   12,000
    To record net income per Beach Branch books

    Intracompany Inventory Profit   3,500
        Beach Branch Net Income   3,500
    To record confirmed intracompany profit

2. Beach Branch Books

a. Cash   5,000
        Home Office Current   5,000
    To record receipt of cash from home office

194

b. Shipments from Home Office   25,000
       Home Office Current   25,000
   To record receipt of merchandise from home office

c. No entry

d. Home Office Current   2,600
       Cash   100
       Shipments from Home Office   2,500
   To record shipment of merchandise to Mountain Branch

e. Home Office Current   8,000
       Cash   8,000
   To record cash transfer to home office

f. Depreciation expense   1,000
       Home Office Current   1,000
   To record depreciation on equipment kept on home office books

g. Income Summary   12,000
       Home Office Current   12,000
   To close income summary

3. Revenue Test:

Segment	Total Revenue	Percent of Total
A	$ 5,000	5.0%
B	25,000	25.0%
C	8,000	8.0%
D	62,000	62.0%
	$100,000	

Segments B and D are reportable under the revenue test.

Identifiable Asset Test:

Segment	Ident. Assets	Percent of Total
A	$ 10,000	6.7%
B	30,000	20.0%
C	10,000	6.7%
D	100,000	66.7%
	$150,000	

Segments B and D are reportable under the identifiable asset test.

Operating Profit (Loss) Test

Segment	Operating Profit	Operating Loss	Percent of Largest Total
A		$ 2,000	5.0%
B	$10,000		25.0%
C		18,000	45.0%
D	30,000		75.0%
	$40,000	$20,000	

Segments B, C, and D are reportable under the operating profit (loss) test.

4. a. Net income from operations $150,000
        Rental income 30,000
        Expected taxable income $180,000

        Tax on first 25,000 @ 25% .... $ 6,250
        Tax on 180,000 - 25,000 @ 50% 77,500
        Expected income tax expense $83,750

        Expected average annual tax rate = 83,750 : 200,0000 =
        41.875%.

b.

	1st Quarter	Year-to-date
Net income before taxes	$40,000	$40,000
Income tax @ 41.875%	16,750	16,750
Net income	$23,250	$23,250

	2nd Quarter	Year-to-date
Net income before taxes	$30,000	$70,000
Income tax @ 41.875%	12,563	29,313
Net income	$17,437	$40,687

	3rd Quarter	Year-to-date
Net income before taxes	$30,000	$100,000
Income tax @ 41.875%	12,562	41,875
Net income	$17,438	$ 58,125

	4th Quarter	Year-to-date
Net income before taxes	$100,000	$200,000
Actual income tax expense*....		86,250
4th quarter expense (86,250 - 41,875)	44,375	
Net income	$ 55,625	$113,750

*First $25,000 @ 25% .... $ 6,250
(200,000 - 25,000 - 15,000**) @ 50% 80,000
Actual income tax expense $86,250
**Municipal interest

Chapter 12
Foreign Currency Transactions

I.   Foreign Currency Transactions

    A.   A foreign currency transaction is a transaction denominated in a currency other than the entity's functional currency.

        1.   According to <u>FASB Statement No. 52</u> the functional currency is "the currency of the primary economic environment in which the entity operates."

        2.   Domestic companies are assumed to be US companies for whom the functional currency is the US dollar.

        3.   The reporting currency is the currency in which financial statements are prepared.

    B.   A trading transaction is an export or import transaction which results in a receivable or payable denominated in a foreign currency, i. e. a receivable or payable which is to be settled in a foreign currency.

    C.   Three questions arise in export and import transactions denominated in a foreign currency:

        1.   At what US dollar amount should the receivable or payable be recorded?

        2.   Exchange gains and losses arise when receivables or payables are settled at a dollar amount different from the amount at which they were first recorded. What is the proper accounting treatment for such transaction exchange gains and losses?

        3.   To avoid transaction exchange gains and losses, companies enter into hedging transactions. What is the proper accounting treatment for such hedging transactions?

II. Currency Exchange Rates

    A.   Exchange rates represent the number of units of one currency that must be given to obtain a single unit of another currency.

    B.   Exchange rate terminology:

        1.   Free versus official exchange rates

a. Free rates reflect the demand for versus the supply of a currency, i. e. the price of a currency as an economic good.

b. Official rates are established by governments rather than the market forces of demand versus supply.

2. Direct versus indirect exchange rate quotations

a. An exchange rate is quoted directly if it represents the number of domestic currency units that must be given to obtain a single unit of foreign currency, e. g. $.60 = DM 1.

b. An exchange rate is quoted indirectly if it represents the number of foreign currency units that must be given to obtain a single unit of domestic currency, e. g. $1 = DM 1.67.

c. Direct and indirect exchange rates are reciprocals of each other.

3. Spot versus forward rates

a. Spot rates reflect exchange values for immediate exchanges of currencies.

b. Forward rates express the rate of exchange that is agreed upon for delivery of foreign currency units at a specific future date.

III. Export and Import Transactions - Settlements Made Within Year

A. In an export transaction a domestic company sells goods to a foreign company. If the sale is on credit, a receivable is recorded on the domestic company's books.

1. If the receivable is denominated in the domestic currency, i. e. US dollars, the exchange risk is assumed by the foreign buyer, not the US seller. In this case the amount of cash received in dollars on the settlement date exactly equals the dollar receivable recorded on the transaction date. Therefore, no transaction exchange gain or loss results.

2. If the receivable is denominated in the foreign currency, the exchange risk is assumed by the domestic seller. In this case the entries are:

198

a.   To record export credit sale denominated in foreign currency, the receivable is converted into US dollars at the current rate, i. e. the rate in effect at the time of the transaction:

Accounts Receivable (FC)
    Sales

b.   To record collection of receivable denominated in foreign currency, the foreign currency received is recorded at the current rate:

Foreign Currency on Hand
    Accounts Receivable (FC)
If a debit (credit) is needed to balance the entry, an exchange loss (gain) is recorded. The gain (loss) equals the number of foreign currency units multiplied by the Increase (decrease) in the exchange rate.

c.   To record sale of foreign currency for US dollars:

Cash
    Foreign Currency on Hand

3.   A change in the exchange rate results in either a gain or a loss.

a.   If a receivable is denominated in the foreign currency:

(1)   A gain results if the dollar weakens, because more dollars than originally anticipated are obtained for the foreign currency.

(2)   A loss results if the dollar strengthens, because fewer dollars than originally anticipated are obtained for the foreign currency.

b.   If a payable is denominated in the foreign currency:

(1)   A gain results if the dollar strengthens, because fewer dollars than originally anticipated are needed to acquire the foreign currency.

(2)   A loss results if the dollar weakens, because more dollars than originally anticipated are needed to acquire the foreign currency.

B.   An export sale is hedged by selling the foreign currency to be received through an exchange broker at a specified forward rate. The chosen delivery date of the foreign currency is the settlement date of the receivable. On the books of the exporter two transactions must be recorded: the export sale and the hedge.

1.   The export sale is recorded in the same way as discussed above.

2.   The hedge is, strictly speaking, an executory contract and therefore need not be recorded. However, <u>FASB Statement No. 52</u> requires that gains and losses from hedges be recognized. For that reason the hedge is usually recorded as follows:

   a.   To record the contract with the foreign exchange broker:

      Dollars Due from Exchange Broker
         Foreign Currency Due to Exchange Broker

      (1)   The dollar amount due from the broker is agreed upon in the contract. The liability to the broker is denominated in the foreign currency and recorded at the spot rate on the day the contract is drawn up.

      (2)   The exporter is now exposed to an exchange risk on the liability to the broker. This is offset by the exchange risk assumed on the receivable from the customer. These two risks cancel each other out, since a gain on one is exactly offset by a loss on the other. In other words, if the dollar weakens, the receivable increases in value, resulting in a gain. At the same time the liability will increase in value, resulting in a loss.

   b.   To record the settlement of the liability to the broker:

      Foreign Currency Due to Exchange Broker
         Foreign Currency on Hand
      If a debit (credit) is needed to balance the entry, an exchange loss (gain) is recorded. The gain (loss) equals the number of foreign currency units multiplied by the Increase (decrease) in the exchange rate.

      (1)   The gain (loss) in this entry will be identical to the loss (gain) recorded in the entry described in A.2.b., above.

      (2)   The foreign currency delivered to the broker is, of course, the currency received from the customer in entry A.2.b., above.

    c.   To record the receipt of the dollars from the
          broker:

          Cash
                Dollars Due from Exchange Broker

C.   In an import transaction a domestic company buys goods from
      a foreign company. If the purchase is on credit, a payable
      is recorded on the domestic company's books.

      1.   If the payable is denominated in the domestic currency,
            i. e. US dollars, the exchange risk is assumed by the
            foreign seller, not the US buyer. In this case the
            amount of cash paid in dollars on the settlement date
            exactly equals the dollar payable recorded on the
            transaction date. Therefore, no transaction exchange
            gain or loss results.

      2.   If the payable is denominated in the foreign currency,
            the exchange risk is assumed by the domestic buyer. In
            this case the entries are:

            a.   To record import purchase on credit denominated in
                  foreign currency, the payable is converted into US
                  dollars at the current rate, i. e. the rate in
                  effect at the time of the transaction:

                  Purchases
                        Accounts Payable (FC)

            b.   To record purchase of foreign currency at the
                  current rate:

                  Foreign Currency on Hand
                        Cash

            c.   To record settlement of payable by delivery of
                  foreign currency:

                  Accounts payable (FC)
                        Foreign Currency on Hand
                  If a debit (credit) is needed to balance the
                  entry, an exchange loss (gain) is recorded. The
                  gain (loss) equals the number of foreign currency
                  units multiplied by the Increase (decrease) in the
                  exchange rate.

D.   An import transaction is hedged by buying the foreign
      currency to be paid from an exchange broker at a specified
      forward rate. The chosen delivery date of the foreign
      currency is the settlement date of the payable. On the
      books of the importer two transactions must be recorded:
      the import purchase and the hedge.

1. The import transaction is recorded in the same way as discussed above.

2. The hedge is recorded as follows:

   a. To record the contract with the foreign exchange broker:

      Foreign Currency Due from Exchange Broker
         Dollars Due to Exchange Broker

      (1) The dollar amount due to the broker is agreed upon in the contract. The receivable from the broker is denominated in the foreign currency and recorded at the spot rate on the day the contract is drawn up.

      (2) The importer is now exposed to an exchange risk on the receivable from the broker. This is offset by the exchange risk assumed on the liability to the supplier. These two risks cancel each other out, since a gain on one is exactly offset by a loss on the other.

   b. To record the collection of the receivable from the broker:

      Foreign Currency on Hand
         Foreign Currency Due from Exchange Broker
      If a debit (credit) is needed to balance the entry, an exchange loss (gain) is recorded. The gain (loss) equals the number of foreign currency units multiplied by the Increase (decrease) in the exchange rate.

      (1) The gain (loss) in this entry will be identical to the loss (gain) recorded in the entry described in C.2.c., above.

      (2) The foreign currency collected from the broker is, of course, the currency delivered to the supplier in entry C.2.c., above.

   c. To record the payment to the broker:

      Dollars Due to Exchange Broker
         Cash

E. Exchange gains and losses resulting from export and import transactions can be viewed in two ways:

   1. The two-transaction approach sees the export and import as one transaction and the assumption of the foreign exchange risk as another transaction. In this case the purchase or sale of merchandise is recorded at the rate

202

in effect at the time of the transaction. The gain or loss on the settlement of the receivable or payable does not effect the purchase or sale price, but is instead seen as a financial, rather than an operating, item on the income statement. FASB Statement No. 52 supports this view and requires separate disclosure of transaction exchange gains and losses.

2. The one-transaction approach sees the import and export and the future payment or collection as one transaction. In this view the purchase or sale price is determined by the exchange rate in effect at the time of the settlement. No transaction exchange gain or loss is therefore recorded.

IV. Forward Exchange Contracts - Advanced Cases

A. In addition to hedging completed import and export transactions, forward exchange contracts are also used to hedge other types of foreign currency exposure and to speculate.

1. For accounting purposes forward exchange hedging contracts are divided into three groups:

a. Hedges of identifiable foreign currency commitments;

b. Hedges of exposed asset and liability positions (such as receivables and payables from export and import transactions, as discussed above); and

c. Hedges of net investments (ownership interests) in foreign entities.

2. The spot and forward rates used in hedging contracts are usually not the same. When the forward rate is higher than the spot rate, the difference between the two rates is called a premium. When the forward rate is lower, the differences is called a discount.

B. An identifiable foreign currency commitment is hedged to avoid the exchange rate risk between the day an executory contract is entered into and the day the transaction occurs and is recorded. The exchange risk is the same for a contractual agreement to buy or sell in the future at a price denominated in the foreign currency as it is for an actual purchase or sale. However, no entry is made on the domestic company's books for the agreement, therefore no receivable or payable is recorded.

1. An identifiable foreign currency commitment may arise from an export or an import contract. The entries in the two cases are similar.

2. The entries recording a hedge of an export contract and the export transaction are:

   a. To record the hedge:

      Dollars Due from Exchange Broker
      Deferred Discount on Forward Contract or
          Deferred Premium on Forward Contract
          Foreign Currency Due to Exchange Broker

      The receivable from the broker is recorded at the forward rate, because that is the price agreed to by the broker. The liability to the broker is denominated in the foreign currency and is therefore recorded at the spot rate. The difference is the deferred discount (if the forward rate is below the spot rate) or premium (if the forward rate is above the spot rate).

   b. In the financial statements a receivable or payable denominated in a foreign currency must be stated at the spot rate on the balance sheet date. In a hedge of an identifiable foreign currency commitment the gain or loss on this restatement may be deferred. The entries to write the liability up or down are:

      Deferred Exchange Gain or Loss
          Foreign Currency Due to Exchange Broker

      Foreign Currency Due to Exchange Broker
          Deferred Exchange Gain or Loss

   c. On the transaction date the liability to the exchange broker is adjusted to the spot rate on that day with one of the following two entries:

      Deferred Exchange Gain or Loss
          Foreign Currency Due to Exchange Broker

      Foreign Currency Due to Exchange Broker
          Deferred Exchange Gain or Loss

   d. To record the export transaction (see the entry in III.A.2.a., above):

      Accounts Receivable (FC)
          Sales

   e. To close the deferred gain or loss to the sales account:

      (1) in the case of a net gain:
          Deferred Exchange Gain or Loss
              Sales

204

   (2) in the case of a net loss:
    Sales
     Deferred Exchange Gain or Loss

  f. To amortize the deferred premium or discount until
   the transaction date to the sales account:

   (1) in the case of a deferred premium:
    Deferred Premium on Forward Contract
     Sales

   (2) in the case of a deferred discount:
    Sales
     Deferred Discount on Forward Contract

3. After these entries the balance sheet contains a
  receivable and a payable of the same amount, both of
  them denominated in the foreign currency. This
  situation is identical to the hedge of an export
  transaction [see III.B.2.a.(2)].

4. The balance in the sales account will be equal to the
  sales price converted at the spot rate on the day the
  export agreement was made, plus or minus the amortized
  portion of the premium or discount on the forward
  contract. Since the forward rate is known when the
  agreement is made, the net sales price can be
  determined at that time.

C. An exposed asset position is hedged to avoid the exchange
  rate risk.

1. The company's balance sheet contains an asset and a
  liability, both denominated in the foreign currency.
  When the exchange rate for the currency changes, the
  gain recognized when the asset is revalued is identical
  to the loss recognized when the liability is revalued,
  and vice versa.

2. The hedge of an identifiable foreign currency
  commitment becomes a hedge of an exposed asset position
  when the export transaction occurs and is recorded.
  The entries to settle the export and the hedging
  contracts are:

  a. To revalue the receivable and payable for
   financial statement purposes at the spot rate on
   the balance sheet date:

   (1) if the exchange rate decreased:
    Foreign Currency Due to Exchange Broker
     Exchange Gain or Loss
    Exchange Gain or Loss
     Accounts Receivable (FC)

205

        (2)   if the exchange rate increased:
              Exchange Gain or Loss
                    Foreign Currency Due to Exchange Broker
              Accounts Receivable (FC)
                    Exchange Gain or Loss

   b.   To amortize the deferred premium or discount to
        the balance sheet date:

        Deferred Premium on Forward Contract
              Other Income

        Other Expenses
              Deferred Discount on Forward Contract

   c.   To record receipt of the foreign currency in
        settlement of the account receivable:

        Foreign Currency on Hand
              Accounts Receivable (FC)
        If a debit (credit) is needed to balance the
        entry, an exchange loss (gain) is recorded.

   d.   To record delivery of the foreign currency to the
        exchange broker:

        Foreign Currency Due to Exchange Broker
              Foreign Currency on Hand
        If a debit (credit) is needed to balance the
        entry, an exchange loss (gain) is recorded. The
        gain (loss) recorded in this entry is identical to
        the loss (gain) recorded in the previous entry.

   e.   To record payment by broker for the foreign
        currency:

        Cash
              Dollars Due from Exchange Broker

   f.   To amortize balance of deferred premium or
        discount:

        Deferred Premium on Forward Contract
              Other Income

        Other Expenses
              Deferred Discount on Forward Contract

3. The hedge of an exposed asset or liability position
    largely eliminates a domestic company's exchange risk.
    Since the exchange gains and losses are identical, the
    only income statement effect is the amortization of the
    deferred premium or discount.

D. Speculation in foreign currency exchange price fluctuations is undertaken to realize a gain from a favorable change.

1. Accounting for speculative contracts is similar to accounting for exposed asset and liability positions. For example, transaction gains and losses are recorded on intervening financial statement dates and on the settlement date. However, two differences exist:

   a. When speculative contracts are valued for financial statement purposes, the asset and liability are restated at the forward rate for the remaining period of the contract.

   b. Both the receivable and the payable in a speculative contract are initially recorded at the forward rate applicable to the period of the contract. Since the receivable and payable are recorded at the same rate, no discount or premium is recorded on a speculative contract.

2. The entries to record a speculative contract to purchase a foreign currency in the future are:

   a. To record the contract:

   Foreign Currency Due from Exchange Broker
       Dollars Due to Exchange Broker

   b. To restate receivable at the spot rate on a balance sheet date:

   (1) if the foreign currency increased in value:
   Foreign Currency Due from Exchange Broker
       Exchange Gain or Loss

   (2) if the foreign currency decreased in value:
   Exchange Gain or Loss
       Foreign Currency Due from Exchange Broker

   c. To record payment to exchange broker:

   Dollars Due to Exchange Broker
       Cash

   d. To record delivery of foreign currency:

   Foreign Currency on Hand
       Foreign Currency Due from Exchange Broker
   If a debit (credit) is needed to balance the entry, an exchange loss (gain) is recorded.

3. The net gain (loss) on the speculative contract is the difference between the dollars paid to the broker and

the value of the foreign currency when it is delivered (see the previous two entries).

V. Multiple Exchange Rates

    A. If a currency has multiple exchange rates, the following rates are used:

        1. At the transaction date the transaction is recorded at the rate at which the transaction can be settled immediately.

        2. For financial statements the receivables and payables are valued at the rate at which the balances can be settled immediately.

    B. Normally the same rate is used from the transaction to the settlement date.

Test Your Understanding of Chapter 12

True or False

Instructions: Indicate your choice by circling either T, if you think the statement is true, or F, if you think the statement is false.

T F 1. An exchange rate is quoted directly if it states the number of foreign currency units that must be given to obtain a single unit of domestic currency.

T F 2. A firm's functional currency is defined as the primary currency in which the firm does business. All other currencies are viewed as foreign currencies by that firm.

T F 3. Premiums or discounts on speculative forward contracts are not recognized in a firm's accounts at the date the contract is written.

T F 4. Strictly speaking a forward contract is an executory contract which, according to conventional accounting principles, would not call for an accounting entry on the date the contract is signed.

T F 5. When multiple official exchange rates exist, a foreign currency transaction should be measured at the transaction date and each subsequent balance sheet date at the rate at which the transaction could then be settled.

T F 6. The spot rate is the same as the free rate.

T F 7. Exchange gains and losses resulting from forward contracts used as hedges of other general foreign currency transactions should be deferred and amortized.

T F 8. When recording an export sale, both the debit and credit side of the entry should be converted to US dollars at the spot rate on the transaction date.

T F 9. A forward contract is a contract to buy or sell a specific number of units of foreign currency at a specific future date at the current spot rate.

T F 10. If the dollar weakens between the transaction date and the payment date, an importing company will realize a gain on a receivable denominated in the foreign currency.

T F 11. If the dollar strengthens between the transaction date and the payment date, an exporting company will realize a gain on a payable denominated in the domestic currency.

T F 12. An exporting company hedges a sale with terms of n/60. In the balance sheet prepared after 30 days, the balance in the Foreign Currency Payable to Exchange Broker account should be revalued at the 30-day forward rate.

T F 13. When the forward rate of a foreign currency is higher than the spot rate, the difference between the two rates is called a premium.

T F 14. At an intervening balance sheet date the receivable and payable of a speculative contract are valued at the spot rate on the balance sheet date.

T F 15. Transaction exchange gains and losses on hedges of exposed asset and liability positions should be recognized currently in the income statement.

Exercises

1. A US firm, whose functional currency is the US dollar, sold merchandise on account to a foreign customer on 12/1/19x1 for FC 10,000. Payment was received on 1/30/19x2. The US firm uses the calendar year. Relevant spot exchange rates are as follows:

Date	Spot Rate
12/1/19x1	FC1 = $1.50
12/31/19x1	FC1 = $1.30
1/30/19x2	FC1 = $1.20

Required: Prepare the journal entries for the exporting company to record the above transactions.

12/1

12/31

1/30

2. The US firm in exercise 1 entered into a forward contract on 12/1/19x1 to deliver FC 10,000 to a foreign currency broker on 1/30/19x2. The forward contract rate was FC1 = $1.40. The forward contract was designated as a hedge of the merchandise transaction recorded in exercise 1.

Required: Prepare the journal entries for the exporting company to record the transactions relating to the hedge.

12/1

12/31

1/30

3. A US firm, whose functional currency is the US dollar, entered into a speculative forward contract on 10/1/19x1 to purchase FC 10,000 from a foreign currency broker on 4/1/19x2. The six-month forward contract rate is FC 1= $1.80 on 10/1/19x1; the three-month forward contract rate is FC 1 = $1.40 on 12/31/19x1. The spot rate is $1.60 on 12/31/19x1 and $1.50 on 4/1/19x2. The US firm uses the calendar year.

Required: Prepare the journal entries for the speculating company to record the transactions relating to the forward contract. Assume that the firm sells the foreign currency on 4/1/19x2.

10/1

12/31

4/1

Solutions to Chapter 12 Exercises

True or False

1.	F	4.	T	7.	F	10.	T	13.	T
2.	T	5.	T	8.	F	11.	F	14.	F
3.	T	6.	F	9.	F	12.	F	15.	T

1. 12/1/19x1 Accounts Receivable (FC) $15,000
       Sales $15,000
    To record sale to foreign buyer for FC 10,000,
    converted at $1.50 = FC1

  12/31/19x1 Exchange loss   2,000
       Accounts Receivable (FC).   2,000
    To restate receivable of 10,000 FC at $1.30 = FC1

  1/30/19x2 Foreign Currency on Hand   12,000
    Exchange loss   1,000
       Accounts Receivable (FC).   13,000
    To record receipt of 10,000 FC, converted at spot rate
    of $1.20 = FC1

    Cash   12,000
       Foreign Currency on Hand.   12,000
    To record sale of 10,000 FC for US dollars at $1.20 =
    FC1

2. 12/1/19x1 Dollars Due from Broker $14,000
    Discount on Forward Contract..   1,000
       Foreign Currency Due to
        Broker $15,000
    To record hedge of 10,000 FC, spot rate = $1.50, 60-day
    forward rate = $1.40

  12/31/19x1 Amortization Expense   500
    Foreign Currency Due to Broker   2,000
       Foreign Exchange Gain ...   2,000
       Discount on Forward Contract   500
    To amortize discount for 30 days and restate foreign
    currency payable to broker at spot rate of $1.30 at
    year-end

  1/30/19x2 Amortization Expense   500
       Discount on Forward Contract   500
    To amortize discount for 30 days

    Foreign Currency Due to Broker   1,000
       Foreign Exchange Gain....   1,000
    To restate payable to broker at spot rate of $1.20 =
    FC1

```
                Foreign Currency Due to Broker      12,000
                      Foreign Currency on Hand                 12,000
                To record delivery of FC 10,000 to broker


                Cash .......................      14,000
                      Dollars Due from Broker..                14,000
                To record cash received from broker

3.  10/1/19x1   FC Due from Broker ...........      $18,000
                      Dollars Due to Broker ...               $18,000
                To record speculative, 6-month contract for FC 10,000,
                to be delivered on 4/1/19x2


12/31/19x1      Foreign Exchange Loss ........       4,000
                      FC Due from Broker ......                 4,000
                To restate receivable from broker at $1.40 = FC 1


4/1/19x2        Foreign Currency on Hand .....      15,000
                Dollars Due to Broker ........      18,000
                      Foreign Exchange Gain....                 1,000
                      FC Due from Broker ......                14,000
                      Cash ....................                18,000
                To record receipt of 10,000 FC and payment to broker


                Cash .......................      15,000
                      Foreign Currency on Hand                 15,000
                To record sale of FC 10,000 at $1.50
```

Chapter Outline

I. The Functional Currency Concept

A. According to paragraph 5 of <u>FASB Statement No. 52</u> a firm's functional currency is the "currency of the primary economic environment in which the entity operates; normally, that is the currency of the environment in which an entity primarily generates and expends cash."

B. For a US company the US dollars is normally the functional currency. A foreign subsidiary of a domestic parent might be one of two extreme types:

   1. It might be an extension of the parent company, i. e. its day-to-day operations depend on the parent and its cash flows directly affect the cash flows of the parent. In this case the subsidiary's functional currency is the US dollar, even if its most of its cash flows and its books are kept in the foreign currency.

   2. It might be highly independent, i. e. its operations are primarily in the foreign country and its cash flows do not directly affect the cash flow of the parent. In this case the subsidiary's functional currency is its local currency.

C. In Appendix A the FASB Statement provides guidance to determining the functional currency of a foreign subsidiary. Briefly, the six indicators are:

   1. Do the subsidiary's cash flows affect the parent's dollar cash flows on a regular basis?

   2. Are the subsidiary's prices responsive to short-term fluctuations in exchange rates?

   3. Are the subsidiary's products sold in its local market for prices denominated in the local currency or in the parent's environment?

   4. Are costs primarily incurred in local markets or in the parent's country?

   5. Are debts denominated in, and serviced by, foreign currency or the parent's currency?

6. Are the operations and management of the foreign subsidiary independent and are there relatively few intercompany transactions and control arrangements?

D. The above indicators should be used to determine which currency better satisfies the objectives of FASB Statement No. 52 when a foreign subsidiary's financial statements are translated from its functional currency into the parent's reporting currency. These objectives are to:

1. Provide information that is generally compatible with the expected economic effects of a rate change on an enterprise's cash flows and equity, and

2. Reflect in consolidated statements the financial results and relationships of the individual companies as measured in their functional currencies in conformity with US GAAP. This requires that the financial statements of foreign subsidiaries which do not meet US GAAP must first be restated using US GAAP before they are converted to US dollars.

E. Once a foreign subsidiary's functional currency is determined it is not changed unless economic circumstances change significantly.

F. If a foreign subsidiary operates in several economic environments, it can have a different functional currency for each operation.

II. Evolution of Conversion Principles

A. The primary reason for converting the financial statements of foreign subsidiaries is the preparation of consolidated statements.

B. The first method that was widely accepted was the current-noncurrent method described in Accounting Research Bulletin No. 4, "Foreign Operations and Foreign Exchange."

1. Current assets and liabilities are translated at the spot rate on the balance sheet date (the current rate).

2. All other assets and liabilities are translated at the historical exchange rate in effect on the day they were acquired (the historical rate).

3. Conversion gains are deferred, while conversion losses are included in income. Under any conversion method such gains and losses are produced only on assets and liabilities converted at the current rate.

C. The current-noncurrent method was gradually replaced by the monetary-nonmonetary method, even though the latter had no authoritative support. Under this method monetary assets

216

and liabilities are converted at the current rate, and nonmonetary assets and equities are converted at their historical rates. The treatment of conversion gains and losses varied.

The next method developed was the temporal method which emphasizes the conversion of assets and equities so that the accounting principles applied to them are retained. This method was given authoritative support by FASB Statement No. 8. It states that "the objective of translation is to measure and express (a) in dollars and (b) in conformity with US generally accepted accounting principles the assets, liabilities, revenue or expenses that are measured or denominated in foreign currency."

1. Balance sheet accounts carried at prices in past exchanges (past prices) are translated at appropriate historical rates.

2. Balance sheet accounts carried at prices in current purchase or sale exchanges (current prices) are translated at the current rate.

3. Conversion gains and losses are included in income.

FASB Statement No. 8 was superseded by FASB Statement No. 52 which endorses the current method. Statement 52 describes the conversion process as translating the foreign subsidiary's financial statements from its functional currency into the reporting currency. The objective of the translation is to preserve the economic results and relationships existing in the foreign subsidiary's functional currency statements.

1. Under the current method translation means:

    a. All assets and liabilities are converted at the current rate.

    b. Translation gains and losses are not recognized in the income statement but are accumulated in a separate account in stockholders' equity, entitled the Cumulative Foreign Exchange Translation Adjustment account.

2. Differences among the foreign entity's local currency, its functional currency and the parent's reporting currency affect the process as follows:

    a. If the foreign entity's functional and local currencies are the same, translation means conversion at the current rate.

    b. If the foreign entity's functional and reporting currencies are the same and its transactions are

217

recorded in its local currency, translation means use of the temporal method.

    (1)   The FASB refers to the temporal method as remeasurement.

    (2)   Remeasurement gains and losses are recognized in the income statement.

III. Translation--Subsidiary's Functional and Reporting Currencies the Same

A.   If the foreign subsidiary's functional and reporting currencies are the same, but its transactions are recorded in the local currency, translation of its financial statements uses the temporal method or remeasurement.

B.   If the domestic parent acquires all of the stock of a foreign company, then the foreign subsidiary's balance sheet at acquisition is translated into dollars at the rate on the day of acquisition. This rate is known as the historical rate at acquisition. The historical rates for assets and equities acquired afterwards are the spot rates on their acquisition dates. After acquisition the following exchange rates are used when remeasurement is used for foreign financial statements:

    1.   Monetary assets and monetary liabilities are converted at the current rate.

    2.   All other balance sheet items and direct charges and credits to retained earnings are converted at their historical rates.

    3.   Income statement items should be converted at their historical rates. However, when this is impractical, the FASB permits the use of a weighted average rate. Depreciation is converted at the historical rate, since that rate is available from the conversion of the depreciable assets on the balance sheet.

    4.   The dollar amount of the beginning retained earnings is the same as the dollar amount of the ending retained earnings in the prior period's statements.

    5.   The remeasurement gain or loss is included in income. It is computed as follows:

        a.   It is the plug figure which balances the debits and credits in the dollar trial balance.

        b.   It can be calculated by computing the company's exposed net monetary asset or exposed net monetary liability position and multiplying this amount by the change in the exchange rate. This process is similar to calculating transaction exchange gains and losses on receivables and payables in the previous chapter.

C. If the domestic parent makes a long-term loan denominated in the foreign currency to the foreign subsidiary and the proceeds are used for the acquisition of fixed assets, Statement No. 52 calls for special treatment of the transaction gains and losses on the loan. Since the loan is a monetary item, it is translated at the current rate; however, the gain or loss resulting from the difference between the current rate and the historical rate (i. e. the rate used for the assets acquired with the loan) is not included in the income statement but in the Cumulative Foreign Exchange Translation Adjustment account in the stockholders' equity section of the balance sheet.

IV. Translation--Subsidiary's Functional and Reporting Currencies Different

A. When the subsidiary's transactions are recorded in its functional currency, the current rate method is used to convert the statements to the reporting currency, i. e. the US dollar.

B. If the domestic parent acquires the stock of the foreign company, the foreign subsidiary's balance sheet is converted at the then current rate. In the future this rate is only used to convert elements of contributed capital.

1. Subsequent to acquisition all assets and liabilities are converted at the current rate.

2. Contributed capital and direct charges and credits to retained earnings are converted at their historical rates.

3. Income statement items should be converted at their historical rates; however, as under the remeasurement rules, a weighted average rate may be used when historical rates are impractical. This applies also to depreciation and cost of goods sold.

4. As under the remeasurement method, the dollar amount of the beginning retained earnings is the same as the dollar amount of the ending retained earnings in the prior period's statements.

5. The translation gain or loss is included in the Cumulative Foreign Exchange Translation Adjustment account in the stockholders' equity section. The beginning dollar balance in this account is the same as the ending dollar balance in the prior period's statements. The current year's translation gain or loss is computed as follows:

219

        a.   It is the plug figure which balances the debits and credits in the dollar balance sheet.

        b.   It can be calculated by computing the company's beginning and ending net asset position.

           (1)   The beginning net asset position is multiplied by the difference in exchange rates between the prior and the current balance sheet.

           (2)   The change in net assets for the year is multiplied by the difference in exchange rates between the average rate used in the income statement and the current rate used in the balance sheet.

    C.   No special treatment is specified for long-term payables denominated in the foreign currency, since all such translation gains and losses are accumulated in the Cumulative Foreign Exchange Translation Adjustments account.

V.   Income Statements and Balance Sheets--Temporal and Current Rate Methods

    A.   Inventories valued at the lower of cost or market require special calculations if the foreign subsidiary's records are not kept in its functional currency, i. e. when remeasurement is used.

        1.   Cost is computed by multiplying the cost in the foreign currency by the rate in effect when the inventory was acquired.

        2.   Market is computed by multiplying the market value (replacement cost, ceiling, or floor) in the foreign currency by the spot rate on the balance sheet date (i. e. the current rate).

        3.   The lower of the above two amounts is used in the dollar balance sheet.

    B.   Foreign branches generally use the home office's reporting currency as their functional currency. In these cases the temporal method is used to convert the branch's account balances. The reciprocal balances, however, are stated at the dollar balances on the home office books.

    C.   When multiple exchange rates exist, the rate used in converting a foreign entity's financial statements usually is the rate used in dividend payments because it governs the conversion of cash flows from the foreign entity into the reporting currency.

D. Income tax allocation relating to foreign currency translation is appropriate in the following cases:

1. When a taxable transaction exchange gain or loss is included in income in a different period for financial statement purposes than for income tax purposes (interperiod income tax allocation),

2. When potential future tax effects partially offset the increases or decreases in an entity's net assets from translation adjustments (interperiod income tax allocation),

3. When some of the current period's income taxes are applicable to transaction exchange gains and losses and translation adjustments in shareholder's equity (intraperiod income tax allocation), and

4. When temporary timing differences of foreign assets and liabilities occur after a change in exchange rates (interperiod income tax allocation).

E. Statement No. 52 requires the following specific disclosures related to foreign currency translation in the financial statements or related footnotes:

1. The remeasurement gain or loss included in net income and

2. An analysis of the period's change in the Cumulative Foreign Exchange Translation Adjustment account disclosing as a minimum:

   a. the beginning balance of this account;

   b. the aggregate change in this balance from translation adjustments and gains and losses from transactions that are

      (1) designated as, and are effective as, hedges of a net investment in a foreign entity, and

      (2) intercompany foreign currency transactions of a long term investment nature;

   c. the income taxes for the period allocated to translation adjustments; and

   d. the amounts transferred from Cumulative Foreign Exchange Translation Adjustments and included in determining net income for the period as a result of the sale or liquidation of an investment in a foreign entity.

221

Test Your Understanding of Chapter 13

True or False

Instructions: Indicate your choice by circling either T, if you think the statement is true, or F, if you think the statement is false.

T F   1. The functional currency is the currency of the primary economic environment in which the entity operates.

T F   2. Under the functional currency approach all elements of the financial statements are measured in the reporting currency.

T F   3. If a foreign subsidiary's prices are responsive to changes in the exchange rate, its functional currency may differ from its local currency.

T F   4. If the foreign subsidiary's costs are mainly incurred in local markets, its functional currency is probably the local currency.

T F   5. Consolidated statements should reflect the financial results and relationships of the individual companies as measured in their local currencies.

T F   6. The current-noncurrent method replaced the monetary-nonmonetary method.

T F   7. The functional currency approach of Statement No. 52 results in maintaining the financial relationships found in the separate statements of the subsidiaries.

T F   8. The conversion gains and losses produced by the temporal method depend on the foreign entity's foreign currency exposure.

T F   9. Regardless of the translation method used, the sources of exchange gains and losses in the translation process are assets and liabilities that are translated at the current rate.

T F   10. As exchange rates fluctuate so that fewer dollars are received (or given) in exchange for one unit of foreign currency the dollar is said to weaken against the foreign currency.

T F   11. Under the temporal method an exposed net monetary liability position produces a loss if the dollar strengthens.

T F   12. The temporal rate method is used in translating foreign financial statements from their functional currencies into the reporting currency.

T F 13. A foreign subsidiary's functional and reporting currencies may be the same, even if its transactions are recorded in its local currency.

T F 14. Under the temporal method depreciation expense is converted at the weighted average rate for the period.

T F 15. Under the temporal method the lower of cost or market valuation of the inventory of a foreign subsidiary should be converted to dollars at an appropriate historical rate if cost is lower and at the current rate if market is lower.

Exercises

1. On 1/1/19x1 Domestic Company purchased 100 percent of the outstanding stock of Foreign Company for $150,000. Foreign Company is located in South America where the local currency is the peso. Foreign Company keeps its books in pesos. Its trial balance on 1/1/19x1 was as follows:

Foreign Company
Trial Balance (in pesos)
January 1, 19x1

Cash	80,000	
Accounts receivable (net)	220,000	
Inventory (at LIFO cost)	275,000	
Property, plant, and equipment (net)	425,000	
Current liabilities		200,000
Long-term liabilities		300,000
Contributed capital		350,000
Retained earnings		150,000
	1,000,000	1,000,000

On 12/31/19x2 Foreign Company had the following trial balance:

Foreign Company
Trial Balance (in pesos)
December 31, 19x2

Cash	70,000	
Accounts receivable (net)	330,000	
Inventory (at LIFO cost)	325,000	
Property, plant, and equipment (net)	255,000	
Current liabilities		190,000
Long-term liabilities		235,000
Contributed capital		350,000
Retained earnings		175,000
Revenues		750,000
Cost of goods sold	600,000	
Depreciation expense	85,000	
Other operating expenses	35,000	
	1,700,000	1,700,000

Additional information:

1. Revenues, purchases of merchandise and operating expenses all occurred evenly throughout the year.
2. The beginning retained earnings balance was $45,000 under the current rate method and $49,250 under the temporal method.
3. Foreign Company maintains a perpetual inventory system. The beginning inventory balance was 300,000 pesos. Assume all inventory layers are added uniformly through the period.
4. Using the current rate method the beginning balance in the cumulative translation adjustment account was $51,250.
5. No acquisitions or retirements of property, plant, and equipment occurred during the year.
6. No contributed capital transactions have occurred since 1/1/19x1
7. Selected exchange rates for one peso are as follows:

1/1/19x1	$0.25
Average for 19x1	0.30
12/31/19x1	0.35
Average for 19x2	0.40
12/31/19x2	0.45

Required: Complete the worksheet below to convert the Foreign Company's 12/31/19x2 trial balance into dollars assuming that the local foreign currency unit is the functional currency.

	Balance (in pesos)	Rate	Balance (in dollars)
Cash	70,000		
Accounts receivable (net)	330,000		
Inventory (at LIFO cost)	325,000		
Property, plant, and equipment (net)....	255,000		
Current liabilities .	(190,000)		
Long-term liabilities	(235,000)		
Contributed capital .	(350,000)		
Retained earnings ...	(175,000)		
Revenues	(750,000)		
Cost of goods sold ..	600,000		
Depreciation expense	85,000		
Other operating expenses	35,000		
Cumulative translation adjustment at beg. of year			
	-0-		
Addition to cumulative translation adjustment			-0-

224

2. Using the data from Exercise 1 complete the worksheet below to convert the Foreign Company's 12/31/19x2 trial balance to dollars assuming the US dollar is the Foreign Company's functional currency.

	Balance (in pesos)	Rate	Balance (in dollars)
Cash	70,000		
Accounts receivable (net)	330,000		
Inventory (at LIFO cost)	325,000		
Property, plant, and equipment (net)....	255,000		
Current liabilities .	(190,000)		
Long-term liabilities	(235,000)		
Contributed capital .	(350,000)		
Retained earnings ...	(175,000)		
Revenues	(750,000)		
Cost of goods sold ..	600,000		
Depreciation expense	85,000		
Other operating expenses	35,000		
Exchange gain or loss			
	-0-		-0-

True or False

1.	T	4.	T	7.	T	10.	F	13.	T
2.	F	5.	F	8.	T	11.	F	14.	F
3.	T	6.	F	9.	T	12.	F	15.	F

Exercises

1.

	Balance (in pesos)	Rate	Balance (in dollars)
Cash	70,000	0.45	31,500
Accounts receivable (net)	330,000	0.45	148,500
Inventory (at LIFO cost)	325,000	0.45	146,250
Property, plant, and equipment (net)........	255,000	0.45	114,750
Current liabilities	(190,000)	0.45	(85,500)
Long-term liabilities ...	(235,000)	0.45	(105,750)
Contributed capital	(350,000)	0.25	(87,500)
Retained earnings	(175,000)	x	(45,000)
Revenues	(750,000)	0.40	(300,000)
Cost of goods sold	600,000	0.40	240,000
Depreciation expense	85,000	0.40	34,000
Other operating expenses	35,000	0.40	14,000
Cumulative translation adjustment at beg. of year			(51,250)
Addition to cumulative translation adjustment			(54,000)
	-0-		-0-

2.

	Balance (in pesos)	Rate	Balance (in dollars)
Cash	70,000	0.45	31,500
Accounts receivable (net)	330,000	0.45	148,500
Inventory (at LIFO cost)	325,000	Note 1	86,250
Property, plant, and equipment (net)........	255,000	0.25	63,750
Current liabilities	(190,000)	0.45	(85,500)
Long-term liabilities ...	(235,000)	0.45	(105,750)
Contributed capital	(350,000)	0.25	(87,500)
Retained earnings	(175,000)	x	(49,250)
Revenues	(750,000)	0.40	(300,000)
Cost of goods sold	600,000	0.40	240,000
Depreciation expense	85,000	0.25	21,250
Other operating expenses	35,000	0.40	14,000
Exchange gain or loss ...			22,750
	-0-		-0-

Note 1:
Inventory conversion:

1/1/19x1 inventory.......	275,000	0.25	68,750
19x1 layer	25,000	0.30	7,500
19x2 layer	25,000	0.40	10,000
	325,000		86,250

Chapter 14
Additional Topics in
International Financial Reporting

Chapter Outline

I. Consolidated Financial Statements and the Equity Method for Domestic Parents and Foreign Subsidiaries--General Comments

   A. The first step in applying the equity method to or consolidating a foreign subsidiary is the conversion of the foreign financial statements into the domestic currency. This procedure was discussed in the previous chapter.

   B. A foreign subsidiary must be consolidated with its parent under <u>FASB Statement No. 94</u>, unless the parent's ability to control it is impaired.

II. Consolidations and Equity Method--Temporal Method

   A. Consolidations and equity method with no long-term intercompany payable presents only one intercompany account on the parent's books, namely the investment account.

      1. Differentials under the temporal method are calculated, allocated, and amortized using the historical exchange rate.

         a. The parent's share of the subsidiary's net assets at the spot rate on the day of acquisition (which becomes the historical rate) is subtracted from the parent's cost to determine the differential.

         b. The fair value and book value of the subsidiary's assets and liabilities are remeasured in dollars, and the differential is allocated to the differences between them. The unallocated differential becomes the goodwill.

         c. The allocated differences and the goodwill, both expressed in dollars, are amortized over their estimated remaining lives.

      2. Parent company entries under the equity method are the same for a foreign and domestic subsidiary.

         a. After the foreign subsidiary's net income has been remeasured, the parent records its share by debiting (crediting) the investment account and crediting (debiting) its equity in subsidiary earnings (loss).

b. The amortization of the differential is debited to the equity in subsidiary earnings and credited to the investment account.

3. The working paper entries are identical to entries consolidating a domestic subsidiary with the exception that the entry eliminating the investment account eliminates the remeasured amounts of the beginning equity balances. The entries are:

   a. The first entry eliminates the equity in subsidiary earnings and restores the investment account to its balance at the beginning of the year.

   b. The second entry eliminates the beginning balances in the investment account and the subsidiary's equity accounts. As mentioned above, the equity balances eliminated are the remeasured amounts.

   c. The differential is allocated to the assets and liabilities.

   d. The amortization of the differential is recorded.

4. Since the foreign subsidiary's net income under the temporal method includes the remeasurement gain or loss, such gains and losses are also included in consolidated net income.

B. Consolidations and equity method with a long-term intercompany payable present two intercompany accounts on the parent's balance sheet: the investment account and the long-term debt.

   1. If the long-term loan is denominated in the foreign currency, the gains and losses resulting from conversion in future years are accumulated in the Cumulative Foreign Exchange Translation Adjustments account in the equity section of the balance sheet.

   2. Parent company entries include additional entries relating to the Cumulative Foreign Exchange Translation Adjustment.

      a. The loss (gain) resulting from the conversion of the parent's long-term receivable at the current rate is debited (credited) on the parent's books to a Cumulative Foreign Exchange Translation Adjustment account and credited (debited) to the long-term receivable.

      b. The parent recognizes its share of the subsidiary's net income or loss with the usual entry.

228

c.   The amortization of the differential is recorded with the usual entry.

d.   In addition, the Cumulative Foreign Exchange Translation Adjustment recorded on the subsidiary's books is also recorded on the parent's books with an offsetting entry to the investment account.

   (1)   If the Cumulative Foreign Exchange Translation Adjustment account was credited on the subsidiary's books, it is also credited on the parent's books.

   (2)   If the subsidiary recorded a gain on its long-term payable, the parent must record a loss on its long-term receivable, and vice versa. The loss was debited in entry a, above, and is now credited with an offsetting debit to the investment account.

e.   Since a credit to the Cumulative Foreign Exchange Translation Adjustment account on the foreign subsidiary's books increases its total equity, a debit to the investment account restores the equality between the parent's investment and the subsidiary's equity.

f.   As a result of the above entries the Cumulative Foreign Exchange Translation Adjustment account on the parent's books has a zero balance.

g.   The translation gain or loss on the long-term receivable is not included in consolidated net income, but it is included in the investment account balance.

3.   The working paper entries in this case are as follows:

a.   The entry eliminating the equity in subsidiary earnings also eliminates the translation gain or loss from the investment account. If the investment account was debited for a translation gain, it is now credited and the Cumulative Foreign Exchange Translation Adjustment account is debited. This debit offsets the credit balance in the account in the subsidiary's balance sheet. As a result the consolidated balance sheet will not show a balance in the cumulative foreign exchange adjustment account.

b.   The entries eliminating the subsidiary's equity, allocating the differential, and amortizing the differential are the same as in A. 3., above.

229

       c.   In addition, the long-term receivable on the parent's books is eliminated against the long-term payable on the subsidiary's books.

    4.   In subsequent years the beginning balance in the Cumulative Foreign Exchange Translation Adjustment account in the subsidiary's balance sheet is eliminated along with the beginning balances in its equity accounts and the beginning balance in the investment account.

III. Consolidations and Equity Method--Current Rate Method

    A.   The calculation of the differential at acquisition is done in the foreign subsidiary's functional currency. For this purpose the parent's dollar investment is converted into the subsidiary's functional currency at the spot rate at acquisition.

        1.   As a result the difference between the parent's cost and its share of the subsidiary's net assets is the differential calculated in the subsidiary's functional currency.

        2.   The differential is then allocated to the differences between book value and fair value of the subsidiary's assets and liabilities computed in its functional currency with the balance allocated to goodwill.

        3.   Differential amortization is determined in the functional currency.

        4.   The differential amortization is converted into the reporting currency (i. e. the dollar) at the weighted average rate for the period.

            a.   Even when the amount of amortization is constant in the foreign currency, it varies in dollars when the weighted average rate changes.

            b.   Under the temporal method the amount of amortization is calculated in dollars and therefore remains constant.

        5.   The translation gain or loss related to the differential is calculated in the reporting currency. This calculation is similar to the calculation of translation and remeasurement gains and losses, discussed in the previous chapter.

            a.   The differential balance at the beginning of the year and changes caused by amortization during the year are calculated in the same manner as the net asset position and changes in it were calculated.

b.   These amounts are then multiplied by the difference in the current rate between the beginning and end of the year.

c.   Alternatively the beginning and ending balance of the differential can be multiplied by the differences in the current rate between the beginning and average rate and between the average and ending rate, respectively.

B.   Parent company entries are as follows:

1.   The parent recognizes its share of the subsidiary's net income (excluding the translation gain or loss) by debiting the investment account and crediting equity in subsidiary earnings.

2.   The differential amortization, as calculated in the functional currency and converted at the weighted average rate for the period, is debited to equity in subsidiary earnings and credited to the investment account.

3.   The parent records its share of the translation gain (loss) recorded on the subsidiary's books in the Cumulative Foreign Exchange Translation Adjustment account with a credit (debit) to its Cumulative Foreign Exchange Translation Adjustment account and an offsetting entry to the investment account. This entry adjusts the investment account for increases or decreases in the subsidiary's equity due to translation gains and losses accumulated in the Adjustment account.

4.   The translation gain (loss) on the differential is recorded with a credit (debit) to the Cumulative Foreign Exchange Translation Adjustment account and an offsetting entry to the investment account.

5.   The ending balance in the investment account can be determined as follows:

Beginning balance,

Add (deduct) parent's share of subsidiary's net income (loss) converted at the weighted average rate for the period,

Deduct (add) amortization of debit (credit) differential computed in the functional currency and converted at the weighted average rate for the period,

Add (deduct) parent's share of the subsidiary's translation gain (loss),

231

Add (deduct) translation gain (loss) on differential,

Equals ending balance.

C. The working paper entries are as follows:

1. The equity in subsidiary earnings and the balance in the Cumulative Foreign Exchange Translation Adjustment account are eliminated with the offsetting entry to the investment account.

2. The beginning balances of the subsidiary's equity and the beginning balance in the investment account are eliminated and the beginning balance of the differential is established.

3. The beginning balance of the differential is allocated to the undervalued and overvalued assets and liabilities, to the goodwill and to the translation gain or loss on the differential, as computed in A.5., above. For this entry the total translation gain or loss has to be divided among the assets and liabilities to which the differential is allocated. This entry can also be done in two entries:

    a. The translation gain (loss) is established with a credit (debit) and an offsetting entry to the differential.

    b. The differential balance is then allocated to the assets and liabilities, including goodwill.

4. Differential amortization is recorded in the usual way.

D. Consolidated net income is computed as follows:

Parent's net income from its own operations,

Add (deduct) parent's share of the subsidiary's net income (loss), excluding translation gains and losses,

Deduct differential amortization.

E. The elimination of the investment account in subsequent years includes the elimination of the subsidiary's cumulative foreign exchange translation adjustment account, since that account forms part of the subsidiary's equity. In addition, the beginning balance of the differential is established net of the parent's translation gains or losses on the differential balance.

F. Long-term intercompany payables and receivables may be denominated in the foreign currency or in dollars.

232

1. If they are denominated in the foreign currency, they pose no problem, since the transaction gains and losses related to this type of debt do not require special treatment.

2. If they are denominated in dollars, a problem arises since the payable on the subsidiary's books is converted at the current rate while the parent's receivable is stated in dollars. Any difference between the two balances should be treated as a receivable or payable until the debt is settled.

V. Consolidated Statement of Cash Flows

A. FASB Statement No. 95 allows both a direct and an indirect approach to preparing the statement of cash flows. Both approaches report cash flows from operating activities, investing activities, and financing activities.

B. The consolidated statement of cash flows under the temporal method uses the dollar balances from the subsidiary's income statement and balance sheet which were converted by using the temporal method.

1. The working paper for the consolidated statement of cash flows is prepared as follows:

   a. For cash provided by or used in operating activities the cash inflows and outflows (converted at the weighted average rate) net of the changes in the current receivables and payables (converted at the current rate at the end of the year).

   b. For cash used in investing activities asset acquisitions are converted at historical rates.

   c. For cash provided by financing activities a long-term loan from the parent is converted at the rate in effect when the loan was received.

   d. The remeasurement gain (loss) is added (subtracted) to arrive at the net change in cash and cash equivalents.

2. The reconciliation of net income with net cash provided by operating activities starts with net income, adds depreciation and amortization, adjusts for increases and decreases in current receivables and payables and adds (subtracts) the remeasurement loss (gain) to arrive at net cash provided by or used in operating activities.

3. The remeasurement gain or loss can be allocated to operating, investing, and financing activities by

233

computing the effect of changes in the exchange rate on the three cash flows.

C. The consolidated statement of cash flows under the current rate method uses the dollar balances from the subsidiary's income statement and balance sheet which were converted using the current rate method.

1. In the working paper for the consolidated statement of cash flows the effect of exchange rate changes on cash and cash equivalents must be computed and included in order to account for the increase or decrease in cash and cash equivalents between the beginning and end of the year.

2. In the reconciliation of net income with net cash provided by or used in operating activities the translation gain or loss does not appear, because it is not included in net income.

V. Hedges of Net Investment in a Foreign Entity

A. FASB Statement No. 52 defines hedges of net investments as transactions "designated as, and effective as, economic hedges of a net investment in a foreign entity." An example is a domestic parent selling its foreign subsidiary's functional currency and designating this sale as a hedge of its foreign currency exposure, i. e. the subsidiary's net asset position.

B. The entries made to record a hedge of a net investment are:

1. To record the hedge at the forward rate:
   Dollars Due from Exchange Broker
       Foreign Currency Due to Exchange Broker

2. To record purchase of foreign currency at the spot rate:
   Foreign Currency on Hand
       Cash

3. To record collection from broker:
   Cash
       Dollars Due from Exchange Broker

4. To record delivery of the foreign currency to the broker:
   Foreign Currency Due to Exchange Broker
       Foreign Currency on Hand
   To balance debit or credit Cumulative Foreign Exchange Translation Adjustments

C. Such a hedge will offset, wholly or in part, the translation gains and losses recorded by the subsidiary in its Cumulative Foreign Exchange Translation Adjustment account.

234

D. If the spot and forward rates of the foreign currency differ, the premium or discount is amortized over the life of the forward exchange contract and recognized in the income statement or in the Cumulative Foreign Exchange Translation Adjustment account (provided the net amount of the domestic company's gain or loss and the amortization does not exceed the foreign entity's translation gain or loss).

VI. Elimination of Unconfirmed Profits

A. When parents and subsidiaries engage in transactions resulting in unconfirmed profits, the question arises as to which exchange rate to use. FASB Statement No. 52 advocates using the rate in effect on the date of sale or transfer.

B. Subsequent changes in the exchange rate do not affect the elimination of unconfirmed profits.

VII. Segmental Disclosures Related to Operations of Consolidated Foreign Subsidiaries and Export Sales

A. According to FASB Statement No. 14 regarding segmental reporting an entity's foreign operations include its revenue producing operations which are located outside the firm's home country and which generate revenue either from sales to unaffiliated customers or from intra-enterprise sales or transfers between geographic areas.

B. Segmental disclosure is required if the foreign subsidiaries meet the 10 percent revenue or the 10 percent asset test.

VIII. Disclosures Related to Previously and Currently Unconsolidated Foreign Subsidiaries

A. Accounting Research Bulletin No. 51 allowed an exception to the general rule that subsidiaries are to be consolidated if the assets and net income of foreign subsidiaries are subject to controls and exchange restrictions.

B. FASB Statement No. 94 narrows the exception to cases in which the parent's ability to control the subsidiary is impaired by the foreign government.

C. For previously unconsolidated subsidiaries summarized information about the assets, liabilities, and results of operations must be provided.

D. The Statement does not make clear whether such summarized information is required for currently unconsolidated subsidiaries. In these cases the requirements of APB Opinion No. 18 should be followed. They call for the disclosure of summarized data about the assets, liabilities, and operating results of unconsolidated subsidiaries.

IX. Consolidated Financial Statements--A Worldwide View

A. Important issues in national and transnational financial reporting is whether consolidated statements are to be prepared for companies and their local subsidiaries and whether foreign subsidiaries are to be consolidated.

B. In the US a majority-owned foreign subsidiary is consolidated unless the parent's ability to control the subsidiary is impaired.

C. In other countries these issues may be resolved differently. In general, the relatively highly developed countries tend to consolidate local and foreign subsidiaries, while the less developed countries do not.

D. Consolidated financial statements are prepared because:

1. They are required by policy setting bodies in the private sector, such as the FASB.

2. They are required by law, as will be the case in the European Economic Community beginning in the 1990s.

3. They are advocated by the International Accounting Standards Committee (IASC) as part of its efforts to harmonize financial accounting standards.

a. In 1976 the IASC issued its International Accounting Standard No. 3 on Consolidated Financial Statements.

b. IAS No. 3 was mostly superseded in 1989 by IAS No. 27 which advocates consolidations for a group. It defines a group as a parent and all of its subsidiaries. A subsidiary is defined as a company controlled by another company.

4. The IASC's definition of control includes, in addition to ownership of over half of the voting stock of an affiliate, agreements with other investors and other arrangements permitting the parent to exercise power over the board of directors.

5. Although current US practice defines control as direct or indirect ownership of more than 50 percent of the affiliate's voting stock, FASB Statement No. 94 suggests that the FASB may broaden this definition in the future.

X. An Introduction to International Financial Accounting

A. Financial accounting standard setting in the US is the responsibility of the FASB. The process used by the FASB may be described as a due process procedure. Its goal is to ensure the presentation of information that is useful in making economic decisions.

B.   The international counterpart to the FASB is the IASC. It was formed in 1973 and now represents about 100 accounting organizations from about 75 countries. The functions of the IASC are: (1) to develop international financial accounting standards required for unqualified attestations on financial statements, (2) to promote the worldwide acceptance of these standards, and (3) to work toward the harmonization of financial accounting standards.

C.   IASC standards are approved by its board which consists of thirteen representatives from its member professional accounting organizations and up to four representatives from non-accounting international organizations with an interest in financial reporting. This diversity is designed to provide representation to a variety of interests, similar to the FASB.

D.   The pronouncements of the IASC are called International Accounting Standards (IAS). To date approximately 30 standards have been issued.

E.   The IASC standard setting process is a due process procedure designed to ensure that the interests of affected parties are represented. The IASC's process resembles that of the FASB, although it is not as involved. It includes a steering committee, preliminary drafts exposed for comments by the members, revisions of the drafts, exposure drafts exposed for additional comments, and finally a standard approved by a 3/4 vote of the IASC board.

F.   To gain acceptance of its standards the IASC strategy is for its members to: (1) promote consistency between IASC and national standards, (2) encourage the adoption of IASC standards in countries which do not have their own standards, (3) encourage the elimination of inconsistencies between existing national and IASC standards, and (4) encourage changes in the laws of countries that contain reporting requirements differing from IASC standards.

G.   The IASC was formed primarily to harmonize financial accounting standards. Three concepts of harmonization are:

   1.   Absolute harmonization means one set of accounting standards applies, regardless of the conditions leading to the production of accounting information.

   2.   Circumstantial harmonization means the same set of accounting standards applies when the underlying conditions are similar.

3. Purposive harmonization add the purpose of the accounting information to the underlying set of conditions considered.

H. Despite the benefits of harmonization, the IASC has experienced only limited success in achieving acceptance of its standards. Reasons for this situation include, among others, the incorporation of accounting procedures into law in many countries, the absence of a conceptual framework, and the inability of the IASC to require compliance with its standards.

I. International financial reporting differences are due to educational, socio-cultural, political, legal, and economic differences. Absolute harmonization is opposed because it would ignore these differences. In this view financial accounting develops in response to the evolution of its immediate environment. Since the environment of countries differs, their financial accounting systems also differ. This also means that countries with similar environments have similar financial accounting systems. Three such groups of countries with similar environments are:

1. The British-American model emphasizes a private sector approach to standard setting and the provision of information that is useful in making economic decisions. This model is used by more nations than any other. Countries in this group include, besides Great Britain and the US, British Commonwealth countries.

2. The continental model is a legalistic model. It is based on legal requirements designed to satisfy various governmental information needs. This group includes all western European countries and Japan.

3. The South American model is designed to compensate for the effects of high inflation rates. It aims to satisfy the needs of governmental units and to aid the decisions of individuals. This group includes such high-inflation countries as Argentina, Brazil, Bolivia, and Peru.

J. National financial reporting practices vary significantly, even among countries using the same model. Research has found many differences even among highly developed countries, especially in accounting for general price level changes, accounting for subsidiaries and other investees, the conversion of foreign entity financial statements and interperiod income tax allocation.

K. Transnational financial reporting is of primary concern to multinational companies. The main factors affecting transnational reporting seem to be global financing strategies and transnational investing activities.

1. Multinationals involved in global financing strategies list their securities on foreign stock exchanges and issue bonds in foreign countries.

2. Transnational investing activities are engaged in by parties purchasing the securities of multinationals.

3. The global financing strategies and transnational investing activities create information demands by financial statement users.

L. Multinational companies engage in the following practices to satisfy varying transnational financial reporting demands:

1. They utilize their existing financial statements.

2. They prepare convenience translations of their existing financial statements into the user's language without changing the currency unit or the accounting standards used.

3. The prepare convenience financial statements by translating their existing financial statements into the user's language and currency unit without changing the accounting standards used.

4. They restate financial statements on a limited basis.

   a. This may be done by providing a reconciliation of its existing net income with its net income calculated under the user's accounting standards. Under this method enough information may be given to allow restatement of the multinational's balance sheet.

   b. It may also be done by restating selected financial statement items under the user's accounting standards.

5. They prepare secondary financial statements by recasting their existing financial statements employing the user's language, currency unit, and accounting standards.

6. They prepare financial statements consistent with universally applicable accounting standards by developing one set of financial statements using what the company considers a superior set of accounting standards.

M. For US companies their existing financial statements are often sufficient since English is a widely understood language, the dollar is an internationally known currency, and US financial accounting standards are highly respected.

239

Test Your Understanding of Chapter 14

True or False

Instructions: Indicate your choice by circling either T, if you think the statement is true, or F, if you think the statement is false.

T F 1. The first step in preparing consolidated financial statements for a domestic parent and its foreign subsidiary is the conversion of the foreign company's financial statements into the domestic currency.

T F 2. Under the temporal method the differential at acquisition is computed in the reporting currency.

T F 3. Under the temporal method the differential amortization is converted into dollars using the weighted average rate for the period.

T F 4. Under the temporal method the parent records its share of the subsidiary's translation gain with a debit to the investment account and a credit to the Cumulative Foreign Exchange Translation Adjustment account.

T F 5. Under the temporal method a long-term loan by the parent to its foreign subsidiary which is denominated in the foreign currency is converted using the historical exchange rate.

T F 6. Under the current rate method the foreign subsidiary's translation gain or loss is not included in consolidated net income.

T F 7. When a credit to the Cumulative Foreign Exchange Translation Adjustment account is recorded by the subsidiary, the parent should debit its investment account for its share of such a credit.

T F 8. Under the current rate method the translation gain or loss on the differential is allocated to the Cumulative Foreign Exchange Translation Adjustment account in the working papers.

T F 9. Under the current rate method net income must be adjusted for the translation gain or loss in the reconciliation of net income with net cash provided by operating activities.

T F 10. Gains and losses on hedges of net investments in a foreign entity are not recognized in net income.

T F 11. Under the current rate method unconfirmed profits from intercompany transactions are eliminated at the current rate.

T F 12. Consolidated financial statements are required in all highly developed countries.

T F 13. For segmental disclosures the operations of foreign subsidiaries must meet the 10 percent tests for revenues, operating profit or loss, and assets.

T F 14. The IASC issues International Accounting Standards.

T F 15. Under absolute harmonization one set of accounting standards would apply worldwide.

Exercises

1. On 1/1/19x1 Domestic Company purchased 100 percent of the outstanding stock of Canadian Company for $350,000 cash. Presented below are the trial balances of Canadian Company at 1/1/19x1 and 12/31/19x1.

	1/1/19x1	12/31/19x1
Cash and Receivables	C$140,000	C$210,000
Property, Plant, and Equipment (net)	200,000	180,000
Land	40,000	40,000
Depreciation Expense		20,000
Operating Expenses		550,000
Current Liabilities	(120,000)	(90,000)
Capital stock	(100,000)	(100,000)
Retained Earnings	(160,000)	(160,000)
Service Revenue...............		(650,000)
Totals	-0-	-0-

Additional information:

(1) On 1/1/19x1 fair values of the property, plant, and equipment and of the land were C$240,000 and C$100,000, respectively. The property, plant, and equipment have a remaining life of 10 years. Goodwill, if any, has a 20 year life.

(2) The exchange rates for the Canadian dollar for 19x1 were:

1/1/19x1 spot rate	.8625
12/31/19x1 spot rate	.8876
Weighted average rate	.8765

Required: a. Compute and allocate the differential at acquisition and determine differential amortization for 19x1 assuming that the temporal method is used.

b.   Compute net income using the temporal method.

c.   Use your answers to a and b, above, and make the entries for 19x1 on Domestic Company's books under the equity method.

d.   Compute and allocate the differential at acquisition and determine differential amortization for 19x1 assuming that the current rate method is used.

e.   Compute net income using the current rate method.

f.   Use your answers to d and e, above, and make the entries for 19x1 on Domestic Company's books under the equity method.

Solutions to Chapter 14 Exercises

True or False

1.	T	4.	F	7.	T	10.	T	13.	F
2.	T	5.	F	8.	F	11.	F	14.	T
3.	F	6.	T	9.	F	12.	F	15.	T

Exercises

a.
Domestic Company's cost $350,000
Less Canadian Company's net assets (260,000 x
 .8625) .... (224,250)
Differential $125,750
Less allocation:
  Property, plant, and equipment [240,000 -
  200,000) x .8625] .... (34,500)
  Land [(100,000 - 40,000) x .8625] .... (51,750)
Goodwill .... $ 39,500

Amortization:
Property, plant, and equipment: $34,500 : 10 years = $3,450
Goodwill: $39,500 : 20 years = $1,975

b.
Service revenue (650,000 x .8765)................. $569,725
Less operating expenses (550,000 x .8765) .... (482,075)
Less depreciation expense (20,000 x .8625) .... (17,250)
Net income before remeasurement gain.............. $ 70,400
Remeasurement gain (plug to arrive at net income). 1,612
Net income*....................................... $ 72,012

*Cash & receivables (C$210,000 x .8876) $186,396
Property, plant, & equipment (C$180,000 x .8625).. 155,250
Land (C$40,000 x .8625 34,500
Current liabilities (C$90,000 x .8876) .... (79,884)
Capital stock (C$100,000 x .8625) .... (86,250
Retained earnings (C$160,000 x .8625) .... (138,000)
Increase in equity (equals net income) .... $ 72,012

c.
Investment in Canadian Company   350,000
     Cash   350,000
To record acquisition of 100% of Canadian Company

Investment in Canadian Company   72,012
     Equity in Canadian Earnings   72,012
To record equity in Canadian earnings

Equity in Canadian Earnings   5,425
     Investment in Canadian Company   5,425
To record differential amortization

d. Domestic Company's cost ($350,000 : .8625) .... C$405,797
    Less Canadian Company's net assets ....   (260,000)
    Differential .... C$145,797
    Less allocation:
      Property, plant, and equipment (240,000 - 200,000) (40,000)
      Land (100,000 - 40,000) ....   (60,000)
    Goodwill .... C$ 45,797

    Amortization:
    Property, plant, and equipment: C$ 40,000 : 10 years =
        C$4,000 x .8876 = $3,550
    Goodwill: C$45,797 : 20 years = C$2,290 x .8876 = $2,033

e. Service revenue (650,000 x .8765) $569,725
    Less operating expenses (550,000 x .8765) ....   (482,075)
    Less depreciation expense (20,000 x .8765) ......   (17,530)
    Net income .... $ 70,120

f. Investment in Canadian Company   350,000
          Cash   350,000
    To record acquisition of 100% of Canadian Company

    Investment in Canadian Company   70,120
          Equity in Canadian Earnings   70,120
    To record equity in Canadian earnings

    Equity in Canadian Earnings   5,583
          Investment in Canadian Company   5,583
    To record differential amortization (3550 + 2,033)

    Investment in Canadian Company   7,414
          Cumulative Foreign Exchange Trans-
              lation Adjustment   7,414
    To record translation gain:
    Gain on beginning net assets [260,000 x (.8625-.8765)] = $3,640
    Gain on ending net assets [340,000 x (.8765 - .8876)]   =   3,774
    Total translation gain $7,414

Chapter 15
Formation and Operation of Partnerships

Chapter Outline

I.   Nature of a Partnership

   A.   Aggregate versus entity concept

      1.   Section 6 of the Uniform Partnership Act (UPA) defines a partnership as "an association of two or more persons to carry on as co-owners a business for profit."

      2.   This definition suggests an aggregative, or proprietary, perspective in that a partnership is viewed as the summation of the rights and responsibilities of the individual partners.

      3.   In general, the UPA provides that individual partners are jointly liable for the debts and obligations of the business.

      4.   However, the UPA's dominant theme is that a partnership is a legal entity, separate and distinct from the owners, i. e. the legal concept. Some of the provisions which support this point of view are:

         a.   In the event of liquidation partnership creditors have priority rights to the partnership assets, whereas personal creditors of the partners have priority rights to the partners' personal assets.

         b.   Title to partnership assets may be vested in the partnership name.

         c.   A clear distinction is drawn between the partners' rights to partnership assets and their interests in the partnership entity.

         d.   Continuity of the partnership organization may exist under certain circumstances.

      5.   Partnership accounting practice seems to reflect the aggregative concept. Support for this position comes from law and provisions of the Internal Revenue Code. Two examples illustrate the basic proprietary emphasis of the Code:

         a.   When a partner contributes assets to the partnership, the existing tax bases transfer to the partnership, regardless of current market values.

b. Income taxes are levied on the partners' shares of periodic partnership net income, not on the partnership.

B. Partnership agreement

1. The partnership agreement may be a written or an oral contract. The written contract, called the articles of partnership, or copartnership, is preferable.

2. The articles of partnership should describe the agreed upon rights and responsibilities of the partners and the nature of their relations with outside parties.

3. Although the UPA has been adopted by most states, many of its provisions may be superseded by contrary provisions in the articles of partnership.

4. The articles of partnership should specify the purpose of the partnership, management rights and authority, and causes of dissolution.

5. The partnership agreement should clearly delineate the partners' intent regarding all aspects of the business. Among the more important accounting-related issues that should be addressed in the partnership agreement are the following:

a. The valuation of assets contributed to the partnership should be described.

b. A distinction should be made between initial capital balances and subsequent profits and losses.

c. The basis for dividing partnership profits should be clearly stated. This includes allocations based on capital balances and/or services performed by partners. If this provision is omitted from the partnership agreement, the UPA states that all partners share equally.

d. If capital balances are used in profit distributions, the following questions should be answered:

(1) Is the capital balance used for distribution the initial balance or is it adjusted for subsequent contributions, profits, and/or withdrawals?

(2) If an adjusted capital balance is used, is it the beginning, average, or ending balance for the year?

(3)   If it is the average balance, how is the
average computed?

e.   The UPA provides that losses are to be shared in
the profit-sharing ratio. If partners are to be
shielded from losses, special loss-sharing ratios
should be established.

f.   The bases for calculating the monetary equity of a
withdrawing partner should be described.

g.   If net income and the partners' drawing accounts
are closed to their capital accounts, the closing
sequence should be stated.

II. Partnership Formation

A.   Recording the initial contributions

1.   If a pre-existing business becomes part of a
partnership, its accounting records may become the
foundation for the partnerships' accounting records;
otherwise new accounting records must be set up for the
partnership.

2.   The assets of a pre-existing business are normally
appraised when they are transferred to a new business
entity. Their previous book values may not adequately
reflect their fair values when the new accounting
entity is established.

3.   At formation, the accounting records should contain all
assets contributed by the partners, the liabilities
assumed, and the partners' dollar interest in capital.
Assets contributed to a new partnership should be
appraised to establish their fair market values.

4.   At formation the initial capital balances of the
partners must be agreed upon, especially if assets
other than cash are contributed.

a.   The initial balances may be the differences
between the fair values of assets contributed less
liabilities assumed by the partnership.

b.   If the partners are supposed to have equal capital
balances, two solutions are possible:

(1)   Part of one partner's capital balance may be
transferred to another partner to compensate
for intangible assets contributed. This
method is referred to as the bonus method.

(2)   Alternatively, the intangible assets
contributed by one partner may be recorded on

the partnership books. Since they are generally called goodwill, this method is known as the goodwill method.

B.   Income tax considerations

1.   A partnership is not assessed an income tax on its earnings; however, partnership income is allocated to the partners as if they individually earned it. The partners are then taxed on their share of the profits, whether distributed or not.

2.   Two values particularly relevant to the initial formation of a partnership are:

a.   The tax basis of the assets contributed to the partnership, and

b.   The tax basis of the partners' dollar interest in the partnership.

3.   The tax bases of contributed assets are carried over from a pre-existing business or from individual partners making the contribution. The tax bases usually do not equal the fair market values used for financial accounting purposes.

4.   The tax basis of a partner's interest in capital equals the sum of the tax bases of the assets contributed by the partner, increased by the liabilities of other partners which the partner assumes, and decreased by the partner's personal liabilities assumed by other partners.

5.   The sum of the tax bases of the partnership assets equals the sum of the tax bases of the partners' individual interests in capital.

III. Partnership Operations

A.   Accounting for partnership operations is similar to accounting for other profit-oriented businesses. Net income is determined in the usual manner by relating period revenues and expenses. For this purpose the partnership is treated as a separate accounting entity.

B.   Nature and amount of relative interests

1.   A partner can be both a debtor or creditor to the partnership and also have a capital interest in the partnership. Although these distinctions may seem arbitrary, they can influence the financial statements of the partnership.

248

2. Amounts advanced by a partner that are to be repaid should be classified as a partnership liability. Amounts advanced by the business to a partner that are to be repaid should be classified as a partnership receivable. Partnership net income normally reflects interest expense or interest income resulting from advances.

3. A partner's capital interest is represented by her/his balances in the drawing and capital accounts. The drawing account is debited for the amount of the partner's periodic withdrawal of cash or other assets. The drawing account is credited (debited) at the end of the period for the partner's share of the partnership net income (loss). This is part of the entry closing the income summary account.

4. The capital account initially reflects the dollar investment of a partner. It is subsequently adjusted for the amount of permanent additional investments and withdrawals in excess of the regular drawings. A partner's drawing account may be closed annually to his/her capital account.

C. Allocating net income to partners

1. Allocation of partnership income is not a distribution of cash or other assets; the periodic withdrawal of assets by partners is a separate matter to be determined by the partners.

2. The three most popular bases for allocating partnership net income are:

   a. Specified ratios.

   b. Relative capital investments of the partners.

   c. Service contributions of the partners.

3. In the absence of contrary provisions profits and losses are shared equally under the UPA. If desired, the partners may agree to other ratios, e. g. 3:1 or 75 percent to one partner and 25 percent to the other one.

4. If capital is an income-producing factor, partners may wish to be rewarded for their relative investments of capital. If so, the partnership agreement must state how these capital balances are to be determined. If average or ending capital balances are to be used, the treatment of withdrawals, or amounts available for withdrawal, should be settled. In addition, the interest rate to be used must be indicated. The total partnership profits may be distributed on the basis of capital balances, but it is more common to provide a

reasonable return on capital investments and to distribute the remaining profit on some other basis.

5. Differences in the partners' service contributions may be recognized by including salary allowances in the income allocation process. Whereas salaries paid to executives are expenses of a corporation, the salary allowances of partners are not treated as expenses but as profit distributions.

6. These three bases may be combined in various ways to form an income allocation process. For instance, each partner may receive interest on the average capital balance, some partners may receive varying amounts of salary allowances, and the remainder is distributed in a predetermined ratio.

D. Order of distribution

1. If periodic earnings are insufficient to cover the allowances prescribed in the partnership agreement, two alternatives are possible:

   a. Full allowances are recognized, and the difference between the sum of the allowances and the period's profit or loss is allocated according to the residual profit or loss sharing ratio.

   b. The sequence of distributing allowances (e. g. salaries first, then interest on capital balances) is prescribed, and income is distributed only as long as it is available. The process concludes with an allocation based on the relative proportions of the salary allowances or the interest allowances, depending on which one is involved when income is exhausted.

2. The first of the above two methods is generally used in practice. Since the results under the two methods can be very different, the order of distribution should be stated in the partnership agreement.

E. Correction of prior years' net income

1. Pronouncements of the FASB regarding prior period adjustments do not necessarily apply to partnerships.

2. For a partnership the decision whether to treat an item as a prior period adjustment or as part of current net income makes no difference if:

   a. The present partners also were the partners in the year to which the adjustments relate; and

b. Income is distributed currently in the same way as in the previous period.

3. If income allocation is directly affected by the prior period adjustment decision, the agreed upon will of the partners should dominate over the pronouncements of the accounting rule-making bodies.

4. In general, the following alternatives have some support for treating partnership prior period adjustments:

   a. An immaterial amount may be absorbed in the current period's net income.

   b. A material amount that is not easily identified with a specific prior period may be either absorbed into the current period's income or arbitrarily allocated to prior periods, depending on the partners' decision.

   c. A material amount that is identified with a specific period may involve the recomputation and reallocation of net income for the affected periods.

F. Financial statement presentation

1. Because partners' salaries and interest on capital are not factors in calculating partnership net income, they are traditionally presented in a schedule at the bottom of the income statement to show how income is allocated among the partners.

2. Changes in partners' capital balances are summarized in a separate statement. This statement reports each partner's beginning capital balance, adjustments for additional investments and withdrawals made during the period, and each partner's share of the profit or loss.

3. A partnership balance sheet discloses assets and liabilities in the traditional manner; however, the owners' equity simply reports the ending capital balance for each partner. Because the simplification may obscure useful information, it has been suggested that the equity section be expanded to disclose separately each partner's invested capital and share of accumulated (undistributed) profits.

Test Your Understanding of Chapter 15

True or False

Instructions: Indicate your choice by circling either T, if you think the statement is true, or F, if you think the statement is false.

T F 1. A partnership is an association of two or more persons who are co-owners of a profit-oriented business.

T F 2. Although elements of both the proprietary approach and the entity approach may be found in provisions of the UPA, its dominant position is that a partnership is a legal entity, separate and distinct from its owners.

T F 3. Partnership accounting practice generally reflects the proprietary, or aggregative approach, and is strongly influenced by law and the Internal Revenue Code.

T F 4. Partnerships themselves are not subject to income taxes, however, the individual partners have to pay income taxes on their share of the partnership profit.

T F 5. Articles of copartnership may successfully override certain provisions of the UPA.

T F 6. When an owner contributes assets to the partnership, the assets' tax bases to the partnership equal their previous tax bases to the contributing partner.

T F 7. According to the UPA, a partner must share partnership losses in the same relative proportion that the partner shares partnership profits.

T F 8. If a partnership is started by the combination of two sole proprietorships, it is generally preferable for the contributed assets to be entered on the partnership accounting records at their existing book values at the date of formation.

T F 9. In general, accounting for partnership operations is substantially different from accounting for sole proprietorships or corporations.

T F 10. If a partner invests cash in a partnership, the classification of this transaction as a loan (liability) or as a capital contribution (equity) has no potential significance for the computation of periodic net income.

T F 11. A partner's capital account is ordinarily credited for capital investments and debited for withdrawals in excess of an agreed upon drawing allowance, provided these transactions are intended to be permanent.

T F 12. Interest allowances on partners' capital balances are not deductible in the determination of partnership net income, but interest on partner's loan balances is deductible.

T F 13. Normally, partners' salary allowances are treated as an allocation of net income and not as a determinant of net income. That is, they are not deducted from gross profit during the calculation of partnership net income.

T F 14. If net income is insufficient to cover the partners' agreed upon salary allowances and interest allowances, the UPA specifies that net income is to be allocated in proportion to the partner's ending capital balances.

T F 15. The decision whether to treat an error as a prior period adjustment or as an item in the current period's net income should always reflect the pronouncements of the accounting rule-making bodies and not the desires of the partners.

Exercises

1. On August 1, 19x1, Ann Green and Bob Brown formed a partnership by combining the operations of their separate businesses. The following assets and liabilities were transferred to the AB Company:

| | Ann Green | | Bob Brown | |
	Book Value	Fair Value	Book Value	Fair Value
Cash	$ 10,000	$ 10,000	$ 5,000	$ 5,000
Accounts receivable (net)	30,000	28,000	20,000	20,000
Inventory	50,000	52,000	75,000	80,000
Equipment (net)	100,000	120,000	100,000	125,000
Building (net)	100,000	100,000		
Land	10,000	40,000		
	$300,000	$350,000	$200,000	$230,000
Accounts payable	$ 40,000	$ 40,000	$ 10,000	$ 10,000
Notes payable	80,000	80,000	40,000	40,000

The partners agreed to accept joint responsibility for all liabilities transferred to the partnership.

Required: a. Prepare the journal entry to record the formation of
the partnership using fair market values of the assets contributed.

b. Prepare the journal entry to record the formation of the
partnership using the tax bases of the assets contributed.

. The articles of copartnership for the accounting firm of Debit and
Credit specify that income is allocated as follows:

1) Annual salary allowances of $20,000 and $40,000 for Debit and
   Credit, respectively.
2) A 10 percent interest allowance based on each partner's beginning
   capital balance.
3) Remaining income is allocated in a 2: 1 ratio between Debit and
   Credit.

The beginning capital balances of Debit and Credit were $100,000 and
150,000, respectively. Each partner withdrew $2,000 per month in
9x1.

Required: a. Allocate the partnership net income of $94,000
according to the above plan.

. Using your solution to part a, prepare the journal entries to
  close the income summary and the drawing accounts.

. Allocate the partnership net income of $70,000, assuming that all
  allowances are recognized in full.

Solutions to Chapter 15 Exercises

True or False

1. T	4. T	7. T	10. F	13. T
2. T	5. T	8. F	11. T	14. F
3. T	6. T	9. F	12. T	15. F

Exercises

1. a.

Cash	15,000
Accounts receivable	48,000
Inventory	132,000
Equipment	245,000
Building	100,000
Land	40,000
Accounts payable	50,000
Notes payable	120,000
Ann Green, capital	230,000
Bob Brown, capital	180,000

1. b.

Cash	15,000
Accounts receivable	50,000
Inventory	125,000
Equipment	200,000
Building	100,000
Land	10,000
Ann Green, capital	265,000*
Bob Brown, capital	235,000**

* (10,000 + 30,000 + 50,000 + 100,000 + 100,000 + 10,000) + (.5 x 50,000) - (.5 x 120,000) = 300,000 + 25,000 - 60,000 = 265,000
** (5,000 + 20,000 + 75,000 + 100,000) + (.5 x 120,000) - (.5 x 50,000) = 200,000 + 60,000 - 25,000 = 235,000

2. a.

	Debit	Credit	Total
Salary allowances	$20,000	$40,000	$60,000
Interest allowances ..	10,000	15,000	25,000
	$30,000	$55,000	$85,000
Remainder 2: 1	6,000	3,000	9,000
	$36,000	$58,000	$94,000

2. b.

Income summary	94,000	
Green, drawing		36,000
Brown, drawing		58,000
Green, drawing (36,000 - 24,000) ...	12,000	
Brown, drawing (58,000 - 24,000) ...	34,000	
Green, capital		12,000
Brown, capital		34,000

2. c.

	Debit	Credit	Total
Salary allowances	$20,000	$40,000	$60,000
Interest allowances ..	10,000	15,000	25,000
	$30,000	$55,000	$85,000
Remainder 2: 1	(10,000)	(5,000)	(15,000)
	$20,000	$50,000	$70,000

Chapter 16
Realignment of Ownership Structure

Chapter Outline

I. Basic Legal Provisions

    A.   Under the common law any change in the ownership structure of a partnership causes its dissolution, although a new partnership is often formed. As a consequence of a legal dissolution the partners' equity and taxable income may have to be determined.

    B.   The Uniform Partnership Act defines dissolution as "the change in the relation of the partners caused by any partner ceasing to be associated in the carrying on as distinguished from the winding up of the business."

    C.   Legal dissolution may have many causes, including:

        1.   The partnership's completion of a designated term of existence or a particular undertaking.

        2.   The express will of any partner (if no term of existence is contained in the agreement).

        3.   The death of a partner.

        4.   A court decree.

        5.   The bankruptcy of any partner or the partnership.

    D.   Accounting for three, not mutually exclusive, acts of dissolution is reviewed in the following major sections:

        1.   Admission of a new partner;

        2.   Retirement of a partner; and

        3.   Death of a partner.

II. Admission of a New Partner

    A.   A new partner may be admitted to the partnership by either contributing assets directly to the business thereby increasing partnership net assets, or by buying an ownership interest directly from one or more of the existing partners. In this case assets pass between the old and new partners usually without affecting the partnership's net assets.

    B.   Prior to the admission of a new partner three types of assets should be analyzed:

1. Existing assets on the partnership books should be appraised to establish their current market values. Whether or not these market values are recorded on the partnership books, they should be considered in the negotiations with the new partner(s).

2. Unrecorded partnership assets include identifiable intangible assets and goodwill.

3. The assets to be contributed by the new partner should be valued, including any goodwill contributed by the new partner.

C. The differences resulting from the revaluation of the existing net assets of the partnership should be allocated to the old partners in their old profit and loss ratio.

D. The admission of a new partner with a payment to the partnership can be recorded in several different ways, depending on the market value of the assets contributed and the capital balance credited to the new partner.

1. The net assets contributed by the new partner equal the new partner's interest in the total partnership equity. This case can be handled in two ways:

   a. The existing assets are adjusted to current values with an offsetting entry to the old partner's capital accounts. The new assets are debited at market value and the new partner is credited for this amount. For example: The partnership net assets are valued at $40,000. To obtain a 1/3 interest in the new net assets, the new partner contributes assets worth $20,000. The new partner's capital balance is 1/3 of $40,000 + 20,000 = $20,000.

   b. No entry is made to adjust the old assets to current values. In this case the assets contributed by the new partner are recorded at market value, while the new partner's capital account is credited for his or her interest in the total recorded net assets. The difference between the market value of the contributed assets and the credit to the new partner's capital account is credited to the old partners in their old profit and loss ratio. To continue the above example: If the old assets with a book value of $34,000 are not written up to their fair value of $40,000, the new net assets will equal only $54,000 ($34,000 + $20,000 contributed assets). The new partner's interest is 1/3 of $54,000 or $18,000. The difference of $2,000 is allocated to the old partners in their old profit and loss ratio.

2. The net assets contributed by the new partner exceed
    the new partner's interest in the total net assets of
    the partnership. To continue the above example: IF
    the new partner contributes assets worth $26,000 for a
    1/3 interest, his or her capital interest will be 1/3
    of $66,000 ($40,000 fair value of old net assets +
    $26,000) or $22,000. The implication is that the
    partnership has unrecorded assets, i. e. goodwill.
    This case can be recorded in two ways:

    a. Under the bonus method the difference between the
        debit to the assets contributed at fair value and
        the credit to the new partner's capital account is
        credited to the old partners in their old profit
        and loss ratio. The old partners are said to
        receive a bonus in this instance.

    b. Under the goodwill method the unrecorded goodwill
        is recorded and credited to the old partners in
        their old profit and loss ratio. The amount of
        goodwill is computed by one of the following
        methods:

        (1) Let C equal the total new capital of the
             firm, including the as yet undetermined
             goodwill, and solve the following two
             equations:

             (a) (Fractional interest in capital retained
                  by the old partners) x C = total
                  recorded capital balances of old
                  partners. To continue the above
                  example: 2/3(C) = $40,000; C = $60,000.

             (b) (Fractional interest in capital obtained
                  by the new partner) x C = investment of
                  new partner. In the above example:
                  1/3(C) = $26,000; C = $78,000.

        (2) The implied goodwill is obtained by
             subtracting the new net assets (including the
             assets contributed by the new partner) from
             the total new capital, as computed above. If
             (a) is larger, the new partner is assumed to
             contribute goodwill. If (b) is larger, the
             old partnership is assumed to have goodwill.

        (3) Computation of goodwill in the above example:
             New capital under (b) = $78,000 - $40,000
             (old net assets) - $26,000 (net assets
             contributed by new partner) = $12,000
             goodwill.

        (4) The total goodwill in this case can also be
             obtained by dividing the new partner's excess

259

payment by his or her interest in the partnership. In the above example the excess payment is $4,000 [$26,000 of assets contributed - $22,000 (1/3 of recorded net assets of $66,000)], the new partner's interest is 1/3. $4,000 : 1/3 = $12,000 goodwill.

3.   The new partner's interest in the total partnership net assets exceeds the fair value of the assets contributed by the new partner. The implication in this case is that the new partner is contributing goodwill to the firm. In the above example: The new partner contributes assets worth $14,000 and receives an $18,000 credit to the capital account (1/3 interest in the new net assets of $40,000 + 14,000). This case can again be recorded in two ways:

   a.   Under the bonus method the excess of the credit to the new partner's capital account over the debits to the contributed assets is debited to the old partners' capital accounts in their old profit and loss ratio.

   b.   Under the goodwill method the unrecorded goodwill is computed and credited to the new partner's capital account.

      (1)   The new capital is computed by the two methods described above. To continue the example:

         (a) $2/3(C) = $40,000$; $C = $60,000$; or

         (b) $1/3 (C) = $14,000$; $C = $52,000$

      (2)   The goodwill is the difference between the new capital of $60,000 and the new net assets of $54,000 ($40,000 + 14,000) or $6,000.

      (3)   The total goodwill in this case can also be obtained by dividing the new partner's excess credit to his or her capital account by the interest in the partnership retained by the old partners. In the above example the excess credit is $4,000, the old partners' retained interest is 2/3. Goodwill = $4,000 : 2/3 = $6,000.

4.   Regardless of the method used, after the admission of the new partner the capital balances should be in the agreed upon percentage relationship. In the previous example, the old partners' capital balances amount to 2/3 of the total capital, whereas the new partner's capital balance equals 1/3 of the total capital.

260

E. A comparison of the bonus and goodwill methods reveals that the two methods result in the same effect on the partners' capital balances if two conditions are met:

1. The new partner's profit and loss sharing percentage must equal his or her initial percentage interest in partnership capital; and

2. The new profit and loss sharing percentages of the old partners must be in the same relative proportion as their previous percentages.

3. In addition, these percentages must not change during the amortization period of the goodwill.

F. A new partner may be admitted to the partnership by making a payment to one or more old partners.

1. The new partner may buy all or some of the interest of one old partner. For example, an old partner with a 20 percent interest may sell half or all of the 20 percent to a new partner.

2. Or the new partner may buy a proportionate interest from all the old partners. For example, a new partner may acquire a 25 percent interest in the partnership by buying 25 percent of each old partner's interest.

G. Because the payment by the new partner to one or more old partners is an independent transaction, i. e. a transaction not affecting partnership assets or liabilities, the only required entry on the partnership books is to transfer the amount of the dollar interest in capital conveyed to the new partner (regardless of the selling price) from the selling partner's capital account to a capital account for the new partner.

H. It can be argued that the negotiated cash price of a capital interest should be used as an independent indicator of the partnership's current value. If partnership net assets are adjusted to current values immediately prior to the new partner's entry, the exchange price may reflect the existence of unrecorded assets, e. g. goodwill. Depending upon the relationship between the cash price and the implied value of the partnership, goodwill may be attributed to the existing partners or to the new partner. If the former, goodwill may be recorded by increasing the existing partners' capital balances before capital is transferred to the new partner.

I. If a capital interest is purchased from two or more partners, a problem may arise as to the cash distribution to the selling partners. It can be argued that, since the transaction is presumably independent of the partnership entity, it is not appropriate to use the partners' capital balances or profit and loss percentages as a basis for the cash distribution. However, the final decision about cash distributions remains with the selling partners.

J. The legal status of a new partner is described in the Uniform Partnership Act.

    1. Section 27 of the UPA provides that a partner may convey to another his or her interest in the partnership. Unless the other partners agree, the new partner does not have the authority to participate in partnership management. However, s/he is entitled to receive profits and, in dissolution, an interest in the net assets.

    2. A person gaining partnership status by contributing assets to the partnership assumes the same rights and obligations as the old partners. However, under Section 17 of the UPA, the new partner is liable only for debts incurred after his or her admission to partnership.

K. The tax basis of a new partner depends on how the partnership interest was obtained.

    1. As described in the previous chapter, the tax basis of a partner's interest in capital equals the sum of the tax bases of the assets contributed plus the amount of partnership liabilities assumed, less the amount of personal liabilities assumed by the other partners.

    2. If a new partner invests assets in the partnership, his or her tax basis equals the tax basis of the contributed assets, plus or minus the usual adjustments for assumed liabilities.

    3. If a new partner purchases an interest from one or more existing partners, his or her tax basis equals the price paid to acquire the interest, plus or minus the usual adjustments for assumed liabilities.

    4. The tax basis of the new partner's interest can be different from the tax basis of the selling partner's interest.

III. Retirement or Death of a Partner

A. Retirement of a partner

    1. Under Section 42 of the UPA a retiring partner is entitled to have the value of his or her equity measured at the time of retirement and to receive this amount plus interest on the unpaid balance if settlement is not immediate.

2. A retiring partner becomes a creditor rather than an owner. This change should be reflected in the partnership books, i. e. the value of the equity becomes a liability.

3. However, a retiring partner has the option of retaining a passive interest in the firm and to receive, in lieu of interest, profits from the use of his or her right in the property of the dissolved partnership.

4. The partners must decide whether the bonus or the goodwill method is to be used when the negotiated settlement price does not equal the retiring partner's adjusted capital balance.

B. Sale of an interest to a new partner

1. The recorded capital interest of the retiring partner is transferred to the new partner, regardless of the sale price.

2. If the sale price suggests unrecorded partnership goodwill and the partners elect to recognize the goodwill in the accounts, the recorded amount is normally the total goodwill of the partnership, and not just the amount relating to the retiring partner. The goodwill is recorded by increasing the partners' capital balances before the transfer of the capital interest to the new partner.

3. If goodwill existing on the partnership books attaches primarily to the retiring partner, the sale price may suggest the amount of lost goodwill. In this case the goodwill on the books should be reduced.

C. Sale of an interest to continuing partners

1. If the retiring partner sells his or her interest to the remaining partners outside the partnership, the transaction is comparable to the sale of an interest to a third party.

2. If the retiring partner sells his or her interest to the partnership, the partnership assumes the obligation to pay off the retiring partner. If the sales price exceeds the retiring partner's capital balance, the transaction may be recorded in several ways:

   a. If the net assets are worth more than book value, they should be written up to their current values with appropriate credits to the partners' capital accounts.

b.   If the sales price exceeds the retiring partner's interest in the recorded net assets, the difference may be handled in two ways:

    (1)   Under the bonus method the excess price is debited to the remaining partners' capital balances in their remaining profit and loss ratio.

    (2)   Under the goodwill method the excess price constitutes the retiring partner's share of the goodwill. It can be argued that this is the amount of goodwill to be recorded, since the remaining partners actually pay for this goodwill. However, a better argument states that the goodwill belongs to the partnership and should therefore be recorded. The total goodwill is obtained by dividing the retiring partner's share of the goodwill by his or her interest in the partnership. For example, if a partner with a 20 percent interest will receive $20,000 in settlement of a $15,000 capital balance, the retiring partner's share of the goodwill is $5,000, and the total goodwill is $5,000 : 20 percent = $25,000. This amount of goodwill should be recorded and credited to all partners in their profit and loss ratio. The retiring partner's capital account will then equal the amount of the payment.

D.   Death of a partner

    1.   Although the death of a partner dissolves a partnership under Section 31 of the UPA, this provision can be superseded in many states.

    2.   The partnership agreement should specify the procedures to be followed upon the death of a partner.

    3.   The immediate objective after the death of a partner is to measure the partner's equity interest. The partnership agreement should specify whether payments are to be based on recorded or revalued amounts.

    4.   Cross-insurance and entity insurance are frequently used to meet the partnership's obligation to the deceased's estate.

E.   Legal status of a retiring or deceased partner

    1.   The fact of partnership dissolution does not of itself discharge individual partners from unpaid partnership debts.

2. However, under Section 36 of the UPA a partner can be discharged from any existing debts if the partnership creditors and the continuing partners agree.

3. If proper notice is given past and prospective creditors, the retiring or deceased partner is, at most, liable for debts existing at the date of dissolution.

Test Your Understanding of Chapter 16

True or False

Instructions: Indicate your choice by circling either T, if you think the statement is true, or F, if you think the statement is false.

T F 1. According to common law, a partnership is dissolved upon the admission of a new partner.

T F 2. It is not possible for a business to admit a new partner without recognizing an increase in partnership net assets.

T F 3. Unless partnership assets are revalued before a new partner is admitted, an inequitable allocation of capital and earnings may result.

T F 4. Because a new partner's admission price is normally based on the current market value of partnership net assets, a comparison of this price and revalued partnership capital may imply the presence of unrecorded partnership assets.

T F 5. X and Y are partners sharing profits and losses in a 3:2 ratio. After revaluations partnership capital is $40,000. Z contributes $8,000 for a 10 percent interest in capital. The profit and loss sharing ratio for X, Y, and Z is 2:2:1. If the bonus method is used, the $3,200 bonus is allocated between X and Y according to their new relative profit-sharing ratio, i. e. 2:2 or equally.

T F 6. If existing partners grant a bonus to a new partner upon her admission, the new partner's recorded capital balance is less than her net asset contribution.

T F 7. Goodwill is attributed to a new partner when his net asset contribution is less than his percentage interest in total partnership capital.

T F 8. The implied amount of unrecorded goodwill equals the difference between the largest calculated value of new partnership capital and the total recorded net assets of the new business (including the tangible net assets contributed by the new partner).

T F 9. A prerequisite for equivalence between the bonus and goodwill methods is that the new partner is given the same percentage interest in capital as in profit or loss.

T F 10. If new partner C purchases a one-eighth interest from partner A (capital balance of $24,000) and partner B (capital balance of $16,000) at a total cost of $4,000, C's capital balance on the partnership books is $5,000.

T F 11. It is never appropriate to record partnership goodwill when a new partner purchases an interest in the business directly from one or more existing partners.

T F 12. The cash paid by a new partner to purchase an interest from two or more partners is generally distributed to the sellers in accordance with their relative profit and loss ratio.

T F 13. The tax basis of a new partner's interest in partnership capital equals the sum of the bases of her contributed assets plus the amount of partnership liabilities assumed by the new partner and less the amount of any personal liabilities of the new partner assumed by the existing partners.

T F 14. If a partner conveys his interest in the partnership to a third party, the new partner is entitled to management privileges only with the consent of the continuing partners.

T F 15. At the time of a partner's death or retirement, it is generally appropriate to revalue partnership net assets.

Exercises

1. Ann and Betty are partners sharing profits and losses in the ratio 3:2. On January 1, 19x1, when their capital accounts have balances of $14,000 and $36,000, they admit Carla to the partnership after they increase the values of the land and inventory by $8,000 and $2,000, respectively.

Required:
a. Prepare the journal entry to revalue the assets.

b. Record Carla's admission to the partnership for a payment of $10,000 for a 10 percent interest in the capital and profits. Use both the bonus and the goodwill methods.

Bonus Method

Goodwill Method

c.   Record Carla's admission to the partnership for a payment of
     $10,000 for a 25 percent interest in the capital and profits.
     Use both the bonus and the goodwill methods.

Bonus Method

Goodwill Method

d.   Record Carla's admission to the partnership for a payment of
     $10,000 to each partner for a 20 percent interest in the capital
     and profits. Give two methods of recording Carla's admission.

Goodwill Not Recorded

Goodwill Recorded

2. Dick, Ed, and Fred share profits and losses 2:2:1. On January 1, 19x1 their capital balances are: Dick $50,000, Ed $60,000, and Fred $40,000. On this day Fred retires from the partnership.

Required: a. Assuming that Ed receives $45,000 for his interest in the partnership, record his retirement on the partnership books.

b. Assuming that Ed receives $80,000 for his interest in the partnership, record his retirement on the partnership books under the bonus and the goodwill method.

Bonus Method

Goodwill Method

True or False

1.	T	4.	T	7.	T	10.	T	13.	T
2.	F	5.	F	8.	T	11.	F	14.	T
3.	T	6.	F	9.	T	12.	F	15.	T

Exercises

1. a. Land 8,000
        Inventory 2,000
            Ann, capital 6,000
            Betty, capital 4,000

    b. Cash 10,000
            Ann, capital 1,800
            Betty, capital 1,200
            Carla, capital* 7,000
        To record Carla's admission under the bonus method

        *Ann, capital (14,000 + 6,000) 20,000
         Betty, capital (36,000 + 4,000) 40,000
         Carla's contribution 10,000
        Total partnership capital 70,000
        Carla's interest 1
        Carla's capital balance 7,000

        Cash 10,000
        Goodwill* 30,000
            Ann, capital (3/5 x 30,000) .. 18,000
            Betty, capital (2/5 x 30,000) 12,000
            Carla, capital (.1 x 100,000) 10,000
        To record Carla's admission under the goodwill method

        *.1C = $10,000; C = $100,000
        or .9C = $60,000; C = $66,667
        Implied new capital (larger of above) 100,000
        Less total partnership net assets 70,000
        Goodwill 30,000

    c. Cash 10,000
        Ann, capital (3/5 x 7,500) 4,500
        Betty, capital (2/5 x 7,500) 3,000
            Carla, capital (.25 x 70,000) 17,500
        To record Carla's admission under the bonus method

271

```
        Cash ...............................    10,000
        Goodwill*..........................    10,000
              Carla, capital (.25 x 80,000)              20,000
        To record Carla's admission under the goodwill method

        *.25C = $10,000; C = $40,000
        or .75C = $60,000; C = $80,000
        Implied new capital (larger of above) .......    80,000
        Less total partnership net assets ..........    70,000
        Goodwill ...................................    10,000

    d.  Ann, capital (.2 x 20,000) ........     4,000
        Betty, capital (.2 x 40,000) ......     8,000
              Carla, capital ..............              12,000
        To record Carla's admission without recording goodwill

        Goodwill* .........................    40,000
              Ann, capital (3/5 x 40,000) ..             24,000
              Betty, capital (2/5 x 40,000).             16,000
        *.2C = $20,000; C = $100,000
        Implied new capital .........................    100,000
        Less recorded tangible assets ..............    60,000
        Goodwill ...................................    40,000

        Ann, capital [.2 x (20,000 + 24,000)]     8,800
        Betty, capital [.2 x (40,000 + 16,000)   11,200
              Carla, capital (.2 x 100,000)              20,000

2.  a.  Ed, capital ......................    60,000
              Cash ........................              45,000
              Dick, capital (2/3 x 15,000)..             10,000
              Fred, capital (1/3 x 15,000)..              5,000

b.      Ed, capital ......................    60,000
        Dick, capital (2/3 x 20,000) ......    13,333
        Fred, capital (1/3 x 20,000) ......     6,667
              Cash ........................              80,000
        To record Ed's retirement, allocating the bonus of 20,000 to
        Dick and Fred in their remaining ratio (2:1)

        Goodwill* .........................    50,000
              Dick, capital (2/5) ..........             20,000
              Ed, capital (2/5) ............             20,000
              Fred, capital (1/5) ..........             10,000
        *.4C = $80,000; C = $200,000
        Implied capital .............................    200,000
        Less recorded capital (60,000 + 50,000 + 40,000)   150,000
        Goodwill ...................................    50,000

        Ed, capital (60,000 + 20,000) .....    80,000
              Cash ........................              80,000
        To record Ed's retirement under the goodwill method
```

Chapter 17
Partnership Liquidation

Chapter Outline

I.   The Liquidation Process

A.   The fundamental objectives of a partnership in liquidation are:

1.   To convert the entity's assets to cash with minimum loss in value (realization of assets);

2.   To discharge valid partnership liabilities; and

3.   To distribute any remaining cash and unrealized assets to the partners.

B.   The primary objective of the accounting function during partnership liquidation is to provide helpful information for determining an equitable distribution of partnership assets to creditors and partners.

C.   Accounting emphasis is shifted from measuring periodic income to determining gains and losses from asset realization, properly allocating the gains and losses among the partners, and planning and recording asset distributions to creditors and partners.

D.   To account for a partnership liquidation, provisions of the Uniform Partnership Act (UPA), the partnership agreement, and state and federal insolvency (bankruptcy) statutes are normally relevant.

E.   A liquidating partnership is either solvent or insolvent. Partnership insolvency may be defined two ways:

1.   Recorded partnership assets are not sufficient to cover existing partnership liabilities (the view taken by the authors for discussion purposes).

2.   Partnership assets plus the excess of the partners' individual assets over their non-partnership debts is not sufficient to cover partnership liabilities (a legal view).

F.   In liquidating a solvent partnership two approaches may be taken:

1.   In a simple liquidation all non-cash assets of a solvent partnership are realized before any distributions made to the partners.

2. In an installment liquidation liquidating payments are made to the partners before all the non-cash assets are converted to cash and the total liquidation gain or loss is known.

II. Simple Liquidation

A. Basic distributive rights

1. According to the UPA partnership assets are distributed according to the following priority scheme:

a. To creditors other than partners;

b. To partners other than for capital and profit;

c. To partners in respect of capital;

d. To partners in respect of profits.

2. Since the conversion of all non-cash assets precedes the distribution of cash to the partners, the total liquidation gain or loss is known. Unless a specific liquidation gain and loss ratio is included in the partnership agreement, the gain or loss is allocated in the current profit and loss residual ratio.

3. If current profits are transferred in closing entries to partners' capital accounts, priorities c and d, above, generally are considered as one. An exception exists when a deficit in the income summary account is not offset against capital balances before cash is distributed to individual partners.

4. A schedule of partnership liquidation is the primary statement reporting a summary of the chronological partnership transactions during liquidation. It reports the partnership's financial position at the date liquidation begins (pre-liquidation balances), gains and losses from asset realization and their allocation among the partners according to the profit and loss (P&L) sharing percentages, and the payment of cash to creditors and partners.

B. Partners' debit balances

1. If a partner's capital account is not sufficient to absorb his or her share of the losses, a debit balance will result. Such a debit balance in a partner's capital account represents a valid claim of the partnership against the partner, i. e. a partnership receivable.

2. The UPA requires a partner with a debit capital balance to contribute an amount equal to his or her deficit.

3.   A partner's failure to contribute assets sufficient to remove a capital deficiency results in the deficit becoming a realization loss to be absorbed by the remaining partners in their remaining P&L ratio. For example: if three partners have a P&L ratio of 4:3:3 and the last partner is unable to make up a debit balance, the first two partners absorb the debit balance in the ratio 4:3.

C.   Partners' loans

1.   Although the UPA ranks payments to partners on loans ahead of payments on capital interests, this ranking has little functional significance in a simple liquidation, because a partner's loan is generally not repaid if s/he has a capital deficiency. Such a payment may result in assets being permanently lost to the partnership, e. g. the partner may use the money to pay personal liabilities or otherwise spend it.

2.   To prevent this outcome, most courts have accepted the rules of setoff: a debit balance is offset against the partner's loan balance before any cash is distributed. Setoff is recorded on a schedule of partnership liquidation only after all non-cash assets have been realized.

D.   Liquidation expenses

1.   Any expenses that are directly related to the sale of an assets are normally deducted from the proceeds to arrive at net proceeds.

2.   Expenses that pertain to the general liquidation process should be separately reported on the liquidation schedule. These expenses are allocated to the partners in accordance with their P&L ratio.

3.   If one partner manages the liquidation process for a fee, the fee expense should be debited to all the partners in their P&L ratio, while the fee is credited to the managing partner's capital account. The fee should not be paid in cash, in case the partner's capital balance is insufficient to absorb all losses.

II. Installment (Periodic) Payments

A.   Basic accounting problem

1.   In a simple liquidation all expenses and gains and losses are known before a cash distribution is made to the individual partners. However, if a liquidation is expected to take some time, periodic cash distributions may be made to the partners before all the assets have been realized. The problem is to develop a procedure

for computing the amount of cash that can safely be distributed at periodic intervals, i. e. to prevent an excessive distribution to a partner that may later have to be reclaimed.

2. The accountant often assumes a fiduciary position with regard to the claims of partnership creditors and the individual partners against the available cash. The fiduciary may be held liable for losses resulting from excessive distributions of cash.

B. Periodic computation of safe payments to partners

1. A schedule of safe installment payments is prepared whenever a periodic cash distribution is made during the liquidation process, e. g. monthly. This schedule begins with the current individual partners' pre-distribution balances (i. e. loan balance plus capital balance) from the schedule of partnership liquidation. Then a series of hypothetical events are accounted for:

a. The largest estimated potential loss, which usually equals the current balance of the unrealized non-cash assets, is charged to the partners according to their P&L ratio. If a cash balance is to be retained to cover possible unrecorded liabilities and future liquidation expenses, the estimated potential loss should be increased to include the desired cash balance.

b. On the schedule of safe installment payments the allocation of the largest potential loss may result in a debit balance in a partner's capital account. In this case it is assumed that this balance represents another potential loss that is allocated to the remaining partners in their remaining P&L ratio.

c. The process of potential loss absorption continues until all remaining partners (or one remaining partner) have a combined credit balance equal to the amount of cash available for distribution to the partners. Cash is distributed as indicated by the final balances, after all third party claims have been satisfied.

d. Since cash payments are not made to any partner who could conceivably end up with a debit balance under the worst possible asset realization scenario, the cash payments calculated in this manner are usually referred to as safe payments.

2. After completing an installment liquidation, three conclusions should be drawn:

a. The total cash payments to each partner are equivalent to the amount of a single payment computed under a simple liquidation procedure.

b. After each partner has received some cash in the liquidation process, the capital balances will be in the P&L ratio. When this condition is achieved, all subsequent installment payments are made in the P&L ratio.

c. The order of payments in the schedule of partnership liquidation is consistent with the order of priority established in the UPA.

C. Partners' loans

1. On a schedule of safe installment payments a partner's total equity, i. e. the sum of both loan and capital balances, should be entered.

2. Installment payments to partners should be applied to the loan balance before it is applied to the capital balance.

D. Liquidation expenses and unrecorded liabilities

1. In the absence of anticipated liquidation expenses and unrecorded liabilities, a total potential loss entered on the schedule of safe installment payments equals the book value of the remaining non-cash assets.

2. The actual loss may exceed this amount if liquidation expenses exceed the proceeds from asset realization or if previously unrecorded liabilities are discovered during the liquidation process. These claims rank ahead of partners' claims.

3. To avoid excessive distributions and possible personal liability, the fiduciary should explicitly allow for these contingencies by periodically estimating and including them in the maximum potential loss.

4. The result is a cash balance (after the distribution to the partners) at the end of the period equal to the sum of the estimated liquidation expenses and unrecorded liabilities.

V. Cash Predistribution Plan

A. Purpose of the cash predistribution plan

1. A cash predistribution plan is prepared at the outset of the liquidation process to show the amounts to be distributed to creditors and partners, and the sequence of the payments. Assuming certain amounts of cash

277

become available during the liquidation phase, the plan indicates the priority distribution between creditors and partners and between the partners themselves.

2. Whereas schedule of partnership liquidation and the schedule of safe installment payments are primarily historical, the cash predistribution plan is forward looking.

B. Loss-absorption potential

1. A cash distribution is directly related to the magnitude of each partner's loss-absorption potential. A partner's loss-absorption potential equals the amount of the largest hypothetical loss the partnership may suffer before his capital balance becomes a debit.

2. This value is determined for each partner by dividing his predistribution balance (loan balance plus capital balance) by his P&L percentage.

3. Ranking the loss-absorption potentials indicates the relative strength of each partner's equity position: the larger the loss-absorption potential, the stronger the position.

C. Hypothetical cash distributions

1. After third party claims have been satisfied, available cash should be distributed to the strongest partner as indicated by a comparison of the loss absorption potentials.

2. A cash distribution reduces a partner's loan or capital balance and therefore his loss-absorption potential. Sufficient cash should be distributed to the strongest partner until his revised loss-absorption potential equals the loss-absorption potential of the second strongest partner.

3. The amount of a cash distribution equals the product of the partner's P&L percentage and the dollar difference between his loss-absorption potential and that of the next strongest partner.

4. Other available cash should be distributed to these two partners until their loss-absorption potential equals the loss-absorption potential of the next strongest partner. The amounts of the distributions are calculated as before. The cash distribution is allocated between the two partners according to their relative P&L ratio.

5. The sequence of hypothetical distribution continues until all partners have equal loss-absorption

potentials. Once this point is reached, subsequent cash distributions are made to all partners in their P&L ratio.

D. The predistribution summary

1. After the sequence and amounts of the distribution have been determined, a cash predistribution plan summarizes the results.

2. This plan serves as a guide for cash payments during the liquidation process. The partners can see how much cash is needed from asset realization before each receives a safe distribution.

3. The indicated payments are made from available cash after liquidation expenses are covered. Future liquidation expenses are not included among the priority claims. Also, unrecorded liabilities are not anticipated during the development of the cash predistribution plan. As a result, total priority claims generally exceed the amount listed on the predistribution plan.

V. Insolvent Partnerships

A. Basic rights

1. When a partnership is insolvent, two conditions are possible:

   a. One or more individual partners have enough personal assets to meet the claims of partnership creditors (i. e. legally, the partnership is not insolvent).

   b. The partners do not have enough assets to discharge all existing partnership debts (i. e. the partnership is legally insolvent and, considering the claims of partnership creditors, all partners are individually insolvent). In this case, the order of distributing the partners' personally owned assets depends on the relative rights of the partnership and personal creditors.

2. When a partnership is insolvent both the partnership and the partner's individual assets must be marshaled to determine the basic rights of the creditors.

   a. Partnership creditors have first claim on partnership assets. After their claims are satisfied, the remaining partnership assets are available to the individual partners' creditors.

b. Personal creditors have first claim on personal assets. After their claims are satisfied, the remaining personal assets are available to the partnership creditors. This is true whether a partner has a debit or credit balance in the capital account.

3. When a partner is bankrupt or insolvent, claims against his separate property rank as follows:

a. Those owing to separate creditors;

b. Those owing to partnership creditors;

c. Those owning to partners by way of contribution.

4. If a partner pays more than his share of partnership liabilities, he has a claim in the amount of his credit balance in his capital account, against the partners with debit balances.

B. Accounting analysis of the insolvent partnership

1. The amount of partnership liabilities paid by a personally solvent partner is credited to his capital account. It is usually assumed that partnership creditors will seek a judgment against the most personally solvent partner.

2. The deficit of an insolvent partner is charged to the other partners' capital accounts in their remaining P&L ratio.

3. A solvent partner is required to contribute assets equal to his deficit balance. If his personal net assets are not sufficient to cover the deficit, the remaining debit balance is charged to the other partners in the P&L ratio.

4. Points 2 and 3 conform with provisions of the UPA. However, if the UPA is not controlling and a partner's debit balance is adjudged an individual liability sharing pari passu with other individual liabilities, the partner's personal assets are divided in proportion to the dollar amounts owed to his separate creditors and to the partnership.

Test Your Understanding of Chapter 17

True or False

Instructions: Indicate your choice by circling either T, if you think the statement is true, or F, if you think the statement is false.

T   F   1. During liquidation the accounting objective changes from measuring periodic income to providing information to assist in an equitable distribution of partnership assets between creditors and partners.

T   F   2. In a simple liquidation all partnership non-cash assets are realized and gains and losses allocated, before cash is distributed to the partners.

T   F   3. If partnership liabilities remain unsettled after all non-cash assets have been realized, only partners with debit capital balances are required to contribute additional assets for the settlement of such partnership debts.

T   F   4. Partners X, Y, and Z share profits and losses in a 2:3:1 ratio. During liquidation Y has a debit capital balance. If Y is personally insolvent and the UPA is controlling, this deficit will be shared by X and Z in a 2:1 ratio.

T   F   5. During liquidation all partners' loan balances are paid before any partner receives a cash distribution for capital and profits.

T   F   6. The rule of setoff means that all partnership liabilities are completely satisfied before any cash is distributed to a partner.

T   F   7. In calculating the amount of cash that can safely be distributed to partners at various times during an installment liquidation, the sum of anticipated liquidation expenses, estimated unrecorded liabilities, and the non-cash asset balance is charged to each partner's predistribution balance in the P&L ratio.

T   F   8. A partner's loss-absorption potential equals the excess of his personal assets over his personal liabilities.

T   F   9. A partner's predistribution balance is the sum (or net) of his loan and capital balance.

T   F   10. On a schedule of sale installment payments it is assumed that partnership non-cash assets will be sold for their book values.

T   F   11. A cash predistribution plan suggests that the partner with the largest loss-absorption potential should receive a cash distribution before any other partner.

T F 12. Once all partners receive an installment payment, their
          revised predistribution balances are in their P&L ratio.

T F 13. After partnership assets are exhausted, creditors of an
          insolvent partnership may seek satisfaction from a
          personally solvent partner only if the partner has a debit
          capital balance.

T F 14. If the UPA is controlling, a partner's debit capital balance
          is regarded as a personal liability sharing equal status
          with his personal third-party creditors.

T F 15. The schedule of safe installment payments incorporates the
          rule of setoff.

Exercises

1. On September 1, 19x1, the partners of Susan's Travel Agency decide
to liquidate the business. Partners Sally, Sophie, and Susan share
profits and losses 3:2:5. The preliquidation balance sheet is as
follows:

Cash	$ 50,000	Outside liabilities...	$100,000
Non-cash assets...	500,000	Sally, capital	120,000
		Sophie, loan	12,000
		Sophie, capital	138,000
		Susan, loan	20,000
		Susan, capital	160,000
Totals	$550,000		$550,000

The partners agree to distribute available cash at the end of each
month, after keeping a cash balance large enough to cover estimated
liquidation expenses and unrecorded liabilities.

In September non-cash assets with a book value of $200,000 are sold
for $80,000. Estimated expenses at the end of the month are $10,000.
In October non-cash assets with a book value of $150,000 are sold for
$60,000. Estimated expenses at the end of the month are $4,000.

Required: Prepare a cash predistribution plan.

Susan's Travel Agency
Loss Absorption Potential

Schedule of Loss Absorption

Cash Predistribution Plan

2. Use the information from Exercise 1.

Required: Prepare a schedule of partnership liquidation for September and October and the supporting schedules of safe installment payments.

Susan's Travel Agency
Schedule of Partnership Liquidation

Susan's Travel Agency
Schedule of Safe Installment Payments

Solutions to Chapter 17 Exercises

True or False

1.	T	4.	T	7.	T	10.	F	13.	F
2.	T	5.	F	8.	F	11.	T	14.	F
3.	F	6.	F	9.	T	12.	T	15.	T

Exercises

1.

Susan's Travel Agency
Loss-Absorption Potentials

Partner	Equities	P&L Ratio	Loss-Absorption Potential	Order of Equity Absorption
Sally	$120,000	30%	$400,000	2
Sophie	150,000	20%	750,000	3
Susan	180,000	50%	360,000	1

Schedule of Loss Absorption

	Assumed Losses	Sally	Sophie	Susan
P&L ratio		30%	20%	50%
Preliquidation balances		120,000	150,000	180,000
Potential loss to absorb Susan's equity	360,000	(108,000)	(72,000)	(180,000)
Balances		12,000	78,000	-0-
Potential loss to absorb Sally's remaining equity	20,000	(12,000)	(8,000)	
Balances		-0-	70,000	

Cash Predistribution Plan

Cash distributions:	Total
First $100,000 to creditors other than partners ...	$100,00∢
Next $70,000 to Sophie	170,00∢
Next $20,000 shared between Sally and Sophie 3:2 ..	190,00∢
All further cash payments are shared among Sally, Sophie and Susan 3:2:5	

	Cash	Non-cash Assets	Priority Claims	Sally, Capital
reliq. balances	50,000	500,000	(100,000)	(120,000)
ale of assets & loss allocation	80,000	(200,000)		36,000
alances	130,000	300,000	(100,000)	(84,000)
ayment to creditors.	(100,000)		100,000	
alances	30,000	300,000	-0-	(84,000)
ept. installment payment (see Sched.)	(20,000)			
alances	10,000	300,000	-0-	(84,000)
ale of assets and loss allocation ...	60,000	(150,000)		27,000
alances	70,000	150,000	-0-	(57,000
ct. installment payment (see Sched.)	(66,000)			9,600
alances	4,000	150,000	-0-	(47,400

	Sophie, Loan	Sophie, Capital	Susan, Loan	Susan, Capital
reliq. balances	(12,000)	(138,000)	(20,000)	(160,000)
ale of assets & loss allocation		24,000		60,000
alances	(12,000)	(114,000)	(20,000)	(100,000)
ayment to creditors.				
alances	(12,000)	(114,000)	(20,000)	(100,000)
ept. installment payment (see Sched.)	12,000	8,000		
alances	-0-	(106,000)	(20,000)	(100,000)
ale of assets and loss allocation ...		18,000		45,000
alances	-0-	(88,000)	(20,000)	(55,000)
ct. installment payment (see Sched.)		56,400		
alances	-0-	(31,600)	(20,000)	(55,000)

Susan's Travel Agency
Schedule of Safe Installment Payments

	Sally	Sophie	Susan
P&L percentages	30%	20%	50%
September installment:			
Predistribution balances	84,000	126,000	120,000
Potential loss (300,000 + 10,000)	(93,000)	(62,000)	(155,000)
Potential balances	(9,000)	64,000	(35,000)
Potential loss - debit balances	9,000	(44,000)	35,000
Safe payment to Sophie	-0-	20,000	-0-
October installment:			
Predistribution balances	57,000	88,000	75,000
Potential loss (150,000 + 4,000)	(46,200)	(30,800)	(77,000)
Potential balances	10,800	57,200	(2,000)
Potential loss - debit balance	(1,200)	(800)	2,000
Safe payment to Sally and Sophie	9,600	56,400	-0-

Chapter 18
Accounting for Estates and Trusts

Chapter Outline

I.   Role of the Fiduciary in Estate Administration

    A.   Introduction

        1.   A fiduciary is a person to whom is entrusted the property of another for safekeeping, management, and/or distribution, and who is accountable to interested parties.

        2.   Upon the death of a person, a representative of the deceased assumes custody of his estate. If the deceased has a valid will, he is said to have died testate (he is referred to as the testator). A representative nominated in a will and confirmed by the court is known as an executor. An administrator is a court-appointed representative of a decedent who died without a valid will (i. e. died intestate).

        3.   Various state laws of descent and distribution govern the distribution of the decedent's real property (laws of descent) and personal property (laws of distribution) if a will does not exist or is invalid.

        4.   Probate, surrogate, orphan's, or county courts administer estates. A will must be admitted to probate (i. e. to have its validity proved) before it is an effective instrument of fiduciary authority.

        5.   Letters testamentary are issued to the deceased's chosen representative upon his approval by the court; letters of administration are issued to an administrator. Such letters empower the holder to act as fiduciary.

    B.   Role of the fiduciary in estate administration

        1.   The fiduciary has the responsibility to:

            a.   Take possession of the decedent's property;

            b.   Manage the property with reasonable care;

            c.   Invest estate resources profitably;

            d.   Liquidate the decedent's debts (including estate and inheritance taxes); and

e. Distribute the deceased's property as specified in the will or by law.

2. Although real property usually passes directly by devise to devisees identified in the will, the fiduciary may include this property in the inventory of the decedent's assets.

3. The fiduciary may petition the court to permit the sale of real property to meet the decedent's obligations when personal property is inadequate to do so.

C. Inventory of assets

1. An inventory of the decedent's personal property is submitted to the court by the fiduciary, including property with no value. The complete inventory comprises the corpus or principal of the estate at the date of death.

2. Court-appointed appraisers may assist the fiduciary in assigning values to estate assets.

3. Real property and some personal property may pass directly to the distributee (e. g. household effects, clothing, items of special value to a surviving spouse or minor children). If so, they are not included in the fiduciary's inventory.

4. Assets discovered after the initial inventory is filed are reported in supplementary statements.

D. Claims against the estate

1. Those having claims against the decedent are informed by public notice to file their claims with the court or the fiduciary within a stated period of time.

2. The fiduciary determines the sequence of paying valid claims against the decedent's estate.

3. State statutes provide the priority sequence for settling claims of an insolvent estate. The following sequence is fairly typical:

a. Funeral and administration expenses.

b. Debts that are secured by a lien on the decedent's property.

c. Taxes, including estate and inheritance taxes.

d. Judgments in force that are a lien against property of the decedent at time of death.

e. Provable debts against the estate.

f. Wages due domestics or other employees.

g. Sustenance payments to the widow for a specified period of time.

4. For a solvent estate the order of payment is not critical.

E. Bequests of personal property

1. A testator's bequest of personal property is called a legacy; the recipient is a legatee. Legacies are either specific, demonstrative, general, or residual. (This order reflects their priority in settlement.)

a. A specific legacy is a bequest of personal property that is specifically identified in the will.

b. A demonstrative legacy is a testamentary bequest payable out of a designated fund or specified asset accumulation, e. g. a gift of cash payable out of a designated bank account.

c. A general legacy is a bequest of money or other property without special designation as to source.

d. A residual legacy is the terminal distribution of personal property after all debts have been paid and all other legacies distributed. A residual legatee receives the residue of the estate.

2. A bequest (gift) may be regarded as an advancement in anticipation of the recipient's share of the decedent's property if the decedent died without a will (intestate); however, gratuitous inter vivos transfers are regarded as absolute gifts, not advancements, unless other intent is demonstrated.

F. Role of the fiduciary in trust administration

1. A trust is an arrangement whereby title to property is transferred to a trustee who holds or manages the property for the benefit of others; beneficiaries are those benefiting from the trust.

2. The trust agreement provides for the distribution of trust principal and the income earned thereon. The income beneficiary is called a cestui que trust (he is also a life tenant if he is to receive income for life). The recipient of the principal is a remainderman.

3. A trustee normally has only such authority as is conveyed to him by the trust instrument. This authority usually includes:

    a. The incurrence of those costs and expenses necessary to the preservation of the trust principal.

    b. The sale, exchange or improvements in respect to existing realty.

    c. The settlement, totally or by compromise, of claims against the trust estate.

    d. The making of new investments and disposition of existing investments.

    e. The distribution of property to distributees as provided in the trust agreement.

    f. The making of advances to beneficiaries.

    g. The payment to or expending of income for the benefit of minors.

4. The trustee is charged with exercising that degree of care in respect to trust property as he would exercise as a reasonably prudent business executive acting in his own self-interest.

II. Dual Bases of Accountability

A. Principal (corpus) and income distinguished

    1. Fiduciary accounting records should preserve the distinction between estate principal and its income. Property comprising these classes are specified by the decedent's will or by the court.

    2. In general, principal is the property to be delivered to the remainderman; income is the return in money or property from the use of principal.

    3. The Revised Uniform Principal and Income Act broadly provides for charges against and credits to principal and charges against and credits to income. In general all expenses related to the settlement of a decedent's estate are charged to principal; costs of operating, preserving, and managing income producing property are charged against income.

B. Special problems

    1. Accruals of interest and rent (receivable or payable) at the date of a decedent's death are usually regarded

as estate principal; interest and rent earned or incurred after the date of death normally are elements of income determination. Taxes on real property customarily do not accrue; therefore, the date the tax lien becomes effective, relative to the date of death, determines whether the property tax is charged against principal or income. Income taxes are assigned to the elements making up the specific taxable base.

2. For corporate dividends the Revised Uniform Principal and Income Act basically reflects the position that cash dividends represent estate income and stock dividends are additions to estate principal.

3. Partnership net income computed and allocated to a decedent at date of death represents estate principal. If the books are not closed until after the date of death, there is no consensus as to the treatment of earnings.

4. A will or trust agreement should indicate whether depreciation and depletion amounts are charted against principal or income; otherwise state laws control. Traditional rules for capitalization or expense apply for repairs and maintenance costs.

5. Corporate bonds held by the decedent are usually inventoried at their market values at date of death; a popular position is that any related premium or discount (difference between market value and face value) should not be amortized. For bonds acquired by the fiduciary during tenancy, premiums are usually amortized while discounts are not. Gains and losses from the conversion of securities, regardless when acquired, are treated as estate principal.

6. Expenses clearly identifiable with the conservation, management, and distribution of principal are legitimate charges against principal; expenses pertaining to the earning of income during the period of tenancy are charged to estate income.

III. Fiduciary Accounts and Reports

A. Introduction

1. The fundamental accounting equation is modified to become:

    Estate (Trust) Assets = Accountability

2. Fiduciary accounts should be titled so that they disclose clearly the level of accountability and how accountability has been discharged. Account titles

should clearly differentiate between income and principal.

3. A fiduciary is responsible for all assets entrusted to him; payments of existing claims is one way to discharge that responsibility.

B. Accounting procedures and entry sequence for an estate

1. Estate accounting procedures basically reflect a strong stewardship orientation.

2. Estate books are opened by debiting the accounts for the inventory of assets and by crediting Estate Principal (or Corpus). Separate cash accounts should be maintained for principal and for income.

3. Assets discovered after the initial inventory has been filed are charged to appropriate asset accounts, with an offsetting credit to Assets Subsequently Discovered. This latter account is closed to Estate Principal at the end of the period.

4. Liabilities of the decedent are not recorded until paid by the fiduciary, at which time Debts of the Decedent Paid is debited for the amount of the settlement. This transaction reduces the accountability of the fiduciary.

5. Gains and losses from realization of principal assets are closed to Estate Principal, thereby changing the amount of the fiduciary's accountability.

6. The account Funeral and Administrative Expenses is debited upon payment of such costs; this also reduces the fiduciary's accountability.

7. The fiduciary's accountability for principal is decreased by the distribution of legacies. An account may be opened and debited (at the asset's carrying value) for each legatee receiving a distribution, e. g. Legacy - Ann Green, Legacy - Bob Brown, etc.

8. An income account should be opened and expense accounts should be clearly labeled to distinguish between principal and income charges, e. g. Expenses - income.

9. Payments to income beneficiaries are charged to Distribution to Income Beneficiary.

C. Charge and discharge statement

1. This statement, which is periodically filed with the court, details the particulars of estate administration by listing the estate resources for which the fiduciary

is accountable and by describing how he discharged his accountability during the period. Responsibility for principal and for income is separately reported.

2. The statement typically begins the principal section and the income section with a listing of the related resources for which the fiduciary has responsibility during the period (I charge myself with:). This is followed by descriptions specifying how s/he discharged this responsibility during the period (I credit myself with:). The dollar difference between the two divisions represents the section's balance at the end of the period. Each balance (the balance as to principal and the balance as to income) is supported by an itemized listed of the assets comprising this total.

B. Closing entries

1. A fiduciary closes the estate's accounts after the final charge and discharge statement is delivered to the court.

2. Accounts increasing or decreasing the fiduciary's accountability for principal are closed to Estate Principal; accounts chargeable to income are closed to the Income account.

C. Properties transferred to trustee

1. After the estate is officially closed, remaining assets may be transferred to a trustee for management and care. The trustee usually accepts fiduciary responsibility for the property.

2. Income earned prior to creation of a living trust is part of trust principal; subsequent income is distributable to income beneficiaries.

3. Income earned subsequent to creation of a testamentary trust (i. e. after date of death) is trust income and is distributable.

4. Trustee accounting essentially parallels that of an executor. The accounts should separate trust principal and trust income.

293

Test Your Understanding of Chapter 18

True or False

Instructions: Indicate your choice by circling either T, if you think the statement is true, or F, if you think the statement is false.

T F   1. Letters testamentary are issued by the court to empower an executor to act as a fiduciary.

T F   2. If a person dies without a valid will, he is said to have died intestate, and his fiduciary is a court-appointed administrator.

T F   3. The fiduciary's inventory of assets usually includes all real property and personal property of the decedent at time of death.

T F   4. A legacy is a testator's bequest of real property.

T F   5. At completion of a trust agreement, the recipient of the trust principal is the remainderman.

T F   6. In terms of priority, laws generally provide for the payment of estate taxes and inheritance taxes before the payment of funeral and administrative expenses and debts secured by a lien on the decedent's property.

T F   7. As a rule, expenses such as funeral expenses, estate taxes, fees of attorneys and accountants, and court costs associated with settling the decedent's estate are charged against estate income.

T F   8. If a tax lien on a testator's real property becomes effective before the decedent's death, but the tax bill is received and paid after death, the payment should be charged to estate principal.

T F   9. The Revised Uniform Principal and Income Act essentially indicates that all corporate dividends, cash or stock, received by the fiduciary become estate income.

T F 10. In general, corporate bonds owned by a decedent are inventoried at their market values at date of death.

T F 11. A fiduciary may discharge his responsibility for estate assets by settling valid claims against the estate, paying legacies as provided for in the will, and distributing estate income to income beneficiaries.

T F 12. Assets discovered after the initial inventory has been filed with the courts are regarded as estate principal.

T F 13. In the final report to the courts, the account Assets Subsequently Discovered is closed to Estate Principal.

T F 14. Liabilities of the decedent are usually accrued by the fiduciary and recorded in the accounting records prior to their settlement.

T F 15. Charge and discharge statements reporting the nature of the transactions and events pertaining to principal and income assets and how the fiduciary distributed the assets during a given period of time, are filed with the courts at periodic intervals.

Exercises

1. On March 1, 19x1, Jane Marple died. Her will was admitted to probate on April 1 and Tom Beresford was appointed executor of the estate. Journalize the following events and transactions which occurred between April 2 and June 1:

a. Beresford filed the following inventory with the court:

Cash on deposit, Bank of Turtlepoint	$ 1,700
Common stock, Roulette Corporation:	
500 shares (par $1) at $12	6,000
Automobile	3,800
Household furnishings	1,500
Life insurance, payable to the estate	20,000

b. Funeral expenses of $1,200 were paid by Beresford.

c. The life insurance policy was collected.

d. Notice was published in the local newspaper requesting
    presentation of claims against the decedent. Debts of $1,500
    were validated and paid.

e. Ten Indian Echo bonds (each having a $1,000 face value and paying
    6 percent interest on December 31 of each year until maturity at
    the end of 19x6) were discovered upon a search of the decedent's
    belongings. Current market value of the bonds is $8,000.

f. The Roulette Corporation declared and paid a dividend of $1 per
    share.

g. The automobile was sold for $3,500.

h. Executorial fees of $5,000 were paid to Beresford.

. The household furnishings were sold for $1,600.

. A cash legacy of $10,000 was paid to the sister, Agatha Marple.

. All income earned to June 1 was distributed to Agatha Marple.

. The other remaining assets were distributed equally to Joan and Raymond Marple, the niece and nephew of the decedent.

. The income account was closed.

n.   The remaining accounts were closed.

2.   Tom Watson, executor of the estate of Sherlock Holmes who died on October 6, prepared the following trial balance on December 31, 19x1:

Estate of Sherlock Holmes
Trial Balance
December 31, 19x1

	Debits	Credits
Cash - principal	$12,560	
Cash - income	1,440	
Accrued interest receivable	200	
Investments: Stocks	34,000	
Bonds	10,000	
Household effects	2,800	
Assets subsequently discovered		$ 6,200
Gain on realization		1,400
Estate principal		65,150
Income		2,950
Expenses - income	260	
Debts of decedent paid	4.390	
Funeral expenses	1,000	
Loss on realization	100	
Distribution to income beneficiary	1,050	
Legacy - A. C. Doyle	5,000	
Administrative expenses	2,900	
	$75,700	$75,700

Required: Prepare a charge and discharge statement as of December 31, 19x1 for the estate of Sherlock Holmes.

Estate of Sherlock Holmes
Tom Watson, Executor
Charge and Discharge Statement
October 6 to December 31, 19x1

Solutions to Chapter 18 Exercises

True or False

1.	T	4.	F	7.	T	10.	F	13.	T
2.	T	5.	T	8.	F	11.	T	14.	F
3.	F	6.	F	9.	T	12.	T	15.	T

Exercises

1. a. Cash - principal 1,700
        Commons stock, Roulette Corporation 6,000
        Automobile 3,800
        Household furnishings 1,500
        Life insurance 20,000
            Estate Principal 33,000

    b. Funeral and administrative expenses 1,200
            Cash - principal 1,200

    c. Cash - principal 20,000
            Life insurance 20,000

    d. Debts of decedent paid 1,500
            Cash - principal 1,500

    e. Indian Echo bonds 8,000
        Accrued interest receivable
        ($10,000 x .06 x 2/12) 100
            Assets subsequently discovered 8,100

    f. Cash - income 500
            Income 500

    g. Cash - principal 3,500
        Loss on realization 300
            Automobile 3,800

    h. Funeral and administrative expenses 5,000
            Cash - principal 5,000

    i. Cash - principal 1,600
            Household furnishings 1,500
            Gain on realization 100

    j. Legacy - Agatha Marple 10,000
            Cash - principal 10,000

    k. Accrued interest receivable 150
            Income 150
        (Interest accrued on Indian Echo bonds for March, April, and
        May)

	Distribution to income beneficiary	650	
	Cash - income		500
	Accrued interest receivable ..		150
l.	Legacy - Joan Marple	11,550	
	Legacy - Raymond Marple	11,550	
	Cash - principal		9,100
	Commons stock, Roulette Corp..		6,000
	Indian Echo bonds		8,000
m.	Income	650	
	Distribution to income beneficiary		650
n.	Estate Principal	33,000	
	Assets subsequently discovered	8,100	
	Gain on realization	100	
	Funeral and administrative exp.		6,200
	Accrued interest receivable ..		100
	Loss on realization		300
	Debts of decedent paid		1,500
	Legacy - Agatha Marple		10,000
	Legacy - Joan Marple		11,550
	Legacy - Raymond Marple	11,550	

2.

Estate of Sherlock Holmes
Tom Watson, Executor
Charge and Discharge Statement
October 6 to December 31, 19x1

As to principal:
   I charge myself with:
      Assets per inventory $65,150
      Assets subsequently discovered 6,200
      Gain on realization 1,400 $72,750

   I credit myself with:
      Funeral expenses .... $ 1,000
      Administrative expenses 2,900
      Debts of decedent paid 4,390
      Loss on realization 100
      Legacy - A. C. Doyle 5,000   13,390
   Balance as to principal $59,360

   Consisting of:
      Cash - principal $12,560
      Stocks 34,000
      Bonds 10,000
      Household effects 2,800
                                  $59,360

As to income:
   I charge myself with:
      Income earned .... $ 2,950
   I credit myself with:
      Expenses - income .... $ 260
      Distribution to income beneficiary ... 1,050   1,310
   Balance as to income .... $ 1,640

   Consisting of:
      Cash - income .... $ 1,440
      Accrued interest receivable 200
                                  $ 1,640

Chapter 19
Corporate Liquidation and Reorganization

Chapter Outline

I. Liquidation

   A. Introduction

       1. A corporation's existence may be ended by voluntary or
           involuntary dissolution. While voluntary liquidation
           results from actions taken by the incorporators or
           shareholders, involuntary liquidation is initiated by
           shareholders, creditors, or the state.

       2. Equity insolvency means that a debtor is unable to meet
           his obligations as they mature; bankruptcy insolvency
           occurs when the total fair value of a debtor's property
           is less than the amount of existing liabilities.

       3. The Bankruptcy Reform Act (BRA) of 1978, which became
           effective in October 1979, is the current federal
           bankruptcy legislation.

       4. State insolvency laws pertain to the equitable
           distribution of the resources of a distressed debtor;
           the BRA is the controlling federal statute in such
           proceedings. State insolvency laws conform with the
           federal BRA.

   B. Bankruptcy Reform Act of 1978

       1. One purpose of the BRA is to provide for an orderly and
           equitable distribution of a distressed debtor's
           property among his creditors. When the proceedings are
           over, the debtor is discharged from remaining unpaid
           debts, except for those that specifically are not
           dischargeable.

       2. In general, the BRA:

           a. Broadly defines a debtor;

           b. Prescribes the number and type of entities
               required to file a petition with a bankruptcy
               court for voluntary and involuntary dissolution;
               and

           c. Provides for several United States Bankruptcy
               Courts.

3. In an involuntary bankruptcy case, courts usually are requested to appoint an interim trustee to take possession of the debtor's property and to operate any businesses associated with the property. At a later date a permanent trustee is usually selected by a creditor committee.

4. Among other things a trustee must:

    a. Realize the property of the estate and collect the money;

    b. Account for all property received;

    c. Furnish information about the estate and the estate's administration;

    d. Report on the business operations of the estate (including the filing of required tax statements); and

    e. File with the court a final report and account of administration.

C. Liquidation sequence

    1. Dissolution involves the:

        a. Marshaling and protection of the debtor's property;

        b. Conversion of the noncash assets;

        c. Distribution of proceeds to creditors with provable claims in the order of their priority; and

        d. Formal discharge of the debtor.

    2. The debtor must:

        a. Provide a list of creditors, a schedule of assets and liabilities, and a statement of financial affairs to the court;

        b. Cooperate with a trustee; and

        c. Surrender all property and information about the property to the trustee.

    3. Creditors must file a proof of claim. After notice and hearing, the court determines the magnitude of the claim and the allowed amount.

4. Obligations of one priority class must be fully satisfied before settlement is made with creditors of a lower class. The five classes are arranged below in descending priority sequence:

    a. Administrative expenses, fees and charges assessed against the estate;

    b. Unsecured claims for wages, salaries, or commissions earned within 90 days of the date of the petition's filing (limited to $2,000 per person);

    c. Allowed secured claims for contributions to employee benefit plans arising from services performed within 180 days of the date of the petition's filing (limited to $2,000 per employee);

    d. Allowed secured claims of individuals arising from deposits for purchase, lease, or rental of property or services (limited to $900 per individual);

    e. Allowed unsecured claims of governmental units in respect of taxes.

5. Mutual obligations between an estate and its creditors may be setoff against each other with only the net balance to be received or paid.

6. After a debtor's assets have been equitably distributed among its creditors, the debtor is released from all debts provable in bankruptcy, unless the debtor is not an individual or has committed certain specific acts.

D. Assignment for benefit of creditors

1. Instead of choosing formal bankruptcy proceedings, a debtor may transfer corporate property to designated assignees (often creditors) who perform functions similar to those of a trustee. This transfer is known as an informal assignment for the benefit of creditors.

2. Advantages of assignment often include:

    a. Lower legal expenses;

    b. Fewer constraints as to conversion and distribution of assets; and

    c. The debtor having the authority to appoint the assignee(s).

3. However, unlike bankruptcy, there is no formal discharge of the debtor. Moreover, an assignment constitutes an act of bankruptcy and an assignee must surrender custody of the debtor's property should a bankruptcy petition be filed.

E. The statement of affairs

1. This special report details the book values and the expected realization values of the debtor's assets, and the amounts of the various creditors' claims.

2. The going concern concept is abandoned and a liquidation perspective is adopted (i. e. appraisal and current market values are emphasized).

3. The statement of affairs is oriented toward the legal status of the claims against the debtor.

4. The asset section is arranged so that:

   a. Assets pledged with fully secured creditors are listed and matched directly against the secured claims;

   b. Assets pledged with partially secured creditors are listed and matched against the partially secured claims;

   c. Free assets are listed and the total of their estimated realizable value is added to the amount by which the estimated realizable value of assets pledged with fully secured creditors exceeds the secured claims. The estimated realizable value of the uncommitted assets is then matched against liabilities having priority. The amount of any shortage is termed "estimated deficiency to unsecured creditors."

5. The next section presents the equity accounts and their balances in the following order:

   a. Liabilities having priority;

   b. Fully secured creditors;

   c. Partially secured creditors (because the claims of this group exceed the estimated realizable value of the assets pledged to them, the unsatisfied amount becomes an unsecured claim); and

   d. Other unsecured creditors. Stockholders' equity accounts are listed so that total book value of the equities equals total book value of the assets.

306

6. A deficiency account usually supplements a statement of affairs. It identifies the assets expected to produce gains and losses upon realization. The difference between the expected gains and losses is netted against the book value of the stockholders' equity accounts. This total equals the estimated deficiency to unsecured creditors.

F. Special problems in preparing a statement of affairs

1. If the term "reserve" is used to describe a valuation account, its balance should be deducted from the related assets, with the net amount extended to the book value column. Liability accounts described as reserves should be classified in a manner consistent with their priority or security positions. Reserves which are actually appropriations of retained earnings should be reported as elements of stockholders' equity.

2. A contingent liability should be reported according to its expected outcome during the liquidation period.

3. Accrued interest receivable or payable should be added to the obligation to which it relates.

4. Generally, prepaid insurance is accorded no estimated realizable value; only its book value is reported.

5. A discount on capital stock under certain circumstances may be treated as a free asset.

II. Reorganization

A. General

1. A debtor seeking reorganization has recourse to both nonjudicial and judicial remedies.

2. A financially distressed debtor may try to rehabilitate his unsuccessful business by reorganizing is, rather than by liquidating it.

3. Reorganization is often desirable because a going concern's resources typically are worth more than the amount they would bring in a forced liquidation.

B. Nonjudicial remedies include the four actions presented below:

1. The creditors agree to extend the settlement period for their outstanding obligations.

2. A debtor and his creditors accept a composition settlement. This is a contractual arrangement in which

the creditors agree to accept less than the original contract amount in full settlement of their claims.

3. A debtor may agree to a voluntary assignment for the benefit of creditors. This involves the conveyance of property to a trustee or assignee who converts the property to cash and ratably distributes the proceeds among the creditors.

4. A debtor agrees to relinquish control of his business to a creditor management committee. This committee determines policy regarding rehabilitation, reorganization, or liquidation of the debtor's business.

C. Judicial remedies

1. A debtor may initiate judicial proceedings by filing with a Bankruptcy Court a petition for reorganization under Chapter 11 of the Bankruptcy Reform Act.

2. After a petition has been filed, the court may appoint a trustee to conduct the affairs of the business or allow the debtor to continue. A court appointed trustee provides a full accounting to the court and other parties of interest.

3. The court shall appoint a committee of creditors holding unsecured claims to perform various duties, including:

   a. Investigating and assessing the debtor's business and financial condition;

   b. Assisting in the development of a plan of reorganization; and

   c. Collecting and filing with the court acceptance of the plan.

4. A reorganization plan must be fair and equitable and preserve the priorities of the parties at interest. In most cases the plan must be accepted by two thirds in amount and one half in number of the allowed claims of each class of creditors.

III. Trustee's Accounts

A. An overview

1. A trustee will establish a system of accounts to facilitate his reporting obligations and stewardship duties.

2. The trustee may continue with the books of the debtor corporation (primarily for convenience) or he may open new accounts. Regardless of the decision, it is important for the accounting records to distinguish clearly between obligations and receivables that existed prior to his appointment and those created during the period of receivership.

3. If new books are opened, the accounting records must identify the assets specifically conveyed to the trustee and contain an equity account that summarizes the trustee's accountability for the net assets entrusted to him. Preexisting debts normally remain on the books of the debtor, even if the trustee is responsible for their liquidation.

B. Reciprocal accounts

1. When new books are opened by the trustee, the net assets transferred to his stewardship are recorded at their book values along with an offsetting credit to a controlling account summarizing his net accountability, e. g. XYZ Company - in trusteeship.

2. The net assets transferred to the trustee's care are removed from the corporate records and an account charging the trustee for responsibility is opened, e. g. Anton Baker, trustee.

3. The control accounts XYZ Company - in trusteeship and Anton Baker, trustee, have reciprocal balances.

4. A trustee's control account is debited whenever the trustee pays preexisting debtor liabilities that are not entered in the trustee's books. Further, the trustee's income summary is periodically closed to this account.

5. The corporation's control account is appropriately adjusted to summarize the above trustee transactions and events, thereby preserving the reciprocal nature of the two control accounts.

6. If two sets of books are maintained (i. e. the trustee books and corporate books) and traditional financial statements are required, working papers assist in the consolidation of both sets of records. In this case, reciprocal account balances must be eliminated.

IV. Realization and Liquidation Account

A. An overview

1. A report summarizing the liquidation and distribution activities of the trustee is the realization and

309

liquidation account. Its format is that of a giant T-account.

2. This report discloses:

    a. The book value of the assets and liabilities of the debtor at the outset of the report period;

    b. The operating activities of the trustee;

    c. The proceeds from realization of specific noncash assets;

    d. The distribution of the proceeds; and

    e. The unrealized assets and unsettled liabilities as of the report date.

3. Supporting the realization and liquidation account is a schedule showing the nature and amount of transactions affecting the cash account.

B. Major divisions

1. The realization and liquidation account's three primary divisions report a variety of information about:

    a. The realization of assets;

    b. The liquidation of liabilities; and

    c. Related revenues, expenses, gains, and losses.

2. Information is categorized and disclosed as illustrated in the following general form:

Assets

Assets to be realized:	Assets realized (conversion proceeds):
Assets acquired or discovered:	Assets not realized:

Liabilities

Liabilities liquidated:	Liabilities to be liquidated:
Liabilities not liquidated:	Liabilities incurred:

310

Revenues, Expenses, Gains and Losses	
Supplementary charges:	Supplementary credits:

3. Net income or loss is the algebraic sum of all debit and credit amounts reported in the above categories. If a debit is needed to produce equality between both sides of the account, there has been income for the period; if a credit is needed, there has been a loss. Because some asset credits are expressed in terms of realized amounts, net income or loss is not completely confined to an analysis of the supplementary charges and credits, but also requires a study of changes in the asset categories.

4. It is important to be familiar with the ten categories of the realization and liquidation account. They are listed in the above T-accounts.

C. Special problems

1. Merchandise purchases may be recorded as "assets acquired" or as "supplementary charges;" sales may be recorded as "assets realized" or as "supplementary credits." If there are several such transactions, the latter entries are preferred.

2. An unsettled liability that is listed at its gross amount under "liabilities to be liquidated" is later reported under "liabilities liquidated" at its:

    a. Net amount if a cash discount is taken when paid; or

    b. Gross amount with the amount of the cash discount entered as a "supplementary credit."

    Parallel accounting treatment may be applied to receivable balances and related sales discounts and allowances.

3. Depreciation expense and estimated bad debts are not separately identified as elements of income determination; however, they affect income computation because their related assets are valued net of these amounts at the report date in the category "assets not realized."

4. Accruals subsequently realized at larger amounts than were originally entered as "assets to be realized" are treated in one of two ways:

    a. "Assets realized" is credited for the amount accrued at the start of the period, with the additional amount collected reported as a "supplementary credit;" or

 b. The accrual for the current period is entered as "assets acquired" with an offsetting credit to "supplementary credits;" the total collection is shown as "assets realized." Similar procedures apply for accrued expenses.

5. A settlement discount (i. e. creditors accept less than face value) should be reported as a "supplementary credit," and a settlement premium (i. e. creditors demand more than face value) should be reported as a "supplementary charge."

Test Your Understanding of Chapter 19

True or False

Instructions: Indicate your choice by circling either T, if you think the statement is true, or F, if you think the statement is false.

T F 1. Liquidation is considered voluntary if action is initiated by incorporators; involuntary if initiated by creditors.

T F 2. State insolvency laws have no similarity to the Bankruptcy Reform Act of 1978, the current federal bankruptcy legislation.

T F 3. A trustee in a bankruptcy case is required to account for property received, file tax statements, and give a final report to the court.

T F 4. Dissolution of a bankrupt entity is completed with the formal discharge of the debtor.

T F 5. Each creditor of a bankrupt entity that files a proof of claim receives payment in chronological order of receipt of the claim by the trustee.

T F 6. Assignment for the benefit of creditors is simply another term for voluntary bankruptcy.

T F 7. A statement of affairs is a report that presents asset book values and expected realization values as well as mounts of creditors' claims.

T F 8. The asset section of the statement of affairs is arranged so that assets pledged with fully secured creditors are matched against the secured claims; assets pledged with partially secured creditors are matched against partially secured claims.

T F   9. A deficiency account determines the claims of the unsecured creditors which will go unpaid.

T F   10. Reorganization of a financially distressed business is the first step toward liquidation of the business.

T F   11. An example of a nonjudicial remedy is a creditor agreeing to extend the settlement period for its outstanding obligation.

T F   12. Chapter 11 of the Bankruptcy Reform Act allows a debtor to file a petition for reorganization with a Bankruptcy Court, which then determines the fairness of the reorganization plan and oversees its implementation.

T F   13. A trustee in bankruptcy or reorganization must establish a new accounting system for the debtor corporation if he is to fulfill his duties.

T F   14. The realization and liquidation account is a report, usually in T-account form, which summarized the liquidation and distribution activities of a trustee.

T F   15. Net income or loss during the period of liquidation is determined by comparing only the supplementary charges and the supplementary credits reported in the realization and liquidation account.

Exercises

1. A receiver was appointed as of July 31, 19x1, for Boulder
Corporation. On this date the following balance sheet was prepared:

Assets

Cash			$ 1,550
Accounts Receivable	$18,000		
Notes Receivable	15,000	$33,000	
Allowances for Bad Debts		(450)	32,550
Accrued Interest on Notes Receivable			350
Merchandise			38,000
Prepaid Insurance			520
Prepaid Rent Expense			480
Building (net of depreciation)			35,000
Machinery & Equipment (net of depr.)			45,000
Goodwill			14,000
			$167,450

Equities

Accrued Wages	$ 4,225
Accrued Property Taxes	1,525
Accounts Payable	76,000
Notes Payable	20,000
Accrued Interest Payable	600
Common Stock	133,000
Retained Earnings (Deficit)	(67,900)
	$167,450

It is estimated that conversions of assets will realize cash in the
following amounts:

Accounts Receivable	$11,000
Notes Receivable (with accrued interest)	10,500
Merchandise	30,400
Building	9,000
Machinery and Equipment	27,000

Notes payable of $12,000 are secured by merchandise with a book value
of $22,000. Notes payable of $8,000 are secured by machinery and
equipment with a book value of $10,000. Interest expense is allocated
ratably to all outstanding notes payable.

Required:
a.   Prepare a Statement of Affairs as of July 31, 19x1.

314

Boulder Corporation
Statement of Affairs
July 31, 19x1

Assets

b.   Prepare a supporting deficiency account or report on this date.

                           Boulder Corporation
                            Deficiency Account
                             July 31, 19x1

. Although the Acme Manufacturing Corporation had contributed
capital in the amount of $55,000 and accumulated earnings of $13,051,
the financial condition of the corporation was very unstable. The
company knew that, to continue in business, it had to obtain cash to
meet expenses, since there was a deficiency of quick assets. Balances
as of August 31, 19x1, were as follows:

Cash	$ 325
Trade Receivables	5,536
Raw Materials	14,300
Work in Process	28,950
Finished Goods	6,300
Machinery	41,000
Accounts payable	28,360

The principal creditors decided to advance $7,500 to Acme to meet its
current obligations. Further, a trustee was appointed to conduct the
continuation of operations until the remaining goods could be
completed and sold.

Transactions completed during the trusteeship were:

Cash disbursements:	
for operating expenses	$ 3,500
for trusteeship expenses	1,000
for labor costs	22,500
Raw materials purchased on account......	5,100
Sales on account	71,500
Loss on collections of old receivables..	250
Expenses incurred on account	12,000

Unliquidated account balances at the termination of the trusteeship
period on November 30 were as follows:

Accounts Receivable (new)	$ 4,200
Accounts Payable (new)	105
Raw Materials	3,500
Finished Goods	28,000
Machinery	42,500

Required: Prepare a statement of realization and liquidation. Ignore
the effects of depreciation in the determination of
operating profit.

Acme Manufacturing Corporation
Realization and Liquidation Account
For the Period August 31 to November 30, 19x1

True or False

.	T	4.	T	7.	T	10.	F	13.	F
.	F	5.	F	8.	T	11.	T	14.	T
.	T	6.	F	9.	T	12.	T	15.	F

Exercises

. a.

Boulder Corporation
Statement of Affairs
July 31, 19x1

Book Value	Assets			Estimated Realizable Value
	Assets Pledged with Fully Secured Creditors:			
22,000	Merchandise (Note 1)		$17,600	
	Notes Payable	$12,000		
	Accrued Interest	360	12,360	$ 5,240
	Assets Pledged with Partially Secured Creditors:			
10,000	Machinery & Equipment (Note 2)...		$ 6,000	
	Notes Payable..........	$ 8,000		
	Accrued Interest	240	8,240	-0-
	Free Assets:			
1,550	Cash			1,550
18,000	Accounts Receivable			11,000
15,000	Notes Receivable (10,500 - 350)			10,150
350	Accrued Interest Receivable			350
16,000	Merchandise			12,800
520	Prepaid Insurance			-0-
480	Prepaid Rent Expense			-0-
35,000	Building			9,000
35,000	Machinery & Equipment			21,000
14,000	Goodwill			-0-
	Total Realizable Value			$71,090
	Less Liabilities Having Priority			5,750
	Net Realizable Value			$65,340
	Estimated Deficiency to Unsecured			
	Creditors			12,900
167,900				$78,240

Equities

Liabilities Having Priority:

$ 4,225	Accrued Wages	$ 4,225		
1,525	Accrued Property Taxes	1,525		
	Total	$ 5,750		

Fully Secured Creditors:

$ 12,000	Notes Payable	$12,000		
360	Accrued Interest	360		
	Total	$12,360		

Partially Secured Creditors:

$ 8,000	Notes Payable	$ 8,000		
240	Accrued Interest	240		
		$ 8,240		
	Assets pledged - Machinery	6,000	$ 2,240	

Unsecured Creditors:

$ 76,000	Accounts Payable		76,000

Reserve:

$ 450	Allowance for Bad Debts

Stockholders' Equity:

$133,000	Common stock		
(67,900)	Retained Earnings (Deficit)		
$167,900			$78,240

Note 1: (22,000 : 38,000) x 30,400 = 17,600
Note 2: (10,000 : 45,000) x 27,000 = 6,000

Boulder Corporation
Deficiency Account
July 31, 19x1

Estimated Losses on Realization of Assets:

Accounts Receivable	$ 6,550
Notes Receivable	4,850
Merchandise	7,600
Prepaid Insurance	520
Prepaid Rent Expense	480
Building	26,000
Machinery and Equipment	18,000
Goodwill	14,000
Total	$78,000

Stockholders' Equity:

Common Stock	$133,000
Retained Earnings (Deficit)	(67,900)
	$65,100
Estimated Deficiency to Unsecured Creditors..	12,900
Total	$78,000

2.

Acme Manufacturing Corporation
Realization and Liquidation Account
For the Period August 31 to November 30, 19x1

Debits

Assets to be Realized:

Accounts Receivable (old)	$ 5,536	
Raw Materials (beginning)	14,300	
Work in Process (beginning)	28,950	
Finished Goods (beginning)	6,300	
Machinery	41,000	$ 96,086

Assets Acquired:

Accounts Receivable (new)	$71,500	
Raw Materials (ending)	3,500	
Finished Goods (ending)	28,000	103,000

Supplementary Charges:

Purchases	$ 5,100	
Operating Expenses	15,500	
Trustee's Expenses	1,000	
Labor	22,500	
Raw Materials (beginning)	14,300	
Work in Process (beginning)	28,950	
Finished Goods (beginning)	6,300	93,650

Liabilities Liquidated:

Accounts Payable	$72,355	
Notes Payable	7,500	79,855

Liabilities Not Liquidated:

Accounts Payable		105

Net Income		10,850
		$383,546

<u>Credits</u>

Liabilities to be Liquidated:
    Accounts Payable .... $ 28,360

Liabilities Incurred:
    Accounts Payable $44,100
    Notes Payable   7,500   51,600

Supplementary Credits:
    Sales $71,500
    Raw Materials (ending) 3,500
    Finished Goods (ending) 28,000   103,000

Assets Realized:
    Accounts Receivable $72,586
    Raw Materials (beginning) 14,300
    Work in Process (beginning) 28,950
    Finished Goods (beginning) 6,300   122,136

Assets Not Realized:
    Accounts Receivable .... $ 4,200
    Raw Materials (ending) 3,500
    Finished Goods (ending) 28,000
    Machinery 42,500   78,200

Loss on Conversion   250
                                                $383,546

Chapter 20
Accounting for State and Local Governmental Units—General Fund

Chapter Outline

I. Financial Reports of State and Local Governmental Units--Uses and Objectives

    A. In <u>Statement of Financial Accounting Concepts No. 4</u> the FASB identifies the major distinguishing characteristics of nonprofit enterprises as:

        1. Receipts of significant amounts of resources from resource providers who do not expect to receive either repayment or economic benefits proportionate to resources provided;

        2. Operating purposes that are other than to provide goods or services at a profit or profit equivalent;

        3. Absence of defined ownership interest that can be sold, transferred, or redeemed, or that convey entitlement to a share of a residual distribution of resources in the event of liquidation of the organization.

    B. <u>Governmental Accounting Standards Board (GASB) Concepts Statement 1</u> lists environmental characteristics that distinguish state and local governmental units from other nonprofit entities. It indicates that the objectives of state and local government financial reporting follow from these environmental characteristics and the informational needs of all users of governmental financial reports. It identifies the primary users as the citizenry, the legislatures, and investors and creditors. These groups need information to compare actual results to legally adopted budgets, to assess financial condition and results of operations, to determine compliance with laws, rules, and regulations, and to evaluate efficiency and effectiveness.

    C. The main objectives of general purpose financial reporting by state and local governments are to assess accountability and to make economic, social, and political decisions. The specific objectives are:

        1. To assist government's duty to be publicly accountable and to enable users to assess that accountability by:

            a. Providing information on whether current-year revenues will cover current-year services;

323

b. Showing that resources were obtained and used in accordance with the legally adopted budget and that legal and contractual requirements were complied with;

c. Providing information regarding the service efforts, costs, and accomplishments of the governmental entity.

2. To assist users in evaluating the operating results of the governmental entity for the year by providing information about sources and uses of financial resources, financing activities, and changes—for better or worse—in the entity's financial position.

3. To assist users in assessing the level of services the entity can provide and its ability to meet its obligations as they become due by providing information about the financial position and condition of the entity, about its physical and other nonfinancial resources, and by disclosing legal or contractual restrictions on resources and risks of potential loss of resources.

D. To accomplish the above objectives financial information must possess the qualities of understandability, reliability, relevance, timeliness, consistency, and comparability.

II. Historical Perspective on Authoritative Pronouncements

A. Prior to 1979 the primary source document for principles of governmental accounting was <u>Governmental Accounting, Auditing, and Financial Reporting.</u> GAAFR was published in 1968 by the National Committee on Governmental Accounting of the Municipal Finance Officers Association.

B. In 1979 the National Council on Government Accounting of the Municipal Finance Officers Association issued its <u>Statement 1</u>, "Governmental Accounting and Financial Reporting Principles." This statement lists 12 basic principles of accounting for state and local governments. It superseded GAAFR and still remains an important authoritative pronouncement on governmental accounting.

C. In 1984 the Governmental Accounting Standards Board (similar to the FASB) was established. In its <u>Statement No. 1</u>, "Authoritative Status of NCGA Pronouncements and the AICPA Industry Audit Guide" the GASB sanctioned all seven NCGA pronouncements and the AICPA Audit Guide as authoritative until amended or superseded by a subsequent GASB pronouncement.

D.   Between 1984 and 1989 the GASB issued nine statements, several interpretations and Technical Bulletins as well as <u>Concepts Statement 1.</u>

E.   The AICPA's state and local governmental accounting GAAP hierarchy is in decreasing order of authoritative support:

1.   Pronouncements by the GASB,

2.   Pronouncements by the FASB,

3.   Pronouncements of other bodies, such as AICPA audit and accounting guides and <u>Statements of Position</u>,

4.   Practices or other pronouncements widely recognizes as being generally accepted, and

5.   Other accounting literature, e. g. textbooks and journal articles.

III. Basic Principles of State and Local Governmental Accounting

A.   Accounting and reporting capabilities: Governmental accounting systems must make it possible both:

1.   To present fairly and with full disclosure the financial position and results of financial operations of the funds and account groups of the governmental unit in conformity with generally accepted accounting principles.

2.   To determine and demonstrate compliance with finance related legal and contractual provisions.

B.   Fund accounting systems: Governmental accounting systems should be organized and operated on a fund basis. A fund is defined as a fiscal and accounting entity with a self-balancing set of accounts recording cash and other financial resources, together with all related liabilities and residual equities or balances, and changes therein, which are segregated for the purpose of carrying on specific activities or attaining certain objectives in accordance with special regulations, restrictions, or limitations.

C.   Types of funds: The following types of funds should be used by state and local governments:

1.   Governmental funds

a.   A general fund to account for all financial resources except those required to be accounted for in another fund.

b.   Special revenue funds to account for the proceeds of specific revenue sources (other than expendable trusts or for major capital projects) that are legally restricted to expenditures for specified purposes.

    c.   Capital projects funds to account for financial resources to be used for the acquisition or construction of major capital facilities (other than those financed by proprietary funds and trust funds).

    d.   Debt service funds to account for the accumulation of resources for, and the payment of, general long-term debt principal and interest.

2.   Proprietary funds

    a.   Enterprise funds to account for operations:

        (1)   That are financed and operated in a manner similar to private business enterprises, where the intent of the governing body is that the costs (including depreciation) of providing goods or services to the general public be financed primarily through user charges, or

        (2)   Where the governing body has decided that periodic determination of revenues earned, expenses incurred, and/or net income is appropriate for capital maintenance, public policy, management control, accountability, or other purposes.

    b.   Internal service funds to account for the financing of goods or services provided by one department or agency to other departments or agencies of the governmental unit, or to other governmental units, on a cost-reimbursement basis.

3.   Fiduciary funds, i. e. trust and agency funds, to account for assets held by a governmental unit in a trustee capacity or as an agent for individuals, private organizations, other governmental units, and/or other funds. These include expendable trust funds, nonexpendable trust funds, pension trust funds, and agency funds.

D.   Number of funds: Governmental units should establish and maintain those funds required by law and sound financial administration. Only the minimum number of funds consistent with legal and operating requirements should be established.

E.   Accounting for fixed assets and long-term liabilities:

1.   Fixed assets related to specific proprietary funds or trust funds should be accounted for through those funds. All other fixed assets of a governmental unit should be accounted for through a general fixed assets account group.

2.   Long-term liabilities of proprietary funds and trust funds should be accounted for through those funds. All other unmatured general long-term liabilities of the governmental unit should be accounted for through a general long-term debt account group.

F.   Valuation of fixed assets: Fixed assets should be accounted for at cost. Donated fixed assets should be recorded at their estimated fair value at the time received.

G.   Depreciation of fixed assets:

1.   Depreciation of general fixed assets should not be recorded in the accounts of governmental funds.

2.   Depreciation of fixed assets accounted for in a proprietary fund should be recorded in the accounts of that fund. Depreciation is also recognized in those trust funds where expenses, net income, and/or capital maintenance are measured.

H.   Accrual basis in governmental accounting: The modified accrual or accrual basis of accounting, as appropriate, should be utilized in measuring financial position and operating results.

1.   Governmental fund revenues and expenditures should be recognized on the modified accrual basis. Revenues should be recognized in the accounting period in which they become available and measurable. Expenditures should be recognized in the accounting period in which the fund liability is incurred, if measurable, except for unmatured interest on general long-term debt, which should be recognized when due.

2.   Proprietary fund revenues and expenses should be recognized on the accrual basis.

3.   Fiduciary fund revenues and expenses or expenditures (as appropriate) should be recognized on the basis consistent with the fund's accounting measurement objective. Nonexpendable trust and pension trust funds should be accounted on the accrual basis; expendable trust funds should be accounted for on the modified accrual basis. Agency fund assets and liabilities should be accounted for on the modified accrual basis.

327

4. Transfers should be recognized in the accounting period in which the interfund receivable and payable arise.

I. Budgeting, budgetary control, and budgetary reporting:

1. An annual budget(s) should be adopted by every governmental unit.

2. The accounting system should provide the basis for appropriate budgetary control.

3. Budgetary comparisons should be included in the appropriate financial statements.

J. Transfer revenue, expenditure, and expense account classification:

1. Interfund transfers and proceeds of general long-term debt issues should be classified separately from fund revenues and expenditures or expenses.

2. Governmental fund revenues should be classified by fund and source. Expenditures should be classified by fund, function (or program), organization unit, activity, character, and principal classes of objects.

3. Proprietary fund revenues and expenses should be classified in essentially the same manner as those of similar business organizations, functions, or activities.

K. Common terminology and classification: A common terminology and classification should be used consistently throughout the budget, the accounts, and the financial reports of each fund.

L. Interim and annual financial reports:

1. Appropriate interim financial statements and reports of financial position, operating results, and other pertinent information should be prepared.

2. A comprehensive annual financial report covering all funds and account groups of the reporting entity should be prepared and published.

3. General purpose financial statements may be issued separately from the comprehensive annual financial report.

4. A component unit financial report covering all funds and account groups of a component unit may be prepared.

5. Component unit financial statements of a component unit may be issued separately from the component unit financial report.

IV. General Concepts Related to Fund Accounting

A. Funds and fund accounting in general

1. In governmental accounting the primary accounting unit is the fund. The governmental accounting process summarizes, classifies, records, and reports the transactions of individual funds viewed as separate entities.

2. The transactions of governmental units include revenue transactions, expenditure transactions, and expense transactions. For some funds the focus is on accounting for financial resources expended, i. e. expenditures, while for other funds the emphasis is on accounting for expenses, including depreciation expense.

3. The set of accounts used in recording the transactions of each fund is self-balancing and may contain both proprietary and budgetary accounts. The proprietary accounts resemble accounts for profit seeking entities, such as revenues, expenditures (or expenses), assets, liabilities, allowances, reserves, and residual equities. The budgetary accounts include estimated revenues and appropriations accounts.

4. It is important to distinguish between expendable and nonexpendable funds.

   a. The resources of an expendable fund can be totally expended to achieve the objectives of the fund. Its resources are taxes, fees, licenses, proceeds of bond issues, etc. Its expenditures are for services of employees, materials, fixed assets, etc. Since fixed asset purchases are classified as expenditures, fixed assets are not included in the assets of an expendable fund. Examples of expendable funds are general funds, special revenue funds, capital projects funds, debt service funds, and expendable trust funds.

   b. In a nonexpendable fund the principal, or capital balance, is supposed to be preserved intact. Examples are enterprise and internal service funds (i. e. proprietary funds), which are supposed to generate sufficient revenues to cover their operating expenses, and nonexpendable trust funds established to invest an endowment fund and use the related income for a particular purpose.

B.   Appropriations, allotments, and apportionments

1.   Appropriations are the amounts of resources that can be expended by a fund on various specific activities in a given budget (or fiscal) period.

2.   Allotments (state and local governments) and apportionments(federal government) are internal allocations of appropriations over subintervals of the budget period.

C.   General fixed assets and general long-term debt account groups

1.   Both account groups are self-balancing sets of accounts.

2.   These groups summarize the total general fixed assets and general long-term debt of a governmental unit, i. e. fixed assets and long-term debt not assignable to specific funds.

D.   Budgetary and encumbrance accounting

1.   Until approved a fund budget is an estimate of expenditures for a period with proposed methods of financing.

2.   Once approved the estimated expenditures become appropriations, i. e. amounts that can be spent on specific items. At this time the budget becomes a control device because it reflects mandated legal ceilings on expenditures and, therefore, is instrumental in prohibiting excess expenditures on items for which appropriations exist.

3.   Approved fund budgets are frequently entered in the accounting records in special budgetary accounts.

4.   Actual transactions of the fund are recorded in proprietary accounts.

5.   Expenditure control is enhanced through the use of an encumbrance system which reveals the fund's expected future expenditures. In such a system the account Encumbrances is debited and the account Reserve for Encumbrances is credited for the estimated amount of the order or the contracted amount.

6.   Control is achieved using the balances in related budgetary, proprietary, and encumbrance accounts. If, for example, near the end of the year the budgetary account Estimated Revenues exceeds the proprietary account Revenues, a deficit may occur. On the expenditure side the Appropriations account can be

330

compared with the sum of the Expenditures and
Encumbrances to avoid excess expenditures.

E. Accrual and modified accrual basis accounting

1. The accrual basis is used in proprietary funds
(enterprise and internal service funds) and in
nonexpendable trust funds. It includes the recognition
of depreciation expense and the expensing of inventory
when consumed.

2. The modified accrual basis is used in governmental
funds, including the general fund, in expendable trust
funds, and in agency funds.

   a. Revenue is recognized when it is available (i. e.
   collectible) and measurable.

   b. Expenditures on the modified accrual basis differ
   from expenses on the accrual basis in the
   following ways:

      (1) Depreciation expense is not recorded.

      (2) Unmatured interest on general long-term debt
      is recognized when due.

      (3) Most short-term prepayments (e. g. prepaid
      insurance) need not be allocated between
      periods.

      (4) The cost of inventory is usually recognized
      as an expenditure when acquired.

   c. Interfund transfers consist of:

      (1) Operating transfers in and out are recorded
      by both funds. A debit to Operating
      Transfers Out is made by the first fund, and
      a credit to Operating Transfers in is made by
      the second fund. An example are taxes
      collected by one fund and transferred to
      another fund for disbursement.

      (2) Quasi-external transactions involve a receipt
      (disbursement), or related accrual, which
      would be considered a revenue (expenditure)
      if the transaction were with an external
      entity. An example is a billing by an
      internal service fund.

      (3) Reimbursements are transfers by one fund to
      another to repay the latter for an
      expenditure made. Reimbursements are
      recorded as expenditures by the fund making

the transfer and as reductions in expenditures by the fund receiving the transfer.

    (4) Residual equity transfers are made to establish and eliminate funds.

F.   Intergovernmental revenues include grants, entitlements, shared revenues, and payments in lieu of taxes.

    1.   A grant is a receipt of cash or other assets from another government. The grant is restricted to a specific use.

        a.   Capital grants are restricted for use on fixed asset acquisitions.

        b.   All other grants are operating grants.

    2.   Entitlements are receipts to which a state or local government is entitled according to a formula designed by the organization providing the resources.

    3.   A shared revenue is a receipt by one government unit that is shared on a predetermined basis with other government units.

    4.   Payments in lieu of taxes are amounts paid to one government by another government to reimburse the former for lost revenues because the latter does not pay taxes (e. g. property taxes).

    5.   The accounting treatment for these types of resource flows depends on the type of fund in which the transactions are recorded.

        a.   Proprietary funds and certain nonexpendable trust funds use the full accrual method.

        b.   Other funds use the modified accrual method.

G.   Financial reporting

    1.   State and local governments prepare three types of financial statements:

        a.   Individual fund and account group financial statements report on the financial positions and operating results of individual funds and account groups.

        b.   Combining fund statements present financial data for all funds of a particular type in adjacent columns along with an all funds total column.

c. Combined fund and account group statements are similar to combining fund statements except that each statement of this type usually contains a column for the financial data of each pertinent type of fund or account group or contains a column for each relevant fund or account group.

2. Combined fund and account group statements are referred to as the general purpose financial statements of governmental units.

a. For funds with a governmental measurement objective the general purpose financial statements are the Balance Sheet and the Statement of Revenues, Expenditures, and Changes in Fund Balance.

b. For funds with a proprietary measurement objective the general purpose financial statements are the Balance Sheet, the Statement of Revenues, Expenses, and Changes in Retained Earnings (or Fund Balance in the case of pension trust funds), and the Statement of Cash Flows (except for pension trust funds).

V. Accounting for the General Fund--Basic Considerations

A. The general fund is used to account for all revenues and expenditures not accounted for in another fund. It is also called the operating or current fund and is used to account for the governmental unit's general administration and traditional services. Its primary revenue sources are taxes, such as property, sales, and income taxes; licenses and permits; fines, penalties and forfeits; and fees. Typical general fund expenditures are for services provided by fire, police, and sanitation departments.

B. Recording the budget and a first look at closing entries

1. Recording the budget in the general ledger control accounts is accomplished by posting the following general journal entry:

Estimated Revenues   → Budget acc
    Appropriations
The entry is balanced with a debit or credit to Fund Balance.

2. The entries to these accounts are recorded in the opposite way actual revenues and expenditures are recorded in the proprietary accounts. Throughout the period total actual expenditures and encumbrances are compared with appropriations, the legal ceiling on expenditures, to ensure that expenditures do not exceed the maximum allowed.

333

3. To close these budgetary accounts at the end of the period, the following entries are made:

    Revenues
        Estimated Revenues

    Appropriations
        Expenditures
    Both entries are balanced with a debit or credit to Fund Balance. These closing entries highlight any differences between the budgetary and proprietary accounts for further analysis.

C. Recording actual transactions

    1. The general fund uses the modified accrual basis, i. e. revenues are recognized when available and measurable. On the expenditure side the following should be remembered:

        a. Depreciation expense is not recorded;

        b. Unmatured interest on general long-term debt is recognized only when due;

        c. Most short-term prepayments need not be allocated between periods;

        d. The cost of inventory is usually recognized as an expenditure when the inventory is acquired; and

        e. Fixed asset purchases are accounted for as expenditures.

    2. The actual transactions of the general fund are recorded in its proprietary accounts. These accounts are often control accounts which are supported by subsidiary ledger accounts containing the detailed information.

    3. Expenditures, encumbrances, and revenues are classified by function. Functional classification allows comparisons of specific revenues and expenditures with their related budgeted amounts, which are also classified by function. Comparisons of expenditures and appropriations is especially important, since it is illegal to spend more than the amount appropriated for a given functional item unless supplementary appropriations are enacted.

4.   Revenue from property taxes is recorded when levied with the following entry:

Taxes Receivable
        Revenues
        Allowance for Uncollectible Taxes

The difference between this entry and an entry accruing revenue by a profit seeking entity is the handling of the allowance for uncollectible accounts. An entry is also made in the Property Taxes Revenue account of the revenue subsidiary ledger.

5.   Property taxes which have become delinquent are transferred to a delinquent account. The same is done with the Allowance for Uncollectible Taxes account. The entries are:

Taxes Receivable - Delinquent
Allowance for Uncollectible Taxes   Reverse
        Taxes Receivable
        Allowance for Uncollectible Taxes - Delinquent

Uncollected taxes are written off against the allowance. If delinquent taxes are collected, the related portion of the Allowance for Uncollectible Taxes - Delinquent is closed to Fund Balance.

6.   Wages and salaries are generally not encumbered, 债权, 抵押 instead the liability is recorded with the following entry:

Expenditures   — to Sub leger
        Vouchers Payable

An entry is also made in the Wages and Salaries Expenditures account of the subsidiary expenditures ledger. It should also be noted that governments often use the account Vouchers Payable instead of Accounts Payable.

7.   Operating transfers in and out are recorded as follows:

Due from Other Fund   从哪里来
        Operating Transfers In   去斗之地方
Cash
        Due from Other Fund

Operating Transfers Out
        Due to Other Fund
Due to Other Fund
        Cash

335

8. If the purchase method is used for inventories of materials and supplies, the following entry is made to record the purchase:

Expenditures
        Cash

The first ending inventory is recorded with the entry:

Materials and Supplies
        Fund Balance Reserved for Materials and Supplies

Thereafter increases in the ending inventory are recorded with the same entry, whereas decreases are recorded with the entry:

Fund Balance Reserved for Materials and Supplies
        Materials and Supplies

The balance in Fund Balance Reserved for Materials and Supplies identifies the portion of the fund balance which is unavailable for expenditures because it has already been expended on materials and supplies.

9. Under the consumption method, which may be required or optional, the purchase of inventory is recorded with the entry:

Materials and Supplies
        Cash

In addition, the amount spent on inventory has to be reserved with the entry:

Fund Balance
        Fund Balance Reserved for Materials and Supplies

The amount of inventory consumed is recorded with the entry:

Expenditures
        Materials and Supplies

After this entry the balance in the Materials and Supplies account will equal the ending inventory. The amount of inventory consumed also reduces the fund balance which had been reserved. The entry is for the amount of inventory consumed and is as follows:

Fund Balance Reserved for Materials and Supplies
        Fund Balance

As under the purchase method, the balance in the Fund Balance Reserved for Materials and Supplies identifies the portion of the fund balance which is unavailable

336

for expenditures because it has already been expended on materials and supplies.

D. Recording encumbrances

1. Budgetary control is enhanced through the encumbrance system because future expenditures on existing orders and contracts are recorded by the entry:

    Encumbrances
        Reserve for Encumbrances

    This entry records the estimated amount of the expenditure and is made in memorandum accounts.

2. When the actual amount of the order or contract is known, the above entry is reversed and the actual amount is recorded as an expenditure as follows:

    Reserve for Encumbrances
        Encumbrances
    Expenditures
        Cash (or Vouchers Payable)

E. Closing the budgetary, proprietary, and encumbrances accounts

1. Actual revenues and operating transfers in are closed with the entry:

    Revenues
    Operating Transfers In
        Estimated Revenues
    The entry is balanced with a debit or credit to Fund Balance. If actual revenues plus operating transfers in are more (less) than estimated revenues, Fund Balance is credited (debited).

2. Expenditures and operating transfers out are closed with the entry:

    Appropriations
        Expenditures
        Operating Transfers Out
        Fund Balance

    Since expenditures are not allowed to exceed appropriations, this closing entry should always credit Fund Balance.

3. The open encumbrances are closed with the entry:

    Reserve for Encumbrances
        Encumbrances

337

In addition, a portion of the fund balance must be reserved for the outstanding orders or contracts. This is done with the entry:

Fund Balance
    Fund Balance Reserved for Encumbrances

It should be noted that these two entries are for the same amount.

4.   At the beginning of the following year the above two entries are reversed, as follows:

Fund Balance Reserved for Encumbrances
    Fund Balance
Encumbrances - Prior Year
    Reserve for Encumbrances - Prior Years

F.   Nonencumbrance related reserves and fund balance designations

1.   Other segregations of fund assets may be indicated by establishing other reserves.

2.   In addition to reserves, governmental units often designate a portion of the fund balance for certain purposes. Designated portions of fund balances represent management's expectations for using resources unlike reserves that represent management's prior commitment of fund resources.

3.   In each of these cases these segregations of fund assets are recorded with a debit to Fund Balance and a credit to Fund Balance Reserved or Designated.

4.   As a result of reserves and designations, the fund balance may be split between reserved and unreserved portions.

5.   When the fund assets become again available for general fund purposes, the original entry reserving or designating a portion of the fund balance is reversed.

G.   General fund financial statements

1.   The balance sheet shows only relatively liquid assets, like cash, receivables, inventory, since the fixed assets are recorded as expenditures and shown as assets in the general fixed assets account group. The liabilities consist of short-term obligations, since long-term debts are included in the general long-term debt account group.

2.   The statement of revenues, expenditures, and changes in fund balance is virtually always done comparing actual

338

and budgeted data. It includes sections for revenues, expenditures, other financing sources and uses of funds, and other changes in the fund balance (i. e. those related to changes in reserves).

Test Your Understanding of Chapter 20

True or False

Instructions: Indicate your choice by circling either T, if you think the statement is true, or F, if you think the statement is false.

T F 1. A governmental entity may have a self-balancing set of accounts for each of its separate funds.

T F 2. As with commercial businesses, budgets for a governmental entity usually are not entered in fund accounts.

T F 3. In most operating funds the proprietary accounts Expenditures and Encumbrances are closed along with the budgetary account Appropriations to the Fund Balance account at the end of the budgetary period.

T F 4. An encumbrance may be entered in a fund's accounts as a means of reserving approved spending authority until a certain liability or expenditure is actually incurred and recorded.

T F 5. The balance in the account Reserve for Encumbrances is reported as part of the equity section of a fund's balance sheet.

T F 6. Fixed assets purchased with General Fund resources are recorded as assets in the accounts of the General Fund.

T F 7. In general, the AICPA and the National Council on Governmental Accounting have recommended that accrual accounting be abandoned for governmental entities.

T F 8. According to the FASB a major distinguishing characteristic of nonprofit entities is that they receive significant amounts of resources from people who do not expect to be repaid.

T F 9. A characteristic of governmental accounting is that fund accounting is used as a control device.

T F 10. GASB Concepts Statement 1 states that it is a specific objective of general purpose financial reporting by governmental entities to provide information about sources and uses of financial resources.

T F 11. Prior to 1979 the main source of governmental accounting principles was the AICPA's Industry Audit Guide.

T F 12. In 1984 the GASB was formed by the Governmental Accounting Standards Foundation.

T F 13. Between 1984 and 1989 the GASB issued seven statements.

T F 14. For governmental accounting the pronouncements of the GASB constitute the highest level of authoritative support.

T F 15. The twelve basic principles of state and local governmental accounting are listed in GASB Concepts Statement 1.

Exercises

1. On January 1, 19x2, the trial balance of the General Fund of Podunk City included the following:

> Reserve for encumbrances - prior year $15,000
> Fund balance   54,000

Required: Prepare the journal entries to record the 19x1 General Fund transactions given below:

a.   The approved 19x2 operating budget included estimated revenues of $250,000 and appropriations of $245,000.

b.   Wages and salaries of $80,000 were approved for payment.

c.   Supplies ordered in 19x1 for $15,000 were received and billed at $15,500. All 19x1 purchase orders are now closed.

d. The general tax levy for the year amounted to $220,000; estimated uncollectible accounts amount to $22,000.

e. Payment was made for the approved vouchers in b and c, above.

f. Current taxes of $190,000 were collected.

g. An invoice for $25,000 was received for gas and electric service from the town's utility (an enterprise fund).

h. Fixed assets were purchased for $120,000.

i. The revenue accounts in the General Fund were closed.

j. The expenditure accounts in the General Fund were closed.

2. The trial balance of College Township's General Fund at the end of the fiscal year ended June 30, 19x1, is presented below:

College Township
General Fund Trial Balance
June 30, 19x1

	Debit	Credit
Cash	$ 6,200	
Taxes receivable - current	8,200	
Allowance for uncollectible taxes - current		$ 300
Due from Internal Service Fund	14,150	
Taxes receivable - delinquent	1,450	
Allowance for uncollectible taxes - delinquent		600
Expenditures	146,500	
Encumbrances	3,500	
Estimated revenues	150,000	
Revenues		160,000
Due to Enterprise Fund		11,100
Vouchers payable		3,000
Reserve for encumbrances - prior year ..		2,500
Reserve for encumbrances		3,500
Appropriations		140,000
Fund balance		9,000
	$330,000	$330,000

Required: Prepare the General Fund balance sheet at June 30, 19x1.

Solutions to Chapter 20 Exercises

True or False

1.	T	4.	T	7.	F	10.	T	13.	F
2.	F	5.	T	8.	T	11.	F	14.	T
3.	T	6.	F	9.	T	12.	F	15.	F

Exercises

1. **General Fund Transactions**

a. Estimated revenues $250,000
      Appropriations $245,000
      Fund balance 5,000

b. Expenditures 80,000
      Vouchers payable 80,000

c. Reserve for encumbrances - prior year... 15,000
      Encumbrances - prior year 15,000
  Expenditures 15,500
      Vouchers payable 15,500

d. Taxes receivable 220,000
      Revenues 198,000
      Allowance for uncollectible taxes . 22,000

e. Vouchers payable 95,500
      Cash 95,500

f. Cash 190,000
      Taxes receivable 190,000

g. Expenditures 25,000
      Due to Enterprise Fund 25,000

h. Expenditures 120,000
      Vouchers payable 120,000

i. Revenues 198,000
  Fund balance 52,000
      Estimated revenues 250,000

j. Appropriations 245,000
      Expenditures 240,500
      Fund balance 4,500

2.

College Township
General Fund
Balance Sheet
June 30, 19x1

Assets

Cash		$ 6,200
Taxes receivable - current	$ 8,200	
Less: Allowance for uncollectible current taxes	300	7,900
Taxes receivable - delinquent	$ 1,450	
Less: Allowance for uncollectible delinquent taxes	600	850
Due from Internal Service Fund		14,150
		$29,100

Liabilities, Reserves, and Fund Balance

Liabilities:		
Vouchers payable	$ 3,000	
Due to Enterprise Fund	11,100	$14,100
Reverse for encumbrances - prior year ..		2,500
Reserve for encumbrances		3,500
Fund balance		9,000
		$29,100

Chapter 21
Accounting for State and Local Governmental Units—Other Funds and Account Groups

Chapter Outline

I. Governmental Funds

   A. Governmental funds are called expendable funds because all
       their resources may be spent to accomplish their objectives.
       For local and state governments the governmental funds are:
       the general fund (discussed in the previous chapter),
       special revenue funds, capital projects funds, debt service
       funds, and, until eliminated by GASB Statement 6, special
       assessment funds.

   B. All governmental funds use similar, but not identical,
       accounting practices. They all use the modified accrual
       basis, do not record depreciation, do not recognize interest
       expense until due, do not allocate most short-term
       prepayments between periods, and may use the purchases
       method to account for inventories. Governmental funds also
       do not list fixed assets and long-term debt on their balance
       sheets. The financial statements they prepare are the
       Balance Sheet and the Statement of Revenues, Expenditures,
       and Changes in Fund Balance.

   C. Special revenue funds

      1. These funds account for special revenue sources which
          are used to finance specific activities, such as
          maintaining roads and bridges, operating libraries or
          parks, or accounting for grants.

      2. Each special revenue fund should be accounted for as a
          separate entity; however, the number of special revenue
          funds should be kept at a minimum.

      3. Accounting for special revenues funds is identical to
          accounting for the general fund: their budgets are
          (usually) recorded in budgetary accounts, their actual
          transactions are recorded in proprietary accounts,
          orders and contracts are encumbered, and in the closing
          entries the differences between budgeted and actual
          amounts are closed to the Special Fund Balance.

   D. Capital projects funds

      1. These funds are used to account for the acquisition or
          construction of major fixed assets such as buildings,
          highways, and bridges. They provide a mechanism for
          ensuring that revenues provided for capital projects

are used solely for their intended purposes. The funds typically exist only until their objective is achieved.

2. Budgetary accounts usually are not used in capital projects funds; however, the use of encumbrances is recommended.

3. Acquired capital assets and any long-term debt incurred to finance the capital projects are accounted for in the general fixed assets and general long-term debt account groups.

4. The resources of capital projects funds are:

   a. Transfers from other funds, usually the general fund, which are recorded as Transfers In;

   b. Grants from other governmental units, which are recorded as intergovernmental revenues; and

   c. Proceeds from bond issues, which are credited to a Proceeds from Bond Issue account. The issuance of bonds at a discount is often prohibited. If the bonds are issued at a premium and the premium may be used in financing the capital project, the entire proceeds are credited to the Proceeds from Bond Issue account. If the premium is not available for the capital project, only the par value is credited to the Proceeds account, while the premium is credited to the liability account Premium on Bonds. This amount is transferred to the related debt service fund.

5. At the conclusion of the project the revenue and expenditure accounts are closed to Fund Balance. The balance of this account should then be equal to the amount of any unexpended cash. This cash is transferred to the related debt service fund, and the capital projects fund is officially closed.

E. Debt service funds

1. These funds are used to account for payments of interest, principal, and other related charges on all general long-term debts except debts serviced by proprietary funds or nonexpendable trust funds. These debts include general obligation debt, i. e. debt that is backed by the full faith and credit of the issuing governmental unit, as well as any other debts which are guaranteed through taxes, i. e. all tax-supported debt, and the long-term debt arising from special assessments.

2. Budgetary accounts are often used to record estimated interfund transfers and earnings necessary to service

346

the debt. Appropriations are recorded for expected debt service payments, including principal, interest, and debt service charges.

3. Actual earnings and transfers are credited to Revenues and Transfers In, while payments for interest, debt retirement and service charges are debited to Expenditures with the offsetting credit to liabilities for principal and interest.

4. Bonds are not recorded as liabilities of a debt service fund until they mature, when Expenditures are debited and Bonds Payable are credited. At the end of the period accrued interest is not recorded. Under the modified accrual basis the liability for interest is not recorded until it becomes due.

5. At the end of the year the closing entry debits revenues, transfers in, and appropriations, credits expenditures and estimated transfers in, and debits or credits Fund Balance for the difference.

F. Special assessment funds

1. These funds are usually established to account for projects or supply services which provide general benefits to the public and specific benefits to particular citizen groups who are assessed special tax levies to pay for them.

2. Special assessment funds are no longer prepared under GASB Statement 6. However, they are still required in some jurisdictions.

3. The transactions formerly accounted for in the special assessment fund will be treated as follows under GASB Statement 6:

   a. The construction phase of the project is accounted for like other capital projects.

   b. If the government is liable for the debt if the property owners default, the debt service phase is accounted for like the debt service of other tax-supported debt.

   c. If the government is not liable for the debt but collects the assessments and remits them to the creditors, the transactions should be accounted for in an agency fund.

4. If special assessment funds are still kept, they are accounted for as follows:

   a. Budgets are usually not recorded.

347

b. The contract for the project is recorded as an encumbrance.

c. The acquisition and construction of fixed assets are recorded as expenditures, and the assets are accounted for in the general fixed assets account group.

d. If the project is initially funded by debt, the debt issue and the liability are accounted for and interest expense is accrued within the fund.

e. The assessments are accrued and recorded as revenue and used to pay interest and principal.

f. Interest on assessments due is accrued as revenue. Interest on the liability is accrued as an expenditure.

g. The closing entry debits Revenues and credits Expenditures and takes the difference to Fund Balance. Open encumbrances are closed.

II. Proprietary Funds

A. The proprietary funds are nonexpendable funds, i. e. the principal, or capital, balances must be preserved. The two types of proprietary funds are enterprise funds and internal service funds. The financial statements prepared for proprietary funds are the Balance Sheet, the Statement of Revenues, Expenses, and Changes in Retained Earnings, and the Statement of Cash Flows.

B. Enterprise funds

1. Enterprise funds are frequently used to finance certain services provided for the public, like electric, gas, and water utilities, airports, and bus service.

2. Because accounting for these funds is similar to that used for commercial businesses, the accrual basis is appropriate. Contributed Capital and Retained Earnings replace Fund Balance as the fund's equity accounts.

3. Acquired fixed assets are capitalized and depreciated, and long-term debt is reported and retired in the enterprise fund.

4. Revenue and expense accounts are closed to Retained Earnings at the end of the year.

5. The balance sheet of an enterprise fund reflects the long-term nature of the fund by listing fixed assets and long-term liabilities first.

C. Internal service funds

    1. These funds are established to finance manufacturing or
        service activities performed for the benefit of other
        governmental departments. They bill these departments
        on a user charge basis.

    2. Initial funding may be provided by an advance from
        another fund or by the sale of bonds. An advance from
        another fund is recorded as an Equity Transfer In.

    3. Accounting procedures for internal service funds are
        very similar to those of profit-seeking enterprises.
        They use the accrual basis and capitalize and
        depreciate fixed assets.

    4. Revenue and expense accounts are closed to Retained
        Earnings at the end of the year.

II. Fiduciary Funds--Trust and Agency Funds

    A. These funds are designed to account for money and property
        held by a governmental unit serving as trustee or agent.

    B. Trust funds are classified as nonexpendable trust funds,
        expendable trust funds, and pension trust funds.
        Nonexpendable trust funds are similar to proprietary funds,
        while expendable trust funds are similar to special revenue
        funds.

        1. A nonexpendable trust fund is established to account
            for trust principal provided by a donor with the
            stipulation that the related income is to be used for a
            particular purpose.

        2. An expendable trust fund is established to expend the
            revenue from an endowment fund set up by a donor for
            some specific purpose.

        3. A pension trust fund accumulates contributions to a
            governmental unit's pension plan, invests these
            resources, and makes pension payments to qualified
            participants.

        4. Nonexpendable trust funds and pension trust funds use
            the accrual basis and prepare a Balance Sheet, a
            Statement of Revenues, Expenses, and Changes in
            Retained Earnings (or Fund Balance in the case of
            pension trust funds), and a Statement of Cash Flows
            (except for pension trust funds). Expendable trust
            funds use the modified accrual basis and prepare a
            Balance Sheet and a Statement of Revenues,
            Expenditures, and Changes in Fund Balance.

C.   Agency funds usually account for assets (generally cash) received for, and payable to, other funds. Since they do not have revenues and expenditures, they prepare only a Balance Sheet.

IV. Account Groups for General Fixed Assets and General Long-Term Debt

A.   These groups provide records of the general fixed assets and the general long-term debt of a governmental unit which are not accounted for in proprietary or nonexpendable trust funds.

B.   These account groups are separate accounting, but not fiscal, entities. Their primary financial statement is the Balance Sheet which is often supplemented by a schedule accounting for changes during the year.

C.   The general fixed assets account group records the fixed assets acquired by the general fund, capital projects funds, special assessment funds, and through gifts. They are recorded at cost or, if acquired by gift, at fair values on the date of the gift.

1.   When general fixed assets are recorded, the offsetting credits are to investment accounts which reflect the source of the fixed assets, i. e. Investment in General Fixed Assets - General Obligation Bonds.

2.   Transfers of fixed assets are recorded at book values.

3.   Depreciation may be recorded in the general fixed assets account group. When depreciation is recorded, the investment account is debited and accumulated depreciation is credited.

4.   The disposal of a fixed asset is recorded by debiting the investment account and crediting the asset. If depreciation is recorded, the related accumulated depreciation account must also be removed. Any proceeds from the sale of general fixed assets are usually recorded in the general fund.

D.   The general long-term debt account group records the long-term debt which is not serviced through proprietary or nonexpendable trust funds. It is not used to record proceeds from the sale of bonds or the payment of interest.

1.   When general long-term debt is issued, a liability account in the general long-term debt account group is credited to record the liability. The offsetting debit is to the Amount to be Provided for Payment of Debt account.

350

2.   When funds are designated for the principal reduction
      and become available to a debt service fund, an entry
      is made in the general long-term debt account group
      debiting Amount Available in Debt Service Fund for
      Payment of Debt and crediting Amount to be Provided for
      Payment of Debt.

3.   When the principal is reduced by a payment from the
      debt service fund, an entry is made in the general
      long-term debt account group debiting the liability and
      crediting Amount Available in Debt Service Fund for
      Payment of Debt.

4.   When funds become available in the debt service fund
      which are designated for principal reduction, e. g.
      when revenues exceed expenditures, the Amount Available
      in Debt Service Fund for Payment of Debt account is
      debited and the Amount to be Provided for Payment of
      Debt account is credited.

Financial Reports of State and Local Governments

A.   As discussed in Chapter 20, three types of financial
      statements are used in reporting for state and local
      governments: individual fund and account group statements,
      combining fund statements, and combined fund and account
      group statements. The combined fund and account group
      statements are referred to as the general purpose financial
      statements of governmental units.

B.   Each combined fund and account group statement usually
      contains a column either for the financial data of each
      pertinent type of fund or account group or for each relevant
      fund and account group. These statements present memorandum
      totals for all funds combined (without eliminating the
      effects of interfund transactions).

C.   General purpose financial statements consists of:

      1.   For funds with a governmental measurement objective,
            the Balance Sheet, and the Statement of Revenues,
            Expenditures, and Changes in Fund Balance.

      2.   For funds with a proprietary measurement objective, the
            Balance Sheet, the Statement of Revenues, Expenses, and
            Changes in Retained Earnings (or Fund Balance in the
            case of Pension Trust Funds), and the Statement of Cash
            Flows (except pension trust funds).

D.   The general purpose financial statements of a governmental
      unit are only part, although the major part, of its
      Comprehensive Annual Financial Report.

Test Your Understanding of Chapter 21

True or False

Instructions: Indicate your choice by circling either T, if you think the statement is true, or F, if you think the statement is false.

T F 1. If a new city building is to be constructed and financed by a special bond issue, four separate funds or groups of accounts will record the various components of this transaction and the eventual liquidation of the debt, i. e. a Capital Projects Fund, a Debt Service Fund, the General Fixed Assets Account Group, and the General Long-Term Debt Account Group.

T F 2. While a Special Assessment Fund may be used to account for expenditures for improvements that are financed by tax levies against the benefited properties, an Enterprise Fund may be used to finance and account for services provided exclusively for other governmental departments.

T F 3. Fixed assets purchased by an Enterprise Fund are capitalized and depreciated in the Enterprise Fund.

T F 4. Proceeds from the sale of fixed assets recorded in the general Fixed Asset Account Group are normally recorded as revenue in this group of accounts.

T F 5. The General Long-Term Debt Account Group reports the unmatured principal of outstanding long-term debt obligations that are not recorded in a fund; the currently matured principal and the period's interest payment on the debt are recorded in a Debt Service Fund.

T F 6. Payments for the construction of a new city hall recorded in a capital projects fund are debited to expenditures.

T F 7. The gain or loss on the sale of a fixed asset recorded in the General Fixed Assets Account Group is generally recorded in the general fund.

T F 8. The operations of a municipal sports stadium receiving the majority of its support from admission charges should be accounted for in a special revenue fund.

T F 9. If interest on a general long-term debt is due semi-annually on April 1 and October 1, interest payable for the period April 1 to September 30 is not recorded in the debt service fund until October 1.

T F 10. If the municipal bus company receives subsidies from the city's general fund, it should be accounted for in a special revenue fund.

352

T F 11. Bonds issued by a county airport, an enterprise fund, for the construction of a new runway, should be recorded in the General Long-Term Debt Account Group.

T F 12. The activities of a print shop which does printing for city departments on a user charge basis should be accounted for in an internal service fund.

T F 13. A rich citizen left a million dollars to her hometown for the establishment of a vacation fund. The income is to be used to pay for vacations of needy children. The principal should be accounted for in a nonexpendable trust fund.

T F 14. A special state gasoline tax earmarked to pay for highway construction and maintenance, should be accounted for in an agency fund.

T F 15. Operating transfers in and out are eliminated in the Combined Statement of Revenues, Expenditures, and Changes in Fund Balance.

Exercises

1. On August 1, 19x1, the town of Fairfield authorized the construction of a new municipal museum at a cost of $950,000. The construction is to be financed with a bond issue of $900,000 and $50,000 in general revenues.

Required: In the Capital Projects Fund journalize the following transactions which occurred during the fiscal year ending June 30, 19x2:

a. On August 1, 19x1, a firm commitment was received for the $50,000 due from the city.

b. A construction contract was signed for $920,000.

c. $10,000 was received from the city on August 15, 19x1.

d. The bonds were sold at 101 on September 1. The stated interest rate is 8%, interest is payable March 1 and September 1. The premium must be transferred to the debt service fund and will be applied towards the first interest payment.

e. The contractor submitted a partial billing for $500,000 on February 3, 19x2.

f. The bill submitted by the contractor was paid on March 1, 19x2.

g. On March 1, 19x2, sufficient cash was transferred from the general fund to the debt service fund to make the first interest payment. The interest was paid.

354

h.   On May 1, 19x2, a consultant was hired for $10,000 to inspect the building.

i.   The contractor submitted the final bill for $420,000 on May 15, 19x2.

j.   The consultant submitted a bill for $10,000 on May 20, 19x2.

k.   The balance due was transferred from the general fund on June 6, 19x2.

l.   All outstanding bills were paid on June 15, 19x2.

m. The capital projects fund was closed on June 28, 19x2. The remaining cash was transferred to the debt service fund.

2. Use the information from Exercise 1.

Required: Prepare journal entries to record the events in any other fund or account group affected.

General Fund

a.

c.

g.

k.

Debt Service Fund

d.

g.

n.

General Long-Term Debt Account Group

d.

General Fixed Assets Account Group

n.

357

Solutions to Chapter 21 Exercises

1.	T	4.	F	7.	F	10.	F	13.	T
2.	F	5.	T	8.	F	11.	F	14.	F
3.	T	6.	T	9.	T	12.	T	15.	F

Exercises

1.
Capital Projects Fund

a. Due from General Fund .... $ 50,000
  Operating Transfers In .... $ 50,000

b. Encumbrances 920,000
  Reserve for Encumbrances   920,000

c. Cash 10,000
  Due from General Fund   10,000

d. Cash 909,000
  Proceeds from Bonds   900,000
  Premium on Bonds   9,000
 Premium on Bonds 9,000
  Cash   9,000

e. Reserve for Encumbrances 500,000
  Encumbrances   500,000
 Expenditures 500,000
  Vouchers Payable   500,000

f. Vouchers Payable 500,000
  Cash   500,000

h. Encumbrances 10,000
  Reserve for Encumbrances   10,000

i. Reserve for Encumbrances 420,000
  Encumbrances   420,000
 Expenditures 420,000
  Vouchers Payable   420,000

j. Reserve for Encumbrances 10,000
  Encumbrances   10,000
 Expenditures 10,000
  Vouchers Payable   10,000

k. Cash 40,000
  Due from General Fund   40,000

l. Vouchers Payable 430,000
  Cash   430,000

m.
Proceeds from Bonds	900,000	
Operating Transfers In	50,000	
Expenditures		930,000
Fund Balance		20,000
Fund Balance	20,000	
Cash		20,000

2.

General Fund

a.
| Operating Transfers Out | 50,000 | |
| Due to Capital Projects Fund | | 50,000 |

c.
| Due to Capital Projects Fund | 10,000 | |
| Cash | | 10,000 |

g.
Operating Transfers Out	27,000	
Due to Debt Service Fund		27,000
Due to Debt Service Fund	27,000	
Cash		27,000

k.
| Due to Capital Projects Fund | 40,000 | |
| Cash | | 40,000 |

Debt Service Fund

d.
Due from Capital Projects Fund	9,000	
Operating Transfers In		9,000
Cash	9,000	
Due from Capital Projects Fund		9,000

g.
Due from General Fund	27,000	
Operating Transfers In		27,000
Cash	27,000	
Due from General Fund		27,000
Expenditures	36,000	
Interest Payable		36,000
Interest Payable	36,000	
Cash		36,000

m.
Due from Capital Projects Fund	20,000	
Operating Transfers In		20,000
Cash	20,000	
Due from Capital Projects Fund		20,000

General Long-Term Debt Account Group

d.
| Amount to be Provided for Payment of Debt | 900,000 | |
| Bonds Payable | | 900,000 |

m.   Museum   930,000
           Investment in General Fixed
             Assets - Capital Projects
             Fund - General Fund Revenues   930,000

Chapter 22
Accounting for Colleges and Universities, Hospitals, and Other Nonprofit Organizations

Chapter Outline

I. Financial Reports of Nonprofit Units--Uses and Objectives

   A. The major characteristics distinguishing nonprofit entities from profit seeking enterprises, as expressed by the FASB in SFAC No. 4, were discussed in chapter 20. They are, in brief:

       1. Receipts of resources from resource providers who do not expect economic benefits proportionate to their contributions;

       2. Operating purposes other than to provide goods and services at a profit; and

       3. Absence of defined ownership interests.

   B. In SFAC No. 4 the FASB also lists the broad objectives of general purpose financial reporting by nonprofit entities. They are to provide information that is useful to present and potential resource providers:

       1. In making decisions about the allocation of resources;

       2. In assessing the services provided by a nonbusiness organization and its ability to continue to provide those services; and

       3. In assessing the performance of the managers of nonprofit organizations.

   C. The specific objectives intended to satisfy these general objectives are to:

       1. Provide information about an organization's economic resources, obligations, and net resources;

       2. Periodically provide information about an organization's performance;

       3. Provide information about an organization's methods of obtaining and spending cash and other factors affecting its liquidity; and

       4. Explain and interpret the financial information provided.

II. Authoritative Pronouncements--Colleges and Universities

A. The primary comprehensive college and university related authoritative pronouncements is College & University Business Administration (CUBA). Other significant pronouncements are Audits of Colleges and Universities and SOP 74-8, both by the AICPA.

B. Even though both the GASB and the FASB issue pronouncements on accounting standards for nonprofit organizations, only one significant difference between them has developed so far. SFAS No. 93, "Recognition of Depreciation by Not-for-Profit Organizations," requires nonprofit entities to disclose periodic depreciation expense. GASB Statement No. 8, however, states that the colleges and universities under its jurisdiction should not disclose depreciation expense.

III. Fund Accounting by Colleges and Universities

A. The funds used by universities are: (1) current funds, (2) loan funds, (3) endowment funds, (4) annuity and life income funds, (5) plant funds, and (6) agency funds. These funds are somewhat similar to the funds used by governmental agencies: Current funds resemble the general fund and special revenue funds; loan, endowment, annuity and life income, and agency funds are like fiduciary funds, and plant funds play a similar role to the account groups for fixed assets and long-term debt.

B. Current funds are used to account for the normal operations of universities. They may be unrestricted or restricted.

1. Accounting for unrestricted funds is similar to accounting for the general fund.

a. The financial statements are the Balance Sheet; the Statement of Current Fund Revenues, Expenditures, and Other Changes; and the Statement of Changes in Fund Balance. The current funds are the only university funds to provide a statement that resembles an income statement.

b. Budgetary accounting usually is required, and encumbrances are often used. The entry to record the budget is:

Unrealized Revenues
    Estimated Expenditures
    Unallocated Budget Balance

c. Revenues are usually on the accrual basis.

d. Expenditures, too, are usually on the accrual basis.

362

e. University funds make transfers out and receive transfers in. Such transfers are classified as mandatory, i. e. required by law, or nonmandatory.

f. Assets and equities resemble those of governmental unit general funds or of profit seeking entities. The assets are generally current assets, since fixed assets acquired by unrestricted current funds are accounted for in a plant fund. The liabilities are generally current liabilities.

2. Accounting for restricted current funds resembles accounting for unrestricted current funds.

a. Fixed assets are accounted for in a plant fund.

b. Revenues generally consist of governmental grants and contracts and endowment income. These revenues are recognized only to the extent that related authorized expenditures have occurred. Unearned revenues are initially credited to Fund Balance. The entries are:

(1) To record cash received:

Cash
    Fund Balance

(2) To record expenditures:

Expenditures - Instructional
Expenditures - Research
    Cash

(3) To record revenues equal to the above expenditures:

Fund Balance
    Revenues - Federal Grants
    Revenues - State Grants

C. Loan funds are used for making loans to students, faculty, and staff. Unrestricted loan funds are subject only to the lending policies set by the university's governing board, while restricted loan funds are subject to the lending intentions of donors.

1. The financial statements of a loan fund are the Balance Sheet and the Statement of Changes in Fund balance.

2. Revenues are recorded when the income is earned or the cash is received. Disbursements are debited to investments, loans, or administrative and collection costs. Estimated bad debts are debited to Loan

Cancellations and Write-offs and credited to Allowance for Uncollectible Loans. Uncollectible loans are written off against the allowance.

D. Endowment and similar funds are funds whose principal is invested to provide income which is used as stipulated by the donors.

   1. The characteristics of these funds are:

      a. In a nonexpendable endowment fund the principal must be preserved intact.

      b. In a term endowment fund the principal may be expended, consistent with the donor's wishes, upon the occurrence of some contingent event, like the passage of a certain period of time or the donor's death.

      c. Quasi-endowment funds are established by university boards to administer assets which are to be retained and invested.

   2. The financial statements of these funds are the Balance Sheet and the Statement of Changes in Fund Balance.

E. Annuity and life income funds make payments to their grantors, or other individuals, over specified time periods. e.g. the grantor's lifetime. Annuity funds make fixed payments which include principal, while life income funds distribute only income. At the end of the specified time the balance is transferred to a current or endowment fund, depending on the grantor's wishes. These funds prepare a Balance Sheet and Statement of Changes in Fund Balance.

F. Plant funds prepare a Balance Sheet and a Statement of Changes in Fund Balance. These funds include unexpended plant funds, funds for renewals and replacements, funds for retirement of indebtedness, and investment in plant funds.

   1. Unexpended plant funds are used to acquire plant assets. They usually receive cash from the restricted or unrestricted current fund and from the issuance of bonds.

   2. Funds for renewals and replacements are used when existing plant assets are renewed or replaced.

   3. The fund for retirement of indebtedness is used to record the cash received to retire bonds and their retirement.

   4. The investment in plant fund records the acquisitions of plant assets by the unexpended plant fund, the construction of buildings through bond issues, the

364

renewals and replacements made through the fund for renewals and replacements and the effect of retiring bonds through the fund for retirement of indebtedness. It debits the assets and credits either Bonds Payable or Net Investment in Plant.

G. Agency funds are used to collect, invest, or expend resources provided by others for various purposes. Their only financial statement is the Balance Sheet.

IV. Authoritative Pronouncements--Hospitals

A. Hospitals which are part of governmental units are accounted for as enterprise funds. Nongovernmental hospitals are subject to the AICPA's Hospital Audit Guide and its Statements of Position 78-1, 78-7, 81-2, and 85-1.

B. For nongovernmental hospitals the Hospital Audit Guide and SFAS No. 93 are in agreement, since both require the recording of depreciation.

V. Fund Accounting by Nongovernmental Hospitals

A. Hospital funds are usually classified as (1) general funds, (2) unrestricted endowment funds, and (3) restricted funds. General funds and unrestricted endowment funds are subject only to the hospital's board, while restricted funds must abide by the wishes of donors or grantors.

B. General funds are used in the daily operations of the hospital. They differ from governmental and university funds in that they record all unrestricted assets and liabilities and use the accrual basis for revenues and expenses.

1. The financial statements of the general fund are the Balance Sheet, the Statement of Revenues and Expenses, and the Statement of Changes in Fund Balances.

2. Hospital accounting distinguishes between revenue deductions, such as contractual adjustments, charity services, and discounts and allowances, and expenses, such as fiscal and administrative expenses, nursing services, and other professional expenses. Estimated bad debts are debited to a provision for Bad Debts and credited to an Allowance for Doubtful Accounts. Uncollectible accounts are written off against the allowance. Depreciation is recorded in the general fund, as are accrued receivables and payables.

C. Specific purpose funds must be operated in accordance with the restrictions placed upon them. They resemble special revenue funds in that they raise funds for specific purposes and then disburse them accordingly. They use the accrual basis and prepare a Balance Sheet and a Statement of Changes in Fund Balance.

D.   Endowment funds are established by donations. Their principal is invested to earn income which is spent in accordance with the donor's or the hospital board's instructions. They may have an indefinite or a limited life. Their financial statements are the Balance Sheet and the Statement of Changes in Fund Balance. Income received by them is credited and then transferred to the fund which will spend the money.

E.   Plant expansion and replacement funds account for donations restricted to the acquisition or replacement of plant assets. Investments in securities are accounted for in this fund, but the acquisition of plant assets is debited to Fund Balance. These funds prepare a Balance Sheet and a Statement of Changes in Fund Balance.

VI. Authoritative Pronouncements--Other Nonprofit Organizations

A.   Among other nonprofit organizations are voluntary health and welfare organizations, cultural institutions, political parties, home owners' associations, and professional organizations.

B.   The primary authoritative pronouncement on accounting for voluntary health and welfare organizations is the AICPA's Audits of Voluntary Health and Welfare Organizations. Descriptions of their accounting procedures are contained in the Standards of Accounting and Financial Reporting for Voluntary Health and Welfare Organizations.

C.   The main authoritative pronouncement for other nonprofit entities is the AICPA's Audits of Certain Nonprofit Organizations (ACNO).

VII. Fund Accounting by Voluntary Health and Welfare Organizations

A.   The funds of these organizations are classified as (1) current funds - unrestricted, (2) current funds - restricted, (3) land, building, and equipment funds, (4) endowment funds, and (5) custodian funds.

B.   The custodian fund is accounted for like the agency fund of a university. The other funds use the accrual basis.

C.   The revenues of health organizations include support, which is divided into direct and indirect public support, revenue, and fees and grants from governmental agencies. Their financial statements are the Balance Sheet; the Statement of Support, Revenue, and Expenses, and Changes in Fund Balance; and the Statement of Functional Expenses. Expenses are classified either by program and support expenses or by function for the latter two statements. Depreciation is recorded by these organizations.

D. Donated services are recorded at their fair market values when (1) the services would have been performed by salaried personnel if not donated, (2) the organization directs the donor in providing the services, and (3) the value of the services can be reasonably estimated.

VIII. Other Nonprofit Organizations--Additional Discussion

A. The accounting procedures prescribed for these entities by the AICPA's ACNO are similar to those of health organizations. They use the accrual basis and prepare a Balance Sheet, an Operating Statement, and a Statement of Changes in Financial Position.

B. Under ACNO government-supported museums, libraries, and similar organizations do not have to list art collections, rare book collections, historical treasures, and other assets on their balance sheets and do not have to depreciate them.

C. Under SFAS No. 93 privately-supported institutions must include all tangible assets, except "collections," on their balance sheets at cost or fair market value if donated. However, they are not required to depreciate individual works of art or historical treasures whose useful lives are unusually long.

D. Donated services are recorded if they meet the three tests stipulated for services donated to voluntary health and welfare organizations plus an additional test set by ACNO, namely that the services not be primarily for the benefit of the organization's members. Therefore, donated services are not recorded by such organizations as labor unions, country clubs and professional organizations.

Test Your Understanding of Chapter 22

True or False
Instructions: Indicate your choice by circling either T, if you think the statement is true, or F, if you think the statement is false.

T F   1. A uniform set of accounting principles applies to all nonbusiness organizations except hospitals.

T F   2. The essence of SFAS No. 4, "Objectives of Financial Reporting by Nonbusiness Organizations," is that the primary objective of financial reporting by nonbusiness organizations is to report on the stewardship function.

T F   3. Revenues of an unrestricted fund are recorded when earned with allowances established for estimated uncollectibles.

367

T F 4. Revenues of a restricted fund are recorded when earned without allowances established for estimated uncollectibles.

T F 5. General expenses of all funds of a nonbusiness organization are recognized when incurred, with perhaps the exception of depreciation.

T F 6. A pure endowment fund accounts for resources that are set aside with the restriction that the principal remain intact in perpetuity.

T F 7. An annuity fund is used to account for resources that have been donated to a nonbusiness organization for the specific purpose of providing a designated beneficiary with a cash or other asset annuity for the remainder of the beneficiary's life.

T F 8. To be recordable, donated services must be rendered by an employee of the nonbusiness organization.

T F 9. One distinguishing characteristic of a nonbusiness organization is that ownership interest cannot be sold and owners are not entitled to share in asset distributions in the ordinary sense of the word.

T F 10. In addition to an income statement and a balance sheet, a statement of changes in financial position is a required statement for most funds of nonbusiness organizations.

T F 11. The FASB or the GASB may override provisions of CUBA.

T F 12. The resources in the restricted current fund of a university may be expended only in accordance with the guidelines set by the university's board.

T F 13. The unrestricted fund of a university records expenses, rather than expenditures.

T F 14. University loan funds may extend loans only to students.

T F 15. Bonds issued for the acquisition of plant assets are not accounted for in the Unexpended Plant Fund of a university.

Exercises

1. The Unrestricted Fund of Private University uses three revenue and expenditure control accounts: Instruction, Research, and General; Financial Aid; and Self-Supporting Enterprises.

Required: Journalize the following events which occurred during the current fiscal year:

a. Student fees of $1,500,000 were assessed, of which $1,250,000 have been collected, and $5,000 is estimated to be uncollectible.

b. The book store is self-supporting. Revenues totaled $450,000, of which 90 percent has been collected to date. Salaries of $100,000 were paid. Other operating expenses amount to $325,000, of which $25,000 has not yet been paid.

c. The Director of Financial Aid reported the following:
       Cash scholarships $30,000
       Tuition credits   12,500

d. A mandatory transfer of $25,000 was made for a payment due on the athletic stadium mortgage.

A check for $35,000 is received from the local chapter of the CPA Society to cover part of the cost of research on accounting principles for universities.

2. Alma Mater University has a Restricted Fund which accounts for restricted grants.

Required: Journalize the following events affecting the Restricted Fund which occurred during the current fiscal year:

a. Received a grant of $80,000 to be used exclusively for tuition credits for students during the current year.

b. $79,800 of the grant was applied to the stated purpose during the year.

c. The grant provided that amounts not awarded by year-end are to be refunded to the grantor.

d. The Alumni Society contributed $1,000 to be awarded to a faculty member for excellence in teaching.

370

Solutions to Chapter 22 exercises

True or False

1.	F	4.	F	7.	F	10.	F	13.	F
2.	T	5.	T	8.	F	11.	T	14.	F
3.	T	6.	T	9.	T	12.	F	15.	T

Exercises

1.a.
```
Cash ..............................        1,250,000
Accounts Receivable ...............          250,000
     Revenues - Instruction,
        Research, and General.......                   1,500,000
To record revenues

Expenditures - Instruction, Research,
   and General .....................          5,000
     Allowance for Doubtful Accounts                       5,000
To record estimated bad debts
```

b.
```
Cash ..............................          405,000
Accounts Receivable ...............           45,000
     Revenues - Self-Supporting
        Enterprises ...............                      450,000
To record book store revenues

Expenditures - Self-Supporting
   Enterprises ....................          425,000
     Cash .........................                      400,000
     Accounts Payable .............                       25,000
To record book store expenses
```

c.
```
Expenditures - Financial Aid.......           42,500
     Cash .........................                       30,000
     Accounts Receivable ..........                       12,500
To record results of report of Director of Financial Aid
```

d.
```
Mandatory Transfer for Mortgage
   Payment ........................           25,000
     Cash .........................                       25,000
To record transfer for stadium mortgage
```

e.
```
Cash ..............................           35,000
     Revenues - Instruction,
        Research, and General ......                      35,000
To record receipt of CPA Society check
```

```
2.a. Cash ..............................          80,000
          Fund Balance ................                              80,000
     To record receipt of restricted grant

b.   Expenditures - Financial Aid ......          79,800
          Student Accounts Receivable ..                            79,800
     To record application of grant against fees receivable

     Fund Balance ......................          79,800
          Revenues - Grants ............                            79,800

c.   Fund Balance ......................             200
          Due to Grantor ...............                               200
     To record liability to grantor

d.   Cash ..............................           1,000
          Fund Balance ................                              1,000
     To record contribution for teaching excellence award
```